also by

PETRA WILLIAMS

Flow Blue China
An Aid to Identification
(1971)

Flow Blue China II
(1973)

Flow Blue China
and
Mulberry Ware
Similarity and Value Guide
(1975)

Staffordshire
Romantic Transfer Patterns

Cup Plates and
Early Victorian China

Table setting of "Villa" pattern, transfer printed in olive green and sepia by John Ridgway c. 1841. The dining room is at "Farmington", Louisville, Kentucky.

Petra Williams

Staffordshire
Romantic Transfer Patterns

Cup Plates and
Early Victorian China

Layout and Photographic Illustrations
for the text by
Marguerite R. Weber

FOUNTAIN HOUSE EAST

Jeffersontown, Kentucky

Dedicated
to the
Devotees of Old China
who
collect and preserve
Our Heritage

Foreword

The whole thing started with cup plates. While building my Flow Blue collection as a basis for research for the books I wrote about that subject, I was offered many dealers' lists of earthenwares. Of course, I was aware that glass cup plates had been a major American collecting field since the early days of this century. My friends who collected Flow Blue and Mulberry also cherished cup plates in those colors. Both a famous Pennsylvania dealer and a major one from Maine displayed their cup plates on the walls of their homes. Just as it was obvious that old Flow Blue china would increase in value when its origins were revealed, so it was equally obvious that the cup plates made c. 1840 would soon be rarities.

I always had intended to donate my Flow Blue collection to a museum. I decided that it would be interesting to try to collect cup plates. They are small; they take little display space, and they would afford me a continuing outlet for the collecting urge. Well, in order to buy the Flow Blue cup plates I wanted, I often had to purchase china by lot. Dealers sell to dealers by lot, which means take all or none. So I bought. Lots!

On the lists that accompanied the dishes I purchased I had noticed that cup plates were offered in other than Flow Blue or Mulberry. After a time the growing collection was dominated by small plates in many colors. The trouble with cup plates is that they are rarely marked or backstamped. Here were these lovely little multi-hued plates, most of them under four inches in diameter, printed in engaging patterns that I had never seen before. I kept the group in a box on a closet floor, and when for health reasons I was forced to stay at home in bed, I would take them from their box, fondle them and study the designs.

Whenever it was possible to go to an antiques show or visit a shop, I would look for dishes that resembled the cup plates. There were very few to be found. Years ago I had bought some old pale blue plates of this type for next to nothing, just because the designs were interesting (Gypsy and Brussels). I now realized that again I was in a field that was not popular and of no interest to dealers because they did not know or care about the subject. With the exception of Kamm and part of Laidecker's books, these transfers were not documented. Some New England and a few Midwest and Southern dealers stocked Staffordshire transfer ware, but very few others in the trade knew what we were looking for.

It is difficult for an American writer to do research in the field of English ceramics. Before she published her book in 1892, Alice Morse Earle went to England to do research on the makers of historical American china patterns. On page 323 of her book, "China Collecting

7

in America", she states, "It is impossible to obtain any information in England about this dark-blue earthenware, or 'semi-china', which was made for so many years in such vast quantities for the American market. The Staffordshire pottery works have all changed owners. The plates from which these wares were printed have all been lost or destroyed. The present owners of the pottery works are ignorant of the existence of these printed American pieces ... A careful search throughout the Staffordshire region developed absolutely not one fact about these . . ." She stated then that a collection was being gathered in America to present to the museum at Burslem for the "consequent enlightenment of English collectors and manufacturers."

By the way, in the United States we use the word china to denote both porcelain and pottery. In England, the purists use it only to mean porcelain. One of our readers wrote to a manufacturer in England inquiring about a Flow Blue dish she owned. The reply was that the pattern was old, no record of it existed, and it was of no importance because it was not china.

If it is impossible to travel abroad, one must rely on books and articles that touch on the subject, and by careful scrutiny of actual specimens form an opinion and reach intelligent conclusions. The great English authorities Geoffrey Godden and John Cushion and the cataloguer, Coysh, have access to the British Museum and its collections. They also have entree to the potteries and their records, to the pattern books which show the drawings used by the early potters, the paper transfer pulls, and the few surviving copper plates which were incised with the patterns, together with the biographies of the artists who used their drawings or those of other craftsmen.

It has taken us three years to seek out the actual patterns of our dishes and their makers and there remain many cup plates that are not yet identified.

You may recall that Flow Blue china was overlooked and discredited as recently as 10 years ago. Before that, English writers and other authorities such as Hudson Moore, around the turn of the century, denigrated Flow Blue as unfit for collecting. Even today, one of the most famous English experts has written a letter to one of our clients saying that Flow Blue is "an American phenomenon." Perhaps. But all my dealer friends who travel there say there is very little Flow Blue to be purchased in England. So, somebody over there exported an awful lot of it to the U.S.A. in the last 10 years. Sam Laidecker states in Part I "Anglo-American China" (1938) page 73, "To Englishmen the names we give the pottery they make are very amusing, but they have never minded that fact as long as they got our dollars. It is doubtful if the condition will ever change."

It may interest you to learn that our books were sought out and purchased by the museum at Stoke-on-Trent, and that we received a very kind and congratulatory letter from the curator.

So the Flow Blue market was quiet a decade ago. A few dealers here had purchased Flow Blue china over the years and held it as a personal collection. You all know what happened when the reading public – at least the reading collectors – which craved to own some precious bit of the past at a price it could afford, rushed into the market place and started to buy Flow Blue china. Of course, prices advanced and the old Victorian patterns are now as high as some of the highly esteemed historical Staffordshire. With the advance in cost of the early Flow Blue patterns, collectors began to snap up the later patterns with the result that some of the most popular late Victorian floral designs are now costly!

A word here about "historical" china. This is an American description – so called because the commemorative china was printed in England, in a total of about 800 subjects, of American views as sketched by English artists. American historical events such as the landing of LaFayette were pictured, and as an extension of this, even a picture of LaFayette's home in France was included. Other subjects were pictures of heroes, eagles, and other patriotic emblems.

English economy was in a sad state after the war with Napoleon and export trade was essential. The potteries rose to the occasion and sent hundreds of thousands of pieces of china to us with themes which would appeal to the pride of Americans. Perhaps THIS was the FIRST American phenomenon! This book does not deal with the so-called historical china mentioned above. A few patterns are shown because they seemed to be Romantic designs and were unmarked and you may have the same situation arise. We will not discuss the subjects of Pratt transfers or of Battersea and Bilston products.

When we published our book which included a compendium of Mulberry patterns, dealers were able to date their wares and collectors could understand another field in old china which was not out of their reach.

We feel that Romantic transfer ware which is closely associated with Flow Blue and Mulberry China is another field which the average collector can enter and enjoy. Dishes with Romantic transfer pictures are still to be found. I learned that some patterns are famous among dealers and collectors and are, therefore, expensive. But others are waiting in dusty piles in old shops, under fern plants in old houses, tucked away in attics and pantries. The china was made early in the 1800's, and the designs are of general historic interest. The time is inevitably coming when china so decorated will be recognized as valuable in the antique and collecting markets. We purchased the dishes shown in this book in order to catalogue and photograph them. The Flow Blue collection has left Fountain House and gone to the Margaret Woodbury Strong Museum in Rochester, N.Y., and will soon be on permanent display there. The shelves in the studio here are now filled with old Staffordshire transfer patterns displayed on cup plates and larger dishes.

It is impossible to quote prices for each pattern or even to attempt a price guide for this book. Values differ widely. Some dealers are not knowledgeable about transfer ware and some don't care about it at all. They sell it very cheaply and it still can be found in flea markets. Other dealers have an exaggerated idea of the value of most of their wares and their prices can be shocking.

For an example, we were paying from $30 to $50 for platters. We do not require mint dishes and do not fuss about chips or flakes or even cracks. In a show in Louisville, we found a platter in good condition in a pattern for which we had searched for 2 years. We could not afford the $150 asking price. In checking the dealers' stock, we found all the offerings were overpriced. We did find a smaller platter in the pattern in good condition for $75 at another show. Plates cost us from $3 up to $35, depending on size, pattern and the dealer's knowledge. Cup plates averaged $30. (Flow Blue and Mulberry cup plates have advanced to $50 and $60). The dealers in the Northeast who have specialized in china and carry a large stock of patterns of Staffordshire transfer earthenware set prices that are reasonable and fair.

Most of the large plates photographed bear both a maker's mark and a backstamp which sets forth the pattern name. A few have one or the other. In the case where the mark is missing we have stated that the maker is unknown to us and have catalogued by title. If the maker's name appears, but there is no backstamp, we have coined a name that describes the pattern and have shown this in quotation marks, as a nickname, a substitute for the proper name which is being sought.

The plates are not photographed in proper scale. Cup plates average under four inches in diameter and the larger plates shown are 8, 9, or 10 inches wide and the platters, of course, are much larger. The cup plates are shown as large as the space allows in order to present the pattern details clearly.

The GMK abbreviation refers to Geoffrey Godden's mark numbers set forth in his "Encyclopaedia of British Pottery and Porcelain Mark's." (GMK = Godden mark.) Marks were changed periodically by manufacturers. Instead of trying to date each pattern exactly, which is almost impossible, we have ascribed the years shown by Godden to denote the period a certain mark was used. A few patterns were issued for many years, and different marks, but of the same pottery usually, are indicative of the time spans. Most of the patterns shown in this book date c. 1835 to c. 1855.

Some of the patterns shown here appeared in my previous books and are catalogued again here to point out identifying features which may help to name an unmarked specimen. Also, I want to impress the fact that the same patterns were often made in flowing colors and also in pastel or other shades. For example, the famous Mulberry pattern, "Washington Vase" was made in a Flow Blue too, and the example photographed here is dark violet. One of the Lorraine cup plates photographed is Flow Blue and the other is actually printed in green. Remember to study the border designs. I look for distinguishing details in the rim patterns, and have tried to point them out in this book as often as it seemed necessary. Remember that rim designs can look very different on a platter than on plates. Those on cup plates often omit much of the border. But in almost all cases some small details tell the story that is missing on unmarked items. Central pictures in the well can be misleading. It is the border design that distinguishes the pattern.

The word Staffordshire is explained in the introduction, but we have included some patterns by makers who were not from that district, but were working elsewhere in England. Also because he was making comparable wares in Holland, we have included some of the dishes made by Petrus Regout. To date there is no literature available about Regout. His patterns, when unmarked, are easily mistaken for Staffordshire and are of equally good quality.

As I stated before, this book is the result of trying to identify cup plates. It is probably wise to discuss cup plates as such at this point. Ruth Webb Lee, the famous writer on pressed glass, states in her book, "American Glass Cup Plates", that handleless cups were much too warm to hold with comfort. The cup plate performed multiple services, not only was it a coaster but also it kept the linen clean and the table from being marred. She states, "China or pottery cup plates preceded those in glass and were largely made in Europe. Pressed glass could be made much more cheaply than china in this country, so as machinery for pressing glass was perfected, it is not surprising that among the earliest items made were numerous cup plates." They were first made at Sandwich in May, 1829. A sales sheet shown in her book from the New England Glass Company lists three dozen three-inch cup plates @ $1.50 and three dozen three-and-one-half inch cup plates @ $1.87.

The center well of a cup plate is of a size to accomodate a cup. The proper size according to Mrs. Lee was a diameter of two-and-five-eighths inches up to, but not including, four-and-one-fourth inches. A smaller plate is toy size and the four-and-one-fourth inch size is a toddy

11

plate made to hold a toddy glass or cup. Cup plates were in use from 1826 into the 1850's in this country. With the exception of G. Bernard Hughes' (page 159) "Country Life Pocket Book of China", most English writers and dealers persist in stating that there are no such things as cup plates, there are only toy dishes. Wouldn't Lee, Larson, Wood, Moore, Metz and Sam Laidecker, all of whom described pottery cup plates in detail, be surprised? Maybe this is just another American phenomenon. (See Bibliography.)

This work is not as complete as one could wish, but we feel that we could go on for years seeking out elusive designs. Publishing costs are mounting as inflation soars, and we do not want to publish a book so expensive that the average collector could not afford to own a copy. We had to forego printing the patterns in their wonderful colors for the same reason. How I wish you could see the array of patterns in different shades. You are welcome to visit the collection here at Fountain House East if you will write first and make an appointment.

It probably is very difficult to acquire a whole set now; the china is so old and the descendants of the families that owned it long ago have gone their separate ways, each taking his or her share. This must be coupled with the effects of attrition, breakage and discard. But a group can be assembled in any one color and look very grand indeed. Our collection like Joseph's coat is of many colors and denies the old tradition that only Blue and White Staffordshire and Mason's color designs are worth documenting. So although I realize that much could be added to this study, and I am certain that I will be found in error, I feel that it is better to take the first step, start out and blaze the path, so that others who follow can widen the trail by improving the original course.

My grateful thanks to the following generous dealers, collectors and friends for their contribution to this book: Ralph Schneider, Angus Cory, Elizabeth Bushnell, Nancy Glendenning, Dave Plummer, Ted Malarik, Bonne and Bob Hohl, Elinor and Christopher Goff, Elizabeth Lanham, Doreen Peterson, David Rockwell, James and Nancy Boyd, Marietta Charmoli, The Campbell Museum, Jean Tunis, Elaine and Charles Milligan, Ed Gibson, Debra Pond, Cleo Moffitt, Bettie Modys and the Historical Homes Foundation, Henrietta Soissin, Dee and Herb Sweet, Dave Stewart, Les Holstner, Karen Dillen, Joe Luzon, Jack Kieffer, Dale Mathias, Kenneth Howe, Gerald Casmir, Ed Goodwin and David Friedlander.

By God's grace I have been given time to study part of the past and produce this work about china made long ago; I am grateful for each sunrise in the present, and I look with anticipation and serenity to the future.

Petra Williams

Jeffersontown, Kentucky   12
July, 1978

Contents

Illustration

Frontpiece Table setting of "Villa" plattern, transfer printed in olive green and sepia by John Ridgway c. 1841. The dining room is at "Farmington", built by Judge John Speed after his marriage in 1808 to Lucy Fry. The scheme of Farmington, completed in 1810, has been identified as Thomas Jefferson's plan number 191, now in the archives of the Massachusetts Historical Society. The inset picture at the bottom of the page shows the charming, beautifully preserved Federal style building, owned and operated by Historical Homes Foundation Inc. The collection can be viewed at Farmington, 3033 Bardstown Road, Louisville, Kentucky.

PAGE

PLATE I

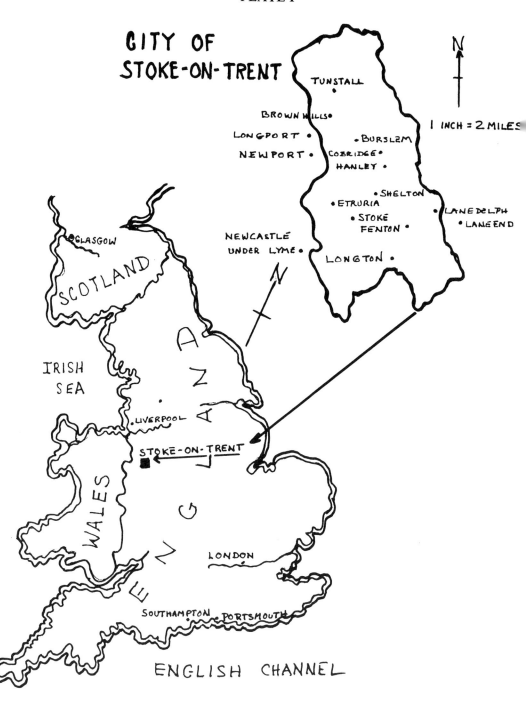

Location of the Staffordshire Potteries.

Introduction

Earthenware, made in England at Staffordshire, and decorated with Romantic transfer patterns in many colors has been ignored by the writers who have documented most of the other products from the potteries. In their enthusiasm for blue and white patterns, the early oriental designs and the so-called American "historical" china, the colorful transfer ware of the early nineteenth century has been relegated to near oblivion. But surely it was an expression of artistry, of fulfillment of customer demand, of successful commercial enterprise. Surely it takes its place in the parade of products affected by the development of the transfer printing process. To understand its place in English pottery history, an understanding of the forces at work in china production is necessary.

Let us go backwards in time to England near the end of the eighteenth century. In 1777 the Mersey and Trent canal was completed. Why was this a great event? Because up to the date the canal was opened, pottery made in the northern part of the county of Staffordshire had to be sent by carriage via the turnpike to the Mersey river at Winsford, or to the Trent River at Willington in order to be shipped to Liverpool. When the canal was finished, it was possible to ship goods to and from the sea at Liverpool for one-seventh the cost of earlier transportation. The Staffordshire potteries became one of the great industries of England. Until that time cheap Chinese porcelain was being shipped all over the world and caused formidable competition for the English potters.

The word "Staffordshire" means different things to different people, but basically it calls to mind the historically important potteries. To antique dealers it may be used in reference to statuettes, Pew figures, dresser boxes or chimney ornaments. It may evoke thoughts of historic scenes on glowing dark blue dinner ware. Dealers, for the most part, do not connect Flow Blue or Mulberry with the word Staffordshire, and yet this is where most of it originated. The buying public is always quite surprised to learn that the specimens in their collection came from a very small district in England. The area located in the northern part of the county of Staffordshire is only about 10 miles long, and according to Ormsbee, comprises less than twelve square miles. From this tiny area came all the dishes we will describe – plus all the useful and decorative Staffordshire items which have been sought by museums and collectors for years. It *was* and *is* made up of many small towns which in 1910 were bound together to form the city of Stoke-on-Trent. The names ring with memories of the great potteries: Tunstall, Burslem, Longport, Cobridge and Hanley, Shelton, Etruria, Stoke, Fenton and Longton.

Let us look at Burslem. In the sixteenth century, many abbeys were located here. The monks were the original potters and thus Burslem was one of the earliest potting centers. Both coal and clay were in abundance here and lead could be obtained nearby. The monks taught their laymen helpers the art of pottery making, and then in 1539 when Henry VIII closed the abbeys and monasteries, their pupils continued to produce useful wares for themselves. In 1600, the crown lands in Burslem and Tunstall were given to the holders who lived thereon, and because these were small parcels not suitable for farming, the holders turned to pottery for a livelihood. In 1616 legal documents for the first time describe men as potters. It must be realized that this was a peasant industry. The potters made clay pipes and butter urns which were glazed inside with lead in order to retain liquids.

In 1690 the Elers brothers from Holland came to work in the district and brought with them the secret of casting salt into the red hot ovens, creating an impervious glaze on the wares which resembled the pitted skin of an orange. This method of glazing was used on common clay and is still used on stoneware jugs and the like. Spies learned the details of the Elers' process and in 1693, Aaron Wedgwood is recorded as making stoneware.".

Mold casting was the next great development and became feasible in 1745 when the secret of making plaster of paris was learned. Molds made possible uniformity and mass production.

In 1761, Josiah Wedgwood added Cornwall stone to an earlier invention of Enoch Booth of Tunstall, who had invented a fluid lead glaze that gave earthenware a light tan color. Wedgwood called his product "creamware." He did not patent his process but gave it to all. Potters had been seeking such a medium in order to make dishes hard enough to stand normal usage, cheap enough to be sold economically, and smooth enough to be decorated attractively. In a letter written by Josiah we learn that by 1762 there were 500 potteries that employed 7000 people in or near Burslem.

In 1800 John and William Turner patented a new hard china. The patent was purchased by Josiah Spode in 1805 and named "stone china." In 1813 Charles James Mason of Lane Delph patented "Iron Stone China" which used scoria — scoria is slag of iron — powdered and mixed with clay, plus oxide of cobalt. This ironstone was sturdy enough to be used for cisterns and bed posts as well as table services and vases. Earthenware, which is the culmination of many of these processes, was and is the body used for transfer printing.

Until the development of transfer printing, decoration had to be done by hand. Cheaper adornment was necessary for mass production. Transfer printing was first used in about 1775 at Battersea, and in

Liverpool by Sadler and Green. A metal plate, usually copper, was deeply engraved with a design which for the most part was copied from a drawing. The color to be used on the finished product was rubbed into the lines of a warmed metal plate, excess paint was removed from the plate with a palette knife; then the surface was wiped clean with a cloth called a boss. A piece of specially made tissue paper was dampened and put over the copper plate. A print was forced onto the paper by an ordinary plate press. The printed paper was then lifted from the copper and carefully placed on the vessel to be decorated, and rubbed down by the women called "transferers" who used soft, soaped flannel. The women were responsible for placing the pattern on correctly, for joining the seams of the borders, and for applying the backstamp. Whether by accident or by direction from the manager, many times the backstamps were ignored. The backstamp appeared on the paper alongside the design, and was supposed to be cut off and applied with the thumb on the reverse of the vessel.

The dish was then placed in water, the paper floated off and the color remained. The piece was heated slightly to dry the color and then was dipped into glaze. It is of interest to note that the pattern disappeared at this point only to reappear after firing when the glaze had become transparent and glasslike.

Blue was a favorite color with the early potters. China trade porcelain had always been popular in that color. In 1784 Josiah Spode printed a Willow plate in dark blue, and in 1787, William Adams started his English and American views in blue. The other great potters of the day followed suit. Blue was the only color certain to survive the high temperature of the glaze process; but by the end of the 18th Century, many other colors were available.

It is at this time in the study of Staffordshire production that our subject appeared. The dishes we are discussing this time were often printed in blue — some in Flow Blue, and some in Mulberry and these were printed with Romantic transfer patterns. They were also printed in red, green, black, brown, purple and yellow. Some patterns evidently were issued in only one color but many were printed in different colors. The old factory sales sheets from the Adams plant called *all* reds "pink," and this name has been used by most cataloguers ever since. But what variations and shades we find! In red there is carmine and pale pink and rose, blood red and henna.

Blues range from darkest navy through a brilliant medium blue to the palest powder blue and turquoise. Greens run from bronze to forest to mint. We find pale lemon yellow and rich gold; the purples could be lavender or orchid, violet, plum or grape; we see browns, tans, chocolate, walnut and sepia, dove grey, steel grey and black. The potters were able to use two colors on a dish by printing the rim with one and the center design with another such as ruby red combined with a soft dark green, and also a surprisingly pleasing combination of brown and purple. The overall effect of the colors is muted when the pastels are grouped, and exciting when the glorious reds are placed together. In our day when we find interiors with decoration of steel, glass and chrome, the Staffordshire transfer ware dishes in sharp black or brown seem sophisticated and undated.

These colors were applied on the useful ware intended for common use. They were used in designs that evoke the Victorian age. The English of the early Victorian era were entranced by foreign travel. The aristocrats sent their young men on European tours of the continent so that they would become educated men of the world. Thus, we find patterns that include castles and rivers and Alpine peaks on the pottery designed for common men who could not afford the voyages, but could enjoy the pictures. The names of the designs give a clue to their aspirations and dreams, "Valencia," "Parisian Chateau," "Gondola," "Rhine," and "Villa." The lure of the Far East was strong, just as it is today and we find oriental fantasies called "Mogul Scenery," "Palestine," "Canton," and "Napier." Some of the artists were content to depict the beauties of their own country and created "Clyde Scenery," "Abbey Ruins," and "Crystal Palace."

Floral designs have been admired by all people of all nations. The English artists for the most part drew realistic flowers, leaves, buds and fruits, but some couldn't help adding an insect, usually a butterfly, in imitation of the Chinese artists.

The Victorians were almost obsessed with the glory of past styles. They favored Gothic adornment in architecture and decoration; they also liked French designs of the Louis XV and XVI periods. They even copied Grecian and Roman design elements. Later on in the century they turned to Japanese naturalistic influences and Art Nouveau became a forceful movement. But at the time the Romantic transfers were being used in great profusion, the typical Victorian purchaser wanted elaborate elegance, plus a touch of romance and history.

We do not know who the artists were; their names do not appear on cheap earthenwares. Only the largest potteries hired their own engravers. Many firms had to purchase from engraving companies such as Sargeant and Pepper of Hanley, who specialized in designing printed patterns and who engraved the copper plates necessary for printing. A popular design might be sold to several firms and we find the pattern such as "Asiatic Pheasants" made by many potters.

As a matter of fact, from what we have learned in this study, although some patterns bear the same name, most of the designs are very different. Of course, there is always the realization that a very popular pattern might be almost copied: that is, the elements could be placed in different locations on the dish and the rim design changed slightly. We find Classic patterns "Corella," "Athena," "Minerva," and others with borders that are very much alike; scenic designs "Epirus," "Aleppo," "Ivanhoe," with rim patterns that seem identical until close study reveals slight differences in the linear borders. Pale blue designs such as "Belvoir," "Garden Scenery," and "Isola Bella" bear a very close resemblance.

Since most of the Romantic transfer ware was produced from 1835 to 1850, we find the names of famous potters on them. The names of the towns of Staffordshire evoke the names of these great men. Here is the list that Simon Shaw made in 1829:

Etruria . . . . . . Wedgwood	Shelton . . . . Hicks and Meigh
Stoke . . . . Spode	Hanley . . . . Meigh
Burslem . . . . Wood	Cobridge . . . . Dillon
Longport . . . . Davenport	Tunstall . . . . Hall
Shelton . . . . Ridgway	Cobridge . . . . Clews
Hanley . . . . Dimmock	Longport . . . . Rogers

Greengates, Tunstall and Stoke . . Adams

These are the names you see on the backstamps of the Romantic transfer patterns. Most of the names live on only as a part of history. Long ago their firms were closed or sold to other companies. As you know, Ashworth still uses Mason's name and backstamp, but that is an exception.

There is a poignancy in handling a dish made by Samuel Alcock in 1830, or one made by the Clews brothers during their short term of 16 years that ended in bankruptcy; one feels a deep admiration for their artistry and for the high quality of the wares produced under almost primitive conditions.

This is also true of the dishes made by the other potters of the early Victorian era. Critics may disparage their wares as mass produced, but much of the successful transfer process was the result of carefully designed patterns, carefully mixed colors, graceful scalloped molds, skilled hand labor, and a canny foreknowledge of how to please the prospective buyers.

Staffordshire potters did indeed capture the world market for their transfer ware. The Staffordshire printed earthenware was sold and shipped to all civilized areas. The durable, inexpensive and charming dishes were a delightful bargain at the time and 150 years later they are still fascinating and well within the means of the average collector. They give us a glimpse into a past time, and create a mental link forged from the realization of the continuity in men's dreams, aspirations, and love of beauty and romance.

Floral Category

Floral Category

The beauty of flowers has always delighted mankind. The English are famous gardeners and landscapers. From the fabulous parks that surrounded the castles and mansions of the aristocracy to the cottage gardens of the working class, their love and care of growing plants is evident. No wonder we find such beautiful transfer prints in this field. In this section of the book we see renditions of formal garden blossoms as well as those of wild flowers. Some are grouped and represent a country, especially the thistle, rose and shamrock of Great Britain. Some of the designs are stylized and this was done surprisingly early in the period. But most are presented in their natural form. Sometimes another element may be added, such as a butterfly, or an urn, or birds, but the outstanding impression is that of the inherent loveliness of flowers.

ALBION

Made by William Ridgway & Co.

Albion is an old name for England. The name means 'White Hills' and describes the hills of chalk which make up the White Cliffs of Dover. The edge of this unevenly scalloped plate is decorated with a wreath of half flowers. A scalloped band of drapery forms a frame for the flowers. Beneath this, the rim is covered with a pattern of diamond trellis and each diamond is centered with a small flower. The bottom of the field is contained by swags composed of tiny rosettes from which short pendants enter the well. The bouquet in the center is composed of flowers which represent the English nation: roses for England, thistles for Scotland, and shamrocks for Ireland.

Marked W.R. & Co., GMK. 3303A, c. 1834-54.

ANTHOS

Made by Edward Challinor & Co.

The rim of this plate is panelled with fourteen divisions, but the outer edge is not fourteen sided. The simple circle is outlined by a white band from which foliated scrolls forming triangles descend across the rim at four points. Between the triangles is a large open rose flanked by leaves and having a small, two-handled vase and three astors at right. The rim design is contained at the well by a band of tooth-like rectangles and an inner wreath of scrolls.

In the center, a very large open rose is set in the foreground, with buds rising at its right and a pair of morning glories at left. A wall or table top projects towards the left, and a vase composed of scrolls is placed on its surface behind the large rose. The vase is tall and opens into a flat shell-like basin filled with flowers and sprigs. A single, large dahlia trails from the basin at left. Anthos is a Greek word, a combination word meaning "flower".

Marked E. Challinor & Co., GMK. 836, c. 1852-62.

APPLE BLOSSOM

Made by William Ridgway, Son & Co.

The edge of the plate is unevenly scalloped and is detailed by six small cartouches, and by six narrow winged half rosettes linked by sprigs. Three large branches of apple blossoms, buds and leaves alternate on the rim with a pair of smaller ones. A wreath of sprigs and pairs of scrolls are placed around the central picture which consists of a large group of apple blossoms, buds and leaves.

Marked W.R.S. & Co., Exact Mark GMK. 3308, c. 1838-48.

ASIATIC PLANTS

Maker Unknown

The white edge of the plate pictured is unevenly scalloped and is outlined by a printed band of dark shell-shapes outlined with white beads. These alternate with six triangular reserves on the rim. Each triangle, filled with small beads, is framed on the side by scrolls, and at the top by scrolls and fleur-de-lis centered with a rosette. The field between the triangles is stippled, and small flowers and sprigs are placed therein. The rim design is contained on the bottom by a white band filled with small triangles.

The well is encircled first by a wreath of beads and stylized leaves in a fine line, and next, by a wavy band, topped with dots and with heavy quatrefoils at the bottom. A leaf design with pendants is placed in the arches formed by the upper band. The plants of the title appear in the center, and consist of several exotic flowers on a single stem. There are branches at right, and some sprigs and berries at left and right.

AURORA
Made by Francis Morley

    The plates photographed display an oddity in that the cup plate bears no border pattern. Both plates have paneled rims, and both are outlined around the edge with a double narrow line. The rim of the larger plate bears a rim design of foliated scrolls, separated by baroque triangular forms. The central designs on both plates are indentical. Both are printed in three colours on the large flowers and on the leaves. The distinquishing feature of this pattern is the foliated scroll in the center, the large, central dahlia, and the wispy buds and sprigs.

    Marked F. Morley & Co., GMK. 2761, c. 1845-58.

AVA

Maker Unknown

The mold used for this plate is slightly scalloped and the upper rim bears a very narrow scalloped ridge. A printed wreath of fleur-de-lis connected by dotted bands accents the outer edge. Three long sprays of oriental-type flowers, buds and leaves are set around the rim and these are separated by a spray of lily leaves with a single flower. The central design is composed of a large vase filled with over-scaled peonies, prunus, leaves and sprigs, set upon a base of two large stylized flowers. An ornate fence is behind the vase and extends to the right and terminates with a spray of wide lily leaves and buds. In the distance at far right are pagodas and mountains.

The cup plate is a duplicate of the larger plate except that the peony tree has fewer blossoms and there is a single pagoda in the distance at right.

Marked Stone Ware.

BERLIN CHAPLET
Maker Unknown

The outer edge of this scalloped plate is embossed and the white embossed ridge is detailed by a narrow dark band of beads, a wider band of oval beads, and a row of dotted spearpoint. Three sprays of different flowers and baroque scrolls are placed around the rim, and part of this design enters the upper part of the well. The central bouquet is composed of baroque scrolls, roses, dahlias, peonies, daisies, forget-me-nots, leaves and sprigs. These form a circular pattern. A small bird is placed at the upper left between two roses.

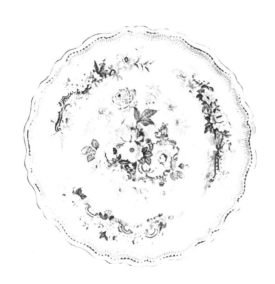

BRITISH FLORA (THE)
Made by John Meir & Son

The outer edges of these plates are unevenly scalloped and are white. The upper part of the rims are stippled. The rim design on the large plate consists of lacy dotted floral ribbon bands which form a wreath around the rim; as they dip towards the well they form an oval reserve on the upper part of the rim which contains three white leaves.

British Flora (cont.)

As the bands advance up the rim they form a shallow swag; under each swag there is a large rose or peony with dark leaves and small sprigs which enter the well. In three spaces on the upper edge there is a triangular design composed of foliated scrolls. Under each of these designs, scrolls are crossed and form a curved X, the bottom of which enters the well.

The rim of the cup plate shows only part of the ribbon design and has a single rose leaf and small flowers in the arched reserves. There is no pattern round the well and no part of the scroll pattern is used.

The center of the large plate is covered with a pair of large open roses, with stems and dark leaves. There are shadowy sprigs and small leaves and flowers surrounding the large blossoms. An overscaled butterfly perches on the roses at center and a small insect is at bottom right.

The triangular pattern in the center of the cup plate consists of a wild rose, small leaves and the insect.

Marked J.M.&S., GMK. 2633, c. 1837-97.

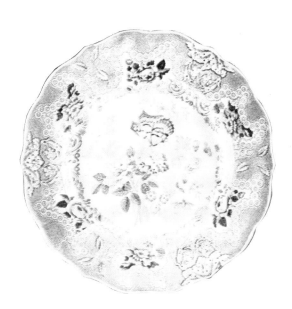

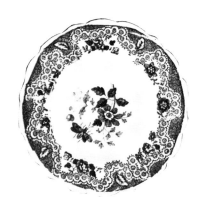

BRITISH FLOWERS

Made by William Ridgway & Co.

The outer edge of this plate is defined by a band of beads and leaf forms connected by small scallops. The well is encircled by the same design turned upside down. Four sprays, consisting of thistles, a large rose and shamrocks are placed around the rim. The central design is composed only of a large rose on a long stem with buds and leaves, and a background stalk topped with small flowers.

Marked W.R. & Co., and (imp.) Opaque Granite China GMK. 3303, c. 1834-54.

CALIFORNIA

Made by Francis Morley & Co.

This plate is slightly lobed and the outer edge is dark. A band of long, shallow scrolls is placed on a ribbon below the dark edge, and tiny leaf forms extend from some of the scrolls and entwine over the band. Four large peonies with dark leaves and tendrils on one side, and an angled scroll design on the other, are placed around the rim. Small buds and leaves and tendrils are placed on the scroll section. The center design contains a large foliated scroll design which forms a platform for a large ruffled peony at left, a smaller ruffled peony at right, and a table top for a small, oriental jar at extreme right. Leaves, prunus flowers and buds are placed over the scroll.

Marked F.M. & Co., GMK. 2760, c. 1845-58.

CASHMERE
Probably Made by John Wedge Wood

The dish photographed is slightly scalloped. The rim design consists of plaid stripes which alternate with a zig-zag filled stripe and one containing a geometrical floral design. Together these resemble a wallpaper pattern. The design enters the well. A wreath of sprigs encircles the central floral composition which contains a peony, passion flowers, smaller flowers, leaves and buds. An exotic bird is perched on each side of the peony.

Marked J.W.W., like GMK. 4276, c. 1841-60.

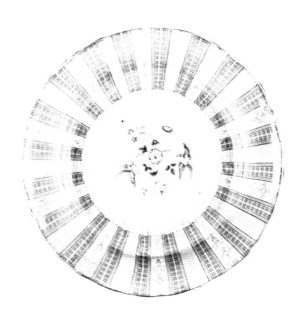

DAVENPORT

Made by William Davenport

The white outer edge of this plate bears an embossed band. A row of printed tiny dots in a double band contain the rim design at the upper edge. Six small pairs of flowers are placed in arches formed on the rim by a baroque scroll pattern which is filled with a pebble diaper design and small flowers. The medallion in the center consists of a frame of baroque scrolls around a bouquet of garden flowers.

Marked (imp.) Davenport and an anchor. Like Mark 1181A, c. 1820-60.

ETRUSCAN FESTOON

Made by William Ridgway & Co.

The rim of the plate shown is printed with symmetrical patterns of light and dark flowers. The light bouquets are placed over a double scroll, centered with a fleur-de-lis and joined by chains to the dark swags below. The dark flowers are placed over an open urn filled with a bouquet and are joined to the other urns by the swags and festoons of dark flowers. The outer edge is decorated with a band of rosettes. The center area, formed by both dark festoons and light quatrefoil swags, is filled with a spray of roses, buds and leaves.

Marked W.R. & Co. The exact mark is GMK. 3303A, c. 1834-54.

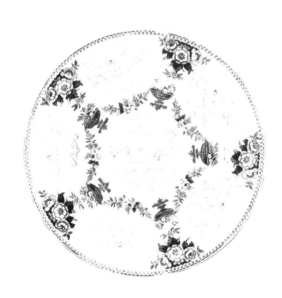

EXCELSIOR

Made by George Wooliscroft

Both the cup plate and the larger dish shown are twelve sided and both have dark rims which are decorated with roses, but there the resemblance ends. The rim of the larger plate is edged with scrolls, that of the cup plate with triple beads placed over a narrow line. The upper well of the larger dish is encircled by a band entwined with leaves and small scrolls under the bands. The cup plate rim is contained by a row of scrolls. Both dishes have designs which contain a vase or urn at left and overscaled flowers at right. These plates are actually printed with a very dark green border and polychrome flowers, leaves and urns.

Marked G. Wolliscroft, GMK. 4308, c. 1851-53.

FLORAL

Made by Spode

The edge of this unevenly scalloped plate is detailed by a band of small C scrolls separated by a dart in their centers. The background of the rim is covered with engraved narrow diagonal lines. Three white large pentagonal reserves, framed with beads arranged in an Indo-Chinese arch form, are set around the rim. They contain stylized exotic flowers and leaves in an Eastern design. The reserves are separated by trios of large realistic flowers, carnation, rose and dahlia, all with stems and leaves.

A larger version of the C scroll and dart wreath surrounds the well and contains the rim pattern. A passion flower, its buds and leaves, and some small sprigs are placed in the center of the well.

Marked (imp.) Spode 54, GMK. 3650, 1820-30.

FRENCH GROUPS

Maker Unknown

The edge of this unevenly scalloped plate is decorated with a dark band set with white dots and carrying spearpoint on the inside. The panelled concave rim contains a design of a cockatoo seated on a branch which is at right of a bouquet of overscaled flowers. A non-crested bird is perched in the center of the bouquet. The bird motifs alternate with flower arrangements similar to the above. A design of large daisies, leaves, columbine and forget-me-nots covers most of the well.

GROSVENOR

Made by Charles Meigh

   This gently scalloped plate has a rim design of five lobed, oval cartouches containing roses and tulips. The space between the floral designs is filled with narrow, concentric lines and a foliated scroll design, vertical oval beads, is placed over this field. The plate photographed is decorated with a dark line around the edge, around the cartouches and at the bottom of the rim design. Eight small, flat fleur-de-lis designs are placed beneath the rim and enter the well. The center design is a bouquet notable for the large rose and bud at left and the clumps of small flowers on a tall stalk at upper right.

   Marked C.M.&S. (imp.) Improved Stone China. GMK. 2620, c. 1851-61.

HAWTHORNE

Made by Davenport

The rim of the plate photographed is embossed with a ridge which is over-printed with a wreath of leaves. Three groups of hawthorne are placed around the rim and a small circular bouquet of the same flower is in the center of the well.

Marked with an impressed anchor and dated. GMK. 1181A, c. 1850-56.

IMPERIAL FLOWERS

Maker Unknown

A band of diamonds and short straight vertical lines interspersed with small flowers and sprigs is set around the edge of these irregularly scalloped dishes. A wreath of somewhat larger flowers, leaves, buds and sprigs encircles the lower part of the rim and enters the well. This floral wreath is omitted on the cup plate. In the center, there is a small bouquet of mixed flowers, a long stem with dark leaves at top and three little African daisy-type flowers in a triangle at right. There are shadowy sprigs around the main flowers.

JAPAN FLOWERS

Made by John & William Ridgway

The scalloped edge of this plate is embossed with a gadroon border. A row of printed scallops with fringe is placed beneath the molded edge. Three sprays of flowers and leaves on a branch alternate with three butterflies around the rim. In the well a very large floral design of a pair of peonies, leaves and buds is placed on a thorny bough at right. A small butterfly and a single blossom are beside the branch at left.

Marked J.W.R. "Stone China". It is GMK. 3260, c. 1814-30.

JESSAMINE

Mark Unconfirmed

The teapot shown has oval side panels printed with three large flowers which resemble camillias and which contain a pair of jessamine blossoms in the center. The outer edges of the panel are diapered with a shell design contained by baroque scrolls. There are small flowers around the base of the pedestal, on the handle, on the upper collar and on the lid. The owners of this piece believe the mark to be that of Bourne, Baker & Bourne and dated in the second quarter of the 19th Century.

It is marked "Opaque China" and B.B.&B.

PAXTON

Made by Francis Morley & Co.

Three groups of lilies are placed around the rim of the plate photographed. Their swirling stems meet and extend into foliated scrolls which form a paisley design over a small stippled teardrop shape. The scrolls continue around the dark outer edge. A single flower and bud with a pair of leaves is placed in the center of the well.

Marked F.M. & Co., GMK. 2760, c. 1845-58.

PORTLAND BASKET
Made by John & William Ridgway

The edge of the plate is deeply scalloped and each indentation is marked with an embossed rosette. Small, printed semi-circles of darts accent the arcs. The border design consists of butterflies and sprigs alternating with a spray of wild roses and forget-me-nots. The classic open vase with pedestal foot in the center scene is filled with a bouquet of garden flowers including a large rose, dark leaves and sprays, and some very small flowers. It is framed by a circle of the same darts used around the scalloped outer edge of the dish. The tureen photographed displays heavy embossed handles and the stand is graced with embossed floral handles. It is possible to discern the classic urn and flowers at the left on the body of the vessel.

Marked J.W.R. & "Opaque China", GMK. 3260, c. 1814-30.

REGINA

Made by Enoch Wood & Sons

A wreath of small ferns encircles the unevenly scalloped edge of the plate photographed. The concave rim is panelled. Three large stylized exotic multi-pattern flowers with buds and sprays alternate around the dish with three smaller plants which resemble a butterfly set on sprigs. A pair of the larger blossom is placed in the center of the well.

Marked E.W.&S., GMK. 4260, c. 1818-46.

"ROSE CHINTZ"

Made by Herculaneum Pottery

The edge of the scalloped cup plate shown is decorated with dark arches which contain tiny stars. Four swags of white laurel leaves are draped around the plate and there are rosettes at their intersections. There are small floral sprays on the rim. In the center there is a large, fully opened rose with dark leaves and several small flowers around it.

Marked with an impressed Liver bird. GMK. 2012, c. 1833-36.

ROYAL FLORA

Made by John Ridgway

The white edge of this plate sets off the irregularly scalloped form. Midway down the rim, a row of flattened "C" scrolls contains a pattern of small white rosettes set in a stippled field. The rest of the rim is filled with trios of flowers, joined to single posies by a narrow band garnished with sprigs. The central floral bouquet is framed by a wreath of the same rosettes used on the rim, set in a narrow, stippled, scalloped band. A wreath of spearpoint is placed on the inside of the band and points toward the center.

Marked J.R., GMK. 3253, c. 1830-41.

SYDENHAM

Made by Francis Morley & Co.

The outer edge of this plate is white and the upper rim is covered with a design of diamonds contained by a vine wreath. Exotic flowers and leaves cover most of the lower rim and enter the well. The largest blossom is a passion flower which is grouped with a pair of morning glories.

Marked F.M. & Co., GMK. 2760, c. 1845-58.

TUSCAN ROSE

Made by John and William Ridgway

The large plate and the two cup plates photographed are scalloped and the outer edges are white and decorated with molded beading contained by a row of printed tiny dark spearpoint. The rim pattern on the large plate consists of floral swags set against a network of fine lines. A chain of oval beads and rosettes encircles the center picture in which a butterfly is perched at top center over a bouquet of overscaled

51

Tuscan Rose (cont.)

flowers which include full blown roses. The bouquet is based in a baroque scrolled basket form. A fancy trellis rises from the basket at right center and small flowers entwine around the trellis. At right there is an overscaled dahlia. Small flowers are placed across the foreground.

One of the cup plates shown bears the exact transfer used on the large plate. The other displays an enlarged version of the basket, and omits the butterfly and trellis as well as the many other small details. The distinguishing features of the pattern are the baroque scroll at right, a part of the basket design, and the chain of ovals and rosettes encircling the well.

Marked J.W.R., GMK. 3260, c. 1814-37.

VICTORIA
Made by Samuel Alcock & Co.

The rim of this scalloped soup plate is covered with a swirling design of curved floral branches of white rosettes, small, dark stylized daisies and many sprigs. In the center, the curving branches are formed into a wreath. A different type of sprig is used around the wreath and one small rosette encircled by sprigs and leaves is placed in the center.

Marked S.A. & Co., GMK. 75, c. 1830-59.

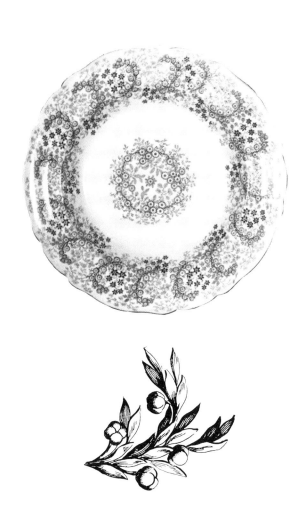

WOODBINE

Made by Thomas Till & Son

The pattern of Woodbine, which is a name for Honeysuckle, consisting of flowers and leaves and tendrils, appears on the side of the pitcher photographed. The bottom pedestal is encircled by a narrow band of the same flowers and the inner and upper rim of the handle carry a larger transfer of the same pattern. The wreath on the rim is contained by a dark band set with small stylized leaves.

Marked T. Till & Son, GMK. 3855, c. 1851.

Classical Category

Classical Category

At about the time the transfer process was being developed, the English government purchased a group of antique statues from a Lord Elgin who had removed them from the Acropolis in Athens following permission from the Turkish government. He was a British ambassador to Constantinople and at the time Athens was part of the Turkish Empire. His government bought the "Elgin Marbles" and placed them in the British Museum.

Josiah Wedgwood had been a pioneer in the introduction of classical designs. In 1767 he became acquainted with a book by a Count de Caylus that showed Egyptian, Etruscan, Greek, Roman, and French antiquities. Wedgwood hired a great sculptor named John Flaxman, educated in antique languages and arts, and between 1775 and 1787 Flaxman created classic designs of great artistry for the firm. Wedgwood copied the Portland Vase which had been found in Rome, and also made a pottery copy of a silver urn which was in Warwick castle. The transfer pattern "Warwick Vase" was made later and appears in this section.

When the artists and engravers made the scenes for the transfer process, they turned to the popular designs stemming from the antiquities and used them in combination with scenic elements. Sometimes the pseudo-copy of an antique figure appears as a statue in a formal stone building, at other times the dominant design is allegorical and the figures appear in a story-telling ambience. Often the classic feature is simply an urn or vase placed in an European garden.

AGRICULTURAL VASE

Made by Ridgway, Morley, Wear & Co.

The scalloped edge of this plate is outlined by a row of printed scallops and a fleur-de-lis design. The same band is used around the bottom of the rim pattern which consists of mossy branches interspersed with two rows of a small stylized four petal flower (shaped like a Maltese cross) with short curved stems flanked by three little leaves.

The scenes on the different items in this pattern differ, but each contains a vase with an agricultural motif. On this dish a large two-handled urn is at left. Its pedestal is decorated with the figures of three reclining sheep. A carving of a man driving his oxen and plow is on the body and the neck is garlanded with peaches, grapes and other fruits. The vase is covered, and a figure of a man holding a scythe stands on the lid. In the background there are flowers and small bushes. The vase is positioned on a grassy bank of a stream and there are bushy trees behind it to the left. Across the water a shepherd seated under a tall elm tends his flock. In the distance there are tall mountains.

Marked R.M.W. & Co., "Improved Granite China", GMK. 3271C, c. 1836-42.

ANTIQUES

Maker Unknown

This plate is gently scalloped and the outer edge is printed with a dark striated field contained by small white scrolls interspersed at eight points with small dark fleur-de-lis which alternate with oval cartouches filled with dots and topped with an acorn form. The rim of the plate is covered with scenes of ancient classic buildings, flights of stairs and tall trees. These are separated by four large double-handled vases.

The center scene is an octagon and contains a picture of two Greek women. One is seated and playing a lyre. The octagonal frame around the center scene consists of a ribbon-like band with small vines set in it and four small rectangular reserves on each of the four sides. The top of the rim design was cut off from the transfer used on the cup plate so that the urns seem to be handleless. However, the octagonal frame is the distinguishing feature of this pattern. The center picture of Europa and the Bull also differs from that on the larger plate, so probably the central scenes differ on the various items of this pattern.

Marked only "Stone China".

ANTIQUE VASES

Mark not located

The border pattern is inside this gravy boat. It consists of trios of flowers set over ferns and alternating scroll patterns. The central picture appears on the side of the vessel and shows five vases and urns set upon a slab which is surrounded by flowers and vines. The two-handled vase at left is elevated on a square step. The large urn at center is filled with sprigs, the design on it shows two women who face each other. Three covered vases are at right.

Marked with coat of arms and "Opaque Pearl".

ARCADIAN CHARIOTS

Maker Unknown

Two views of this small vase are presented so that one can see the temple at right surmounted by a statue, and a chariot at left pulled by a white horse and a black one. There are several persons on the terrace steps leading to the temple. A warrior holding a spear stands in the chariot and looks back toward the temple. In the background, there is a river and in the distance there are other temples and high mountains. Both the base and collar of the vase are decorated with a wide striated band of narrow parallel lines. White vines with small white leaves are placed over this background. The upper edge and the base edge are trimmed with dark triangles. A narrow row of scalloped straight lines forms a fringe under a white band that contains the rim pattern.

ATHENA

Mark Not Located

This plate is slightly scalloped and the rim mold is made so that the inner side is detailed by a molded scallop which projects one-quarter inch below the outer edge. The rim is filled with honeycomb diapering set in oblong reserves that are outlined with beading. These alternate with scrolled oval cartouches which contain a large classic ewer with a single handle at left. The bottom of the rim design is contained by scrolls under the urns and by a beading under the oblong areas. A narrow stitch-like band runs beneath the rim and around the well.

At right in the center, there is a statue of a pair of women, one seated and leaning against the taller who is half stooping. Both have long hair and wear soft, Grecian robes. In front of the statue at the right is a large urn on a square pedestal. In front of this there is a classical vase without handles and behind the two, there is a flat, wide dish on a pedestal. In the foreground at left, there is a balustrade, and behind the railing one sees a formal courtyard. In the distance, there are other balustrades and trees and Alpine peaks. In the right background, there is part of a wall, an urn and tall poplars.

Marked M.T. & Co., dated Oct. 1852.

CLAREMONT

Made by Joseph Clementson

The mold used for this soup plate is ridged around the top of the rim and the outer edge is detailed by a band of printed rope. Right below the ridge, there is a wreath of small flowers, leaves and stems which twines through the upper loops of a large, white, classical U-shaped design. The bottom of the arches meet, and a stylized white acanthus leaf is placed between each loop. Below each acanthus, there is a pendant, and below each hairpin opening, there is a triangular design. These two elements form a wreath around the well. The central picture is of large, classical urns, sprawling realistic roses, architectural effects at right and trees in the background.

Marked J. Clementson, GMK. 910A, dated June 1856.

CORELLA
Made by Edge Malkin & Co.
and by Barker & Son

The rim of the octagonal vegetable dish has oval scroll form cartouches in each corner. Each bears a picture of a tall, double-handled urn set on a platform in the center of a formal garden with balustrades and poplar trees. There is a small, squat dark urn next to it at right. The space between the urns is filled with a horizontal reserve which contains a diaper pattern of dotted circles. At the top, in the center of the horizontal patterns, a pair of scrolls meet under a small, white spade design and a swag of roses.

Gothic, geometric designs composed of straight lines are placed around the well. The scene is dominated by a statue at the right of a woman holding two infants. A tall, dark urn is in the foreground at right and there are smaller jars on either side of it. At left there is a formal garden with balustrades and statues. In the background, a very tall fountain plays in the center of a lake. In the background at left, there are poplar trees, a Gothic castle, and tall mountains. The soup plate shown displays the rim pattern clearly. The center statue is the same and there are minor variations in the background details.

The dish was made by Edge Malkin & Co., c. 1874-80, GMK. 1443. The vegetable dish is marked B.&S., possibly made by Barker & Sons, GMK. 256, c. 1850-60.

DE FETE

Made by Knight, Elkin & Co.

The outer edges of this cup and saucer are white. A row of printed inverted scallops containing beads enhances the edge. The rim is covered with a lambrequin design consisting of a wreath of white flowers entwining around a dark running scroll that bears leaves and a large fleur-de-lis. Eight small spear points are placed between the swags formed by the rim pattern. This can be seen on the cup.

In the center of the saucer, a large white vase, encrusted with rosettes, is filled with a bouquet of passion flowers, sprigs and buds. At left, in the foreground, an oval platter rests against the vase. Behind these objects there are parts of other urns or vases, a balustrade at left, and in the distance the facade of a columned temple surmounted by a statue. At right, in the middleground there is a dark ewer filled with flowers. In the foreground some small pine branches are scattered. In the far distance there is a white wall, a small white tower, and some trees.

Marked K.E. & Co., GMK. 2301, c. 1826-46.

DIOMED

Made by Joseph Clementson

The correct title on this platter is "Diomed Casting His Spear Against Mars". It is also marked "Classical Antiquities". The rim of the octagonal platter bears six reserves filled with various Grecian pots and urns. The reserves are separated by pairs of large foliated scrolls that are joined at the upper rim above the urns and vases. A wreath of acanthus leaves encircles the well. In the center scene, Mars is shown at left in his chariot. Diomed, at right, stands over a fallen comrade and is ready to hurl his spear. The entire background of this plate is coloured and the transfer print is in white.

Marked J. Clementson, GMK. 910A, c. 1839-64, dated 1840.

ETRUSCAN

Made by Hancock & Whittingham

The three vases shown on the side of this pitcher are placed on a platform, part of which projects toward the foreground. One vase, at left, is two handled, the design on it is geometric. The tallest vase has one straight handle, and the squat urn, also two handled, has a design of acanthus leaves. There are architectural effects of balustrades, columns and arches in the background. The rim design is composed of a Greek Key pattern, there are scrolls and stylized acanthus leaves on the handle and under the spout. The outer edge is detailed with a narrow dark band set with small crosses (xs).

Marked with a figure of a horseman. GMK. 1938, 1873-9.

ETRUSCAN VASE
Made by Enoch Wood & Sons

This dish is unevenly scalloped and the edge is detailed by a dark band. A wreath of foliated scrolls winds around the rim. Snail scrolls are set in the loops, and rosettes in the arches, formed by the wreath. Tiny winged fans, like small kites, are set in six places around the upper rim. The coloured rim descends into the well and is confined by a band of bars and rosettes set in squares.

The vase of the title is at left on a stone base that resembles a burial monument. The vase has double scrolled handles and is covered with a fancy lid with a finial; a dark tree is placed behind it. A balustrade is seen next to the stone structure. Beyond it at right there is a lake on which there is a small boat with white sails. In the distance there are buildings, a pair of palm trees and tall mountains. In the foreground, there are bushes at right and a jagged, dark fern at left.

Marked E.W.&S. GMK. 4260, c. 1818-46.

ETRUSCAN VASES

Made by Thomas, John and Joseph Mayer

The sloping rim of this dish, which is a comport, (11-1/2" diameter), is covered with a design of rounded snake-like scrolls that intertwine and present a circular pattern. In the center of each opening there is a quatrefoil. The scrolls are interrupted at four points with oblong reserves that contain a black sketch that seems pen drawn, and which is composed of scrolls and stylized leaves that flank an acanthus. The outer edge bears narrow lines centered with a dash and dot design. The well is surrounded by three bands, the uppermost is filled with very narrow vertical lines, the second contains a leaf and scroll pattern, and the third is a wreath of dentils.

In the center there are three vases on a shelf that is supported by a scrolled pediment. The largest vase is handled and resembles an ewer. A tazza is placed on the shelf in front of the vases at the right. A candlestick is placed at left behind the two-handled urn.

Marked T.J.&J. Mayer and "Longport". GMK. 2570, 1843-55.

HERCULANEUM VASE
Maker Unknown

The edge of this scalloped plate was left white and the transfer on the rim includes a dark, stippled field with short fringe that extends into the white edging. Large quatrefoils centered with a small, dark vase, form links between horizontal ribbons, filled alternately with foliated scrolls or small vases and other artifacts. A deep row of netting fills the rim and is contained at the bottom by a wreath of bold, Gothic designs, the points of which enter the well.

A large vase with Baroque handles, masks below the handles and figures engraved on the body, dominates the central scene which is framed by a row of narrow ribbon scrolls that echo the design on the upper rim. Behind the vase, there are lacy trees, and at left in the distance, there are a Grecian Temple, a dome, a tall tower, a minaret, and other buildings with flat roofs. In the foreground, a vase, very similar to the main design, but smaller, lies on its side amidst some ferns. A round covered jar and some flowers complete the scene.

LACADNIA
Made by Barker & Till

The edge of this plate is decorated with a band of small, square crosses centered with a bead. The rim is covered with a woven diaper design of the same crosses without the bead center. A narrow, dark band contains the rim design at the bottom and a band of hairpin designs, filled with a dark center, encircles the well.

A large statue of a cloaked figure whose hand is holding a sword is at left, and dominates the foreground. The statue rests on a three part pedestal and overlooks the coping of a pool. At extreme left, there are short Gothic columns and tall elm trees. Directly behind the statue, there is a large funeral monument. At right in the distance the spires of a Gothic church rise above a lake. There is a terrace with a railing in the center, and a man, woman and child standing on top of a flight of steps below the statue. Other people are below them near the lake, and a fountain plays behind the terrace railing at right.

Marked B.&T., GMK. 712, registered in 1848.

LAVINIA

Mark Not Located

The upper part of the collar of the pitcher photographed is covered with a stippled ground contained by scrolls at the bottom and a chain of ovals at the upper edge. Floral reserves alternate with small garden scenes beneath the scrolls. The scenes contain a picture of a man who wears a brimmed hat and stands near an urn on a pedestal. A girl, holding a book, is seated on a rug on the grass at right. In the distance there are mountains and trees. The same scene and the bouquets are used on the inside of the pouring lips of the pitcher.

The body of the pitcher is decorated on each side with a scene showing a woman in classic dress, who stands at right near an urn on a pedestal. She is holding a tall, slender, dark vase full of flowers. Classical buildings can be seen at left in the background beyond, a lake or river. Lavinia was the daughter of King Latinus. She was promised in marriage to Aeneas and is described in the epic poem by Virgil.

Marked EMG.

MINERVA

Made by Podmore, Walker & Co.

Both the large plate and the cup plate bear rim designs of four, shield-shaped scenic cartouches set against a background of a diaper pattern of eggcrate, contained by a frame of straight lines and topped in the center by scrolls and a fleur-de-lis. Each scene is the same and shows a woman in a white robe and scarf standing behind a large, two-handled urn. A small vase is at the right. A row of tiny dots is placed beneath the bottom of the rim designs, beneath the cartouches, and a band of triple narrow lines encircles the well and dips under the scrolls framing the cartouches.

In the center there are two women, one is seated, the other stands and holds a cup, or tazza, in one hand. There is a white bird on her shoulder. The women are placed in a paved hall behind two dark urns at right. In the foreground, there is a small, covered urn on top of a pedestal which is part of a railing. Behind the women there are halls, and arches and statues. The cup plate eliminates the urn in the right foreground and some of the background detail.

Marked P.W. & Co., and "Pearl Stone Ware", GMK. 3075, and like GMK. 3080, c. 1834-59.

MYCENE
Made by Hulse, Nixon & Adderly

This plate is ten-sided and the edge is detailed with white beading. Pairs of classical figures from the arts are placed against a stippled ground around the rim. Two depict a sculptoress, the other pair show a female musician. A band of lace-like scrolls decorated with letters that may be Greek enclose the scenic sections at the well and arch up over groups of seashells and seaweed at the upper rim. Small garlands of flowers and sprigs enclose the shell patterns at the well.

The central medallion is framed with the same ribbon design. It contains a picture of a very large two-handled figural urn set against pine and willow branches. There is part of another urn at left. In the background at left, there are steps, a balustrade and some bushes. At right there is part of a wall. Beyond that one sees a small temple and some other buildings on a promontory. There are tall trees and some mountain peaks in the distance.

Marked H.N.&A. GMK. 2133, c. 1853-68.

POMONA

Made by Anthony Shaw

On the rim of the plate shown there are four scroll framed oval cartouches. Each contains a picture of a tall two-handled urn set in a formal garden with stone walls and a poplar tree. A small dark urn is next to it at right. The spaces between the urn designs are filled with horizontal reserves framed in white and with rounded corners. These are filled with a diaper pattern of small squares filled with crosses (x). A pair of scrolls meet at the top center of the reserves at a fleur-de-lis, and a small swag of roses is placed beneath the fleur-de-lis. Gothic geometrical designs of double lines are placed around the well.

A statue of two women, one standing holding a butterfly, and the other kneeling at her feet, dominates the scene. A large dark, two-handled urn is in the foreground at right and a flat open dish is behind it at right. At left there is a two-tiered fountain. In the distance there are trees, a formal garden and a Tuscan castle.

Marked A. Shaw, GMK. 3497, c. 1851-82.

POMPEII

Made by John & George Alcock

The outer edge of this plate is detailed by a row of small triangles with beads placed beneath them. Eight small scroll-framed reserves containing sprigs, or small flowers and sprigs, are placed on the rim which is covered with a repetitive design of three flowers, curving stems and sprigs.

In the center, a large two-handled covered vase sits on a pedestal. Two women are pictured on the sides of the vessel and there is a wreath of acanthus leaves around the bottom of the body. An overscaled sunflower is at left and there are large leaves in the foreground at left. At right in the background, a small vase with cover also is placed on a pedestal. Sprigs are behind both vases and under the sunflower.

Marked J.&G. Alcock, Cobridge, GMK. 68, c. 1839-46.

"ROMAN GARDEN"

Made by Herculaneum Pottery

The embossed edge of this scalloped cup plate was left white and the rim design of roses, passion flowers and trophies is contained by a brocaded band at the top. In the central garden scene a woman (or statue) is seated on a klismos (greek chair) placed on a pedestal at left. She wears a tiara or wreath. There are many flowers in the foreground and a lawn and trees in the background.

Marked (imp.) Herculaneum, GMK. 2007, 1793-1841.

SYDENHAM

Made by Joseph Clementson

The cup plate photographed shows the border design of this pattern in detail. The rim is decorated with cartouches flanked by long, foliated scrolls. Each reserve pictures a statue of a woman and a large, dark handled urn at right. There are a lake, castle and mountains in the left background. These alternate with three small oval cartouches which contain a picture of an urn on a pedestal base. Both reserves are placed in a field of honeycomb diaper pattern. A row of fringe surrounds the well. There is a different scene on each of the various items in this set. The photograph of the sauce tureen and that of the cup plate, shows a statue at right with architectural details at far right. At left a lake can be seen behind a terrace and at left distance there are castles and mountains.

Marked J. Clementson, GMK. 910A, c. 1839-64.

TRIUMPHAL CAR

Made by J.&M.P. Bell & Co.

The platter photographed is slightly scalloped and the rim is decorated with four cartouches framed in foliated scrolls. Two reserves contain a picture of a fountain basin supported by the intertwined tails of a pair of dolphins. The other two, which are much larger, contain a scene of a cherub holding a cupid's bow as he rides in a classical chariot pulled by a pair of tigers or lions. Another cherub is astride one of the animals and holds aloft a crescent shaped object. There are temples and trees in the background of both cartouche scenes. The space between the reserves is filled with small flowers on a stippled ground. The same flowers form a wreath around the well. The punch bowl shown does not present the border design on the outside except for a small portion around the base. The cartouches and flowers are in a band around the inside upper rim. There is a triple row of beading around the edge of the platter and this is enlarged and used around the top of the bowl.

On the platter, a Greek or Roman warrior is pulled in a single chariot by three horses at center. Behind him, there is a large urn on a pedestal and an exotic plant with large leaves. In the right background there are willow trees and a temple. A river divides the scene, and at left there are triumphal arches on pillars surmounted by statues, temples, poplar trees and distant mountains. In the foreground there are small sprigs, bushes and flowers.

The punch bowl presents a picture of a goddess seated in a chariot drawn by lions. She also holds aloft a crescent and may represent Diana. She is escorted by a fawn and dancing maidens with tambourines. At left there are a tall fountain and tall palm trees, and the same exotic wide broad leafed plant that appears on the platter.

Marked J.&M.P.B. & Co., also an impressed bell, GMK. 318 and GMK. 319, c. 1850-70.

"URN AND ROSES"

Made by Copeland and Garrett

The rim and upper well of the scalloped plate photographed is covered with a design of three long scroll-framed oval cartouches which contain part of a garland of roses. The garlands continue across a diamond diaper background and swag beneath three vertical keyhole designs which are set between the long cartouches. The outer edge is trimmed with a twisted rope band. In the center scene a two-handled figural urn is set upon a plinth at left center. The body of the vessel is decorated with figures that resemble Greek gods. At right and in the foreground there are large, realistic roses, buds and leaves on long stems.

Marked as above, and also "New Blanche". Like GMK. 1091, c. 1833-47.

VERSAILLES

Maker Unknown

A Greek key design is placed around the edge of this plate and the rim is covered with a pattern of stylized Greek acanthus leaves which alternate with small bouquets set on triangular bases. Scrolls are placed in a continuous circle under the design elements and a dark band contains the rim pattern. A row of U-shaped arches which are pointed at the bottom, surround the well. In the center of the plate, a trio of urns appears on a platform at right. Realistic roses are placed between them. In the distance at left there are a large castle, poplar trees and part of a formal garden.

Marked J.G. Mark not located.

WARWICK VASE

Made by Enoch Wood & Sons

Four cartouches formed by foliated scrolls, large chrysanthemums, sprigs of small flowers and inverted scallop shells are placed around the rim of the platter shown. Each bears one of two designs of a handled figural vase set against a background of bushes. The cartouches are separated by large pairs of stylized lilies set in ruffled shell forms which are enclosed by scrolls, and filled with vines and berries set against a stippled dark ground. A pair of scrolls is placed beneath the flowers. There are forget-me-nots between and underneath the scrolls. These small flowers and those under the vase pictures form an irregular wreath around the well.

In the center scene the vase of the title is seen at left center mounted on a decorated pedestal that ends in a tomb-like gravestone marker. Grape leaves cascade down from the rectangular plinth, and there are large plants next to the urn and bamboo and elm trees behind it. In back of a balustrade at center and beneath an opuntia cactus plant at right there is a lake. A small boat floats in the water at center. There is a castle set against Alpine peaks in the distance.

Marked E. Wood & Sons, GMK. 4261, c. 1818-46.

WASHINGTON
Made by Enoch Wood & Sons

The plate is unevenly scalloped and the outer edge is detailed with a row of dotted triangles. Three scenic cartouches are placed on the stippled rim and each contains the same scene of pointed mountains, a temple upon a high bluff, another temple at its base, bushes at left, willow trees at right and pieces of broken columns and overscaled flowers in the foreground. Bouquets of flowers, fruits and leaves flanked by small urn shapes separate the scenic reserves. The stippled background has been allowed to end in scallops in the well. These scallops are trimmed with small scrolls and are linked by rosettes placed over a swag of ferns.

The central picture is dominated by a seated statue in the right foreground. This is a figure of a Roman holding a scroll and a pen. Behind the figure, there are a large urn, trees, shrubs, part of a railing and a lake. Across the lake there are castles, towers and tall mountains. This statue was purported to be the statue of George Washington by Italian sculptor Canova.

Marked E.W.&S., GMK. 4260, c. 1818-46.

WASHINGTON VASE

Made by Podmore & Walker

The border of this plate is printed with small scroll-framed medallions in each of which there is a picture of a vase in the foreground, a lake and buildings in the distance. These are separated by scrolled reserves filled with fish net diaper pattern and crowned at the top with flowerets. The well is outlined by a wreath of the same small flowers.

The center picture is dominated by a large covered urn at left. Its handles are made of birds with outstretched wings, and it is decorated with a scene of a deer who flees from 3 small dogs. At right is a smaller urn with long straight handles. The usual Victorian romantic scenic elements are present in the background, tall tropical trees, a lake, and castle-like buildings.

Marked P.W. & Co., and "Pearl Stone Ware" GMK. like GMK. 3080, 1834-54.

WEBSTER VASE

Possibly Made by J.& M.P. Bell

The platter photographed is six-sided and slightly lobed at the corners. The rim is panelled, its outer edge is detailed by a double row of narrow oval scallops and it is covered with a design of trailing branches and buds that resemble mistletoe. In the center of the well, there is pictured a two-handled urn which is set on a square narrow pedestal. The handles resemble a pair of coiled snakes with tails crossed toward the lower body. A grotesque leonine mask flanked by grapes is placed in the center of the vase.

The cup plate shows the vase in more detail, and the animal-like grotesque mask and also the entwined snake handles are clearly discernible. The rim design on the cup plate is taken from the lower part of the transfer used on the platter.

Marked with a tiny dark blue bell. It is like GMK. 319, c. 1842-60.

PLATE II

"Mosque" soup tureen, Made by William Davenport. Collection, The Campbell Museum, Camden, New Jersey, photograph courtesy of the Museum.

Oriental Category

Oriental Category

The first transfer prints made in England reflect the pervasive influence of the Chinese artists who created the patterns traditionally used on the porcelain products exported by the Chinese to the Western countries. One of the earliest plates shown in this book was made before 1800 by Joshua Heath, and although it bears a classic wreath surrounding words of tribute to his King, the border is decorated with a butterfly and fret design borrowed from the Chinese. The Willow patterns were derivatives from the same inspiration. Oriental flowers, baskets, urns, exotic birds, flowering trees and pagodas were depicted on English dishes. Canton china was in great demand in the West and the British potters, with the invention of transfer patterns, now had the opportunity to capture the world market in pottery.

As an extension of the current fascination with the Orient, the artists looked to other sources for Indo-Chinese designs. East-Indian motifs, geometric and arabesque, were evocative of the mysterious lands so far away. Mosques, minarets and desert scenes, men and women in Turkish or Arabian garb, African plants and animals, Japanese stylized patterns, all captured the attention of the engravers and artists involved in the transfer process. The designs were startingly novel and captivating, and the English artists mixed many of the exotic elements with European flowers and trees, and created "Oriental" patterns. The scenes, except for those taken from travel books, were, of course, imaginary. Hence we have in this section a melange of ingenious and charming fantasies.

ALADDIN

Made by John Ridgway

This plate is fourteen sided and the rim is paneled. A wreath of leaves surrounds the outer edge. The rim is covered with a basket weave design. The well is encircled by a deep row of spearpoint placed on the cavetto.

The field in the center is dominated by an elaborate pavilion with unturned tiled rooves at right. A stream of water divides the scene and is crossed by a single arched bridge in the middle ground. At left there are two tall elms and at extreme left there is another building. In the distance there are trees and a tall pagoda tower. In the foreground there are three people in a decorated boat with a curved prow. There is a Rococo reclining throne-like chair in the stern. One man sits and rows the boat, one stands in the middle, and one is seated in the stern.

Marked as above and "Stone Ware", GMK. 3254, c. 1830-55.

AMOY

Made by William Ridgway

The two dishes photographed have borders covered with intertwined dark and white swags. The dark ones are topped with rosettes, the white are tied with a ribbon bow. The bottom of the rim design is scalloped. A wreath of small swags is placed around the upper well of the tureen stand, but this is eliminated on the cup plate.

The scene on the stand shows a boat on a large river that divides the scene horizontally. One man poles the boat, which has an upturned prow and stern, and two figures are seated in the vessel. There are pagodas and temples at right across the stream. On the bank in the foreground, there are two tall trees, some rock forms, bushes and flowers. A man stands at the water's edge and points to the boat. Another man is seated at his feet. There is a small pavilion at left and in the distance one can see two other pagodas and a bridge. The cup plate design omits the boat and the buildings at right.

Marked WR, GMK. 3301, c. 1830-34.

ASIA DISPLAYED

Made by Joseph Heath and Co.

The edge of this scalloped plate is detailed with a double row of beads with small triangles on the outside and scallops on the inside. The upper part of the rim is covered with foliated scrolls and small flowers against a stippled background. In the upper design, there is a distinguishing element. This consists of three foliated shields with dark centers in which there are four distinct white beads. The lower part of the rim carries three sprays of small flowers that alternate with a pair of large flowers, one of which is dark and the other almost white but with a dark center.

The foreground of the central scene shows a man riding a camel. He wears a large turban, and is smoking a long pipe. A water bag is attached to the camel's flank. There are flowers in the foreground and a tree at right. A very ornate domed round building with a tall spire is in the right middle ground. In the background there is water and in the distance there are very tall towers, buildings and mountains.

Marked I.H. and Co. and (imp.) a propeller mark in a circle, GMK. 1994b, 1828-41.

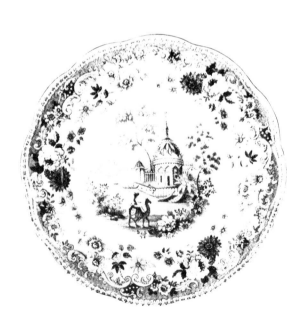

ASIATIC SCENERY

Made by Thomas and John Carey

The white-molded-beaded edge of this platter is enhanced by a printed row of beads set against a very dark band edged in white. The upper rim is covered with a dotted stippled field. Various large white flowers with dark leaves are placed around the rim. These are connected by baroque scrolls. Sprays from the flower groups enter the well.

The scenic transfer is dominated by a large domed building crowned with a crescent, which is placed in the center of the scene. A man stands holding a spear in front of the building and another man wearing a turban reclines on the lawn. At left there are other buildings and tall trees in the background. A white decorative fence extends from the left in front of the building and there are over-scaled flowers in the left foreground. A sailboat with curved prow and stern is in a river at right center. Three men are seated in it. One holds the tiller, one smokes a long pipe, and one is behind a central sail. At right there are tall trees, bushes, and over-scaled flowers. Across the river in the background, there are other bushes and trees.

Marked Careys. GMK. 772, 1823-42.

ASIATIC SCENERY

Made by Job and John Jackson

The edge of this scalloped plate is outlined with a wreath of scrolls placed over a stippled rim, in which three groups of flowers centered with a large lily alternate with three smaller ones that feature a wild rose. In between the flower patterns that appear on the upper rim are small pairs of forget-me-nots. Tiny rosettes and scrolls are placed over these.

The central scene is framed by a lace-edged, uneven scalloped line that is placed over the lower part of the rim. A wreath of passion flowers, cabbage roses, and sprigs encircles the upper well. In the center picture two turbaned men sit on a platform in the left foreground. One is smoking a hookah (a water pipe). Over-scaled flowers cascade over the platform. A large domed temple is at the left, and a tall elm tree rises beside it. A river divides the scene, and on the left bank there are several people on a raised platform decorated with a round open pavilion. Domed temples, minarets and exotic trees are in the right background.

The edge of the cup plate is detailed with embossed beading. The stippled rim is decorated with small sprigs, a pattern of three lilies under a dark trefoil, pairs of small white flowers under a shallow triangle composed of scrolls, and five-petaled white flowers with sprigs and leaves which are placed beneath a wide dark scroll containing three white dots at the left. A distinguishing feature appears in that the stippled background is allowed to dip into the well, and gives a lace-like effect around the center on larger plates in this pattern. The central scene covers the well and is dominated by a large mosque. In the foreground there are two persons at left. One sits on a bundle and the other stands near him holding a lance. There are over-scaled flowers in the right foreground.

Marked Jacksons Warranted, GMK. 2156, 1831-35.

ASIATIC SCENERY (JACKSON) (cont.)

ASIATIC VIEWS

Made by Francis Dillon

A row of small, dark, printed triangles is placed around the white edge of this scalloped plate. The upper part of the rim is stippled. Three large vignettes formed by scrolls and flowers, and flanked by bold embellished C scrolls at the top of the rim contain a picture of a camel with his head to the left. A man with pole stands in front of the beast. There are two scrawny pine trees at left and buildings with towers in the background. Pairs of large peonies and dahlias with dark leaves, buds, and fern fronds fill the spaces between the scenic reserves.

An open air pavilion composed of columns and arches, and topped with a large dome is at left in the central scene. There are smaller buildings nearby. A tall bamboo rises from behind the building and arches across the top center of the scene. In the foreground, a man is seated on a dromedary. Two men stand near him at left. At right a large dark urn filled with over-scaled flowers is placed on a square base surrounded by bushes and small flowers. In the middle of the scene an arched bridge crosses a stream. A small boat containing two men can be seen in front of the arch. In the distance there are minarets and other buildings.

Marked (imp.) Dillon. Also marked F.D. GMK. 1288 and 1288a, 1834-43.

ASIATIC VIEWS

Made by Podmore Walker and Co.

The edge of this saucer is decorated with a row of small white triangles. On the rim three scenic cartouches are set in frames that have a shell design at center bottom and are flanked by a pair of ruffled large C scrolls at top. These reserves contain a picture of a man who holds a pole and stands by a camel. In the distance there are buildings and towers. At left there is a pine tree. Pairs of large flowers with buds and springs alternate with the reserves.

The scenes differ on various articles of this pattern. The saucer shows a very tall open structure at right. It has a domed and flared top. There are other buildings next to it and a tall palm tree is placed behind it. At left there is an urn filled with branches and over-scaled flowers which is placed on a high pedestal. In the foreground a man is seated on a camel at left and two other persons stand together in front of him. One of the figures carries a banner over his shoulder. In the distance there are towers, a river, and a mountain.

Since Dillon also made this pattern, it could be speculated that Podmore Walker and Co. obtained the pattern when Dillon ceased manufacture in 1843.

Marked P.W. and Co. GMK. 3075, 1834-59.

AURORA
Made by Beech and Hancock

The plate photographed has a rim printed with random foliated scrolls placed over a stippled background. The outer edge is outlined with a narrow scalloped line, and the inner edge of the rim is detailed with double narrow scalloped lines. A row of scrolls on the cavetto surrounds the well.

The central scene shows two women in Oriental costume. They are in the foreground on a grassy bank covered with flowers. One is standing and holds a flower. The other is seated in a wicker yard chair. Behind them there is a small arched bridge over a stream. On the right bank there is a fancy gazebo with a lookout tower on its roof. A tall elm rises from its gnarled base at extreme right. At left there is a garden house and behind it one sees a fir tree and a tall maple. In the distance there are a turreted castle, hills, and trees. Clouds above complete the circular design. The outstanding feature in this pattern is the rim design in which the white scrolls all seem to flow toward the right.

Marked Beech Hancock and Co. with a printed eagle. GMK. 311, dates 1851-55. The same pattern is also found marked Beech and Hancock, dated 1857-76 and later, J.B. which is 314 and stands for James Beech who took over the Beech and Hancock works in 1877.

BELZONI

Made by Enoch Wood and Sons

Four different, unevenly scalloped plates are photographed to show the differences in the central design. The rims of all, with the exception of one cup plate, are edged with small diamonds and contain scenic reserves flanked by large ruffled C scrolls. Each scene is the same and shows two hunters standing at right. One is shooting a bow and arrow. The other, who is taller, is pointing toward some trees at left. The base of the tree and the hunters are printed in a very dark color. Tall light trees and mountains are in the background.

The largest plate shown, however, contains two different reserves on the rim. It shows the hunters, and the other two scenes show a man holding a spear who leads a donkey that carries a woman and a pair of large baskets. There is a villa at left behind them and bushes on either side of the scene. The spaces between the scenic reserves on all the plates are decorated with a large bunch of grapes flanked by small flowers, set against a stippled ground.

The three small plates (one a 6" plate, the other two are cup plates) contain a central scene of the man described above who is leading the laden donkey. The largest plate shows a man on horseback who holds a pennant on a spear. He is aiming an arrow at two ostriches which are in the right foreground. A small dog is at left and chases the big birds. There are three other horsemen carrying pennants in the background.

Marked E.W. and S. GMK. 4260, 1818-46.

BELZONI (cont.)

BLUE PHEASANTS

Made by George Miles and Charles James Mason

One of the pheasants of the title, which resembles a parrot, is at right. He perches on a coral formation that is placed over a large peony. The other bird is at center left under another large flower and a jagged leaf. The border design consists of stylized lotus blossoms flanked by dark fret patterns and an Indo-Chinese motif seen at the top corners on the platter shown. The outer edge is covered with a band filled with a honey comb diaper pattern.

Marked (imp.) Masons Patent Ironstone, GMK. 2539, c. 1818.

BOSPHORUS

Made by J. Jamieson and Co.

The outer edge of this octagonal platter is gently scalloped and is defined by a band of printed, rounded triangles and a white chain. The dark background of the rim sets off the border wreath of large white flowers, lilies and roses, with very dark leaves, that are joined by smaller daisies. The bottom of the leaves and some sprigs enter the well. On the plates in this pattern these form an irregular wreath.

The center scene is divided by a waterway, the strait that is called the Bosphorus which connects the Black Sea and the Sea of Marmora. On the left bank there is a domed mosque-like building and tall minarets. In the distance there are peaked mountains. Tall trees rise at right and in the foreground there are two men, one standing, smoking a pipe, the other seated on a tiered platform. There is a curved wall and a tall post topped with an urn behind the men.

The same pattern can be found marked Marshall and Co. who in 1854 took over the Bo'sness Pottery which is in Scotland. This pattern was made in Scotland, not in Staffordshire, but is of the same quality and type.

Marked I. Jamieson and Co. Bo'sness and (imp.) "Porcelaine Opaque", 1836-54. The same pattern can be found marked John Marshall who took over the business in 1854.

BYZANTIUM

Made by William Ridgway

The scalloped rims of both plates shown are covered with concentric lines that are filled with dashes and give a small checkerboard effect. A ring of interlinking ovals containing rosettes encircles the middle of the rim. Dark lines contain the rim design at both top and bottom. At the well there is a white circle and then a row of slanted hairpin loops from which beads depend.

The center scenes on both plates show nomad tents in the foreground placed in the shade of two very tall trees at left. On the larger plate two persons sit on a rug in the center foreground. There are no figures depicted on the little plate. Below the hill there is a flat roofed castle and in the distance beyond there is water on which there are ships. Minarets, domes, and a city wall are in the background. The city is Constantinople, the former name of which was Byzantium.

Marked W.R. and Co. GMK. 3303, 1844-54.

CANTON

Made by William Davenport and Co.

This plate is decorated with a band of dark triangles and beads and the upper part of the rim is stippled. A lattice pattern, consisting of three curved lines, like long C scrolls, is placed over the stippling. Small dark leaves appear in the trellis. At the point where the C scrolls touch toward the bottom of the rim, they terminate in a triangular design, ending in a rosette flanked by scrolls that enter the well. Five large flowers are placed in the openings created by the trellis arches. Small stylized flowers and dark leaves are placed around the large blossoms, and a few enter the well.

In the central scene on this plate, a large ovoid urn is placed on a pedestal. It has two handles and holds floral sprays. It is at right and sits on a stone platform. There are large flowers at the base of the platform. In the middle distance there are a man and a woman in pseudo-Oriental costume. Behind them there is a gateway and a gazebo with a dragon roof. Tall lacy trees appear in the distance.

Marked Davenport, GMK. 1185, 1820-60.

CANTON VIEWS

Made by Elkin, Knight, and Bridgewood

The gadroon edge of this scalloped plate was left white. A row of printed foliated scrolls is placed against the stippled upper rim. Three sprays of flowers and scrolls alternate with three floral swags which frame a daisy set against the upper rim. The well is encircled by a band of small triangles set in double scallops.

In the central scene, two men are in a boat in the middle of a river. One poles the craft, the other is seated. At right there are three small pavilions and a tower. A tall tree rises behind the buildings. At left there is an island with trees. In the distance, there are two other islands, one with palm trees. A small boat with a mast is in the distance. In the foreground there are flowers, rocks, and a large bush.

Marked E.K.B. GMK. 1464, c. 1827-40.

CHAPOO

Made by Ralph Hall and Co.

The edge of this fourteen-sided plate and that of the platter, is decorated with a band of spearpoint and the rim is covered with concentric lines that curve and point and form triangles, thus forming an effect of vertical divisions. A dark band of the same type with a bead placed under each angle encloses the rim design at the bottom of the rim. A wreath of scrolls is placed around the cavetto.

The central scene on the dinner plate shows a large pagoda at right. A stream or river divides the picture, and there are towers, poplar trees, and other plants on the left bank. In the distance there are mountains. In the middle of the scene, there is a flat bridge and three Oriental figures, one seated, two standing are on the bridge. A pair of tall elms rise in the middle of the scene. A pool of water, some rocks and bushes are in the foreground. The platter contains the same basic design elements.

Marked R.H. and Co., GMK. 1890a, 1841-9.

CHAPOO (cont.)

CHINESE

Made by John Ridgway and Co.

This plate is fourteen-sided and the paneled rim is covered with a design of six rows of crosses set in dark squares and graduating in size from the edge of the rim to the well. Between the geometric patterns there are vertical sprays of flowers set against six rectangular spaces. The border is distinctive. A vine decorated with clovers encircles the cavetto.

In the central scene, which differs on the various articles of this pattern, a two-story temple is at right. A tall, slender tower is placed behind it. At left there is an open garden house with upturned roof which is approached by a flight of steep steps. A river divides the scene and an arched bridge topped with a small shelter built like a gazebo connects the two buildings. In the foreground a man is seated on the lawn and two other figures stand facing him. In the distance there are a sampan on the river and pagodas in the distance.

Marked J.R. and Co., and a printed Chinese mark. GMK. 3259, 1830-55.

"CHINESE BAROQUE"
Made by Josiah Wedgwood

The upper part of the rim of this plate is very dark. A row of scrolls and large leaves is placed next to the dark area. Trios of large flowers set on a stippled field enclosed by baroque scrolls are placed in three places around the rim. A pair of flowers set over a lattice filled scroll and flanked by small flowers, alternate with the larger group.

The central scene is dominated by a large pavilion set in the middle of the picture. A bridge with carved railing and containing two arches is placed in front of the structure. Two small dark figures, one carrying a parasol, are placed behind some bushes and a rocky bank in the foreground. At right there are trees which include two palms. At left there are bushes, a lake, and a sailboat. In the distance, one sees a pagoda, two smaller buildings, and a pair of pine trees. Stylized clouds complete the picture.

Marked (imp.) Wedgwood and "S.S." GMK. 4075, 1830-40.

CHINESE CHILDREN'S GAMES

Made by Charles Meigh

The paneled rim of this scalloped child's plate (4¾ inch diameter) is covered with fine printed dots. Small vertical designs of alternating single flowers with two leaves and a beaded diamond on top of a rosette are placed around the rim. A row of beads contains the design at the edge, and a line of lacy scallops is placed at the bottom of the floral design but the dotted field continues a bit past the scallops.

In the center, two little boys in Chinese garb are blowing bubbles, and a third child at right tries to catch a bubble. The first two are on a platform and a piece of drapery is swagged over tree branches above them. In the foreground there are a basin, a flat dish, and some grassy sprigs.

Marked with an Oriental cartouche, GMK. 2618, 1835-49.

CHINESE FOUNTAINS

Made by Elkin, Knight, and Bridgwood

The molded, scalloped, white edge of the platter shown is embellished with embossed flowers which were also left white. A row of printed darts enhances the embossed design. The upper part of the rim is stippled. Bouquets of large flowers, four of which support a small bird at left, are joined by foliated C scrolls around the rest of the rim, sprays and leaves from these enter the well.

A band of beads, dots, and darts frames the central scene which is dominated by a tall fountain and a large circular basin. An over-scaled scroll design is placed behind the fountain at left, and tall flowering branches rise behind the scroll. At right this design is balanced by a scroll and the same flowering branches. A woman holds a water jug and stands in the center of the scene. There is a lake behind her and in the distance there are an ornate gazebo and adjoining building, trees and hills. Over-scaled flowers and leaves are placed across the foreground.

Marked E.K. and B., GMK. 1464, 1827-40.

"CHINESE GARDEN"

Made by Francis Dillon

A band of beads is placed around the outer edge of this saucer and around the outside rim of the cup. Three horizontal designs that incorporate a half of a flower at top flanked by stylized lilies set over a pair of scrolls and filled with a snail diaper pattern, alternate around the rim with three flowers that resemble butterflies set over a small fan and stylized white flowers. These are flanked by a shell diaper design. Small loops are placed under the diaper pattern, and festoons of small flowers are draped to the center of the scrolls under the half flowers. The stippled rim is cut in scallops at the well.

In the center scene a personage in turban is seated on a grassy lawn at center. He leans on a footstool and is holding a cup. A child stands at right holding a basket. In the background there is a gazebo with a loop on its roof. Another person with a black hat and vest stands in the gazebo entrance. There are dark bushes, a balustrade, and lacy trees in the background, and a round jar filled with flowers in the foreground.

The side of the cup contains a fishing scene. In the bottom of the cup the only design is the gazebo with the figure in black hat and vest.

Marked (imp.) Dillon, GMK. 1288, 1834-43.

111

CHINESE JUVENILE SPORTS

Possibly made by Thomas Barlow

The outer edge of this scalloped dish was left white, and a band of printed ovals is set under the white border. Large poppies surrounded by dark leaves and small flowers alternate with pairs of dahlias similarly treated against a stippled pebbled pattern on the rim. The flowers are separated by a shield design composed of foliated scrolls and filled with a darker version of the background pattern. Garlands of small flowers and sprigs are placed beneath the shield design, and these drape into the well.

A circle of spearpoint frames the central scene, which shows two boys and a girl in Chinese costume, who are whipping a top. They stand on a brick paved platform. Some grapes, peaches, and leaves are placed on the platform in the foreground. Behind the children there is a wall with scalloped top and two palm trees. At right there is a garden house. A flight of stairs leads downward in the middle. There are people at the garden house and on the stairs. In the background there is a lake and in the distance across the water there are pagodas and mountains.

Marked B. GMK. 267, 1849-82.

CHINESE LANDSCAPE

Made by James and Ralph Clews

The white edge of this scalloped plate is beaded. A dark line follows the curves, and a row of printed stars and beads is set within this. The rim is decorated with a bird design at three places. This consists of a bird perched on a scroll, another Asiatic-type smaller bird at the left, and a large cabbage rose at right. These alternate with triangular patterns of scrolls and feathers, flanked by bunches of grapes. A small bird is perched at the left in the second design.

The scene in the well is encircled by a wreath of small oval beads. An open garden house on an island is in the center of the picture. The edge of its upturned roof is scalloped and hung with small round bells. A lattice shed is attached to the house at left and there is a fence at right. In the foreground there is a boat with upturned prow and a sheltered canopy at rear. A man stands in it holding a pole. Another is seated beside him. The man who stands in the boat is holding out his hand to another person who is standing on the bank in front of the garden house. In the foreground there are large rocks and some shrubs.

Marked Clews Warranted Staffordshire, GMK. 919, 1818-34.

113

CHINESE MARINE

Made by Thomas Minton

The gadroon edge of this scalloped plate was left white. The rim pattern follows the scalloped outline with dark scrolls and small flowers. Three ovals appear at the top of the rim and are placed over a very large dahlia with buds and leaves on a dark stem which is attached to the oval at left. Three triangular forms at the top rim are connected at the left to a vertical pair of small flowers by dark C scrolls that resemble hooks. A trio of dahlias also appears in three places.

A band of oval beads frames the central scene, which is dominated by a large open arch in the center. Two figures stand on a platform under the arch which is approached by a long platform that appears from the left. In the distance at right there is a large horizontal two-story building. A pair of domed buildings with upturned rooves are on the hills behind the long structure. A river divides the scene and leads to a larger body of water in the background. At left there are hills and trees and there are mountains in the background. Near the platform a pair of very tall trees rises from the left wall of the platform and there are over-scaled flowers along this wall. At right in the foreground there are grassy hillocks, some rocks, and some exotic bushes.

Marked M and "Opaque China", like GMK. 2685, 1822-36.

CHINESE PASTIME

Made by Davenport

These plates are unevenly scalloped and the outer edges are decorated with a double row of small beads. The upper part of the rim is dark and is contained by small white scrolls. The rest of the rim background is stippled with a lighter color. At six points there are stylized round flowers flanked by a pair of foliated scrolls. Two star-shaped flowers and tiny buds are placed under these. In the six spaces between the white floral patterns, triangles are formed, and they contain a dark pair of flowers and leaves. A pair of round stylized flowers are on either side of the base of these triangles. The rim pattern is contained by a row of diamonds, centered with tiny quatrefoils and fringed with small tassels which gives a spearpoint effect.

The scenes differ on the various items on this pattern. One is with children playing with a hoop and a pinwheel, and another with a man pulling a carriage containing a lady with a sunshade. The sides of the sugar bowl show boys spinning a top with the aids of whips. In the inside of the sugar bowl, there is a scene of a man holding a bird in his hand. The top of the sugar bowl shows a gardener with coolie hat tending a potted plant. The cup plate contains the same picture as the sugar lid but omits the buildings. It contains the same rim design as the larger plates.

Marked as above, exact GMK. 1186,1820-60.

CHINESE PASTIME (cont.)

"CHINESE RUINS"

Made by William Davenport

The edge of this gently lobed dish is outlined with a row of dotted beads. A wreath of leaves, geometric rock formations topped by ferns, and slanted palm trees circles the rim.

The central design is stylized. Tall tropical trees line either side of this scene, which is dominated by a towering wall of a ruined building in the right background. There is a fence in the foreground, and another in the left and central background. In the center on a small mound, a man stands holding a parasol and talks to another man who is sitting on the ground. In the foreground there are ferns and triangular jagged rock forms.

Marked (imp.) Davenport over an anchor, GMK. 1181, 1795-1810.

"CHINOISERIE AFTER PILLEMONT"

Made by William Adams & Sons

The two cup plates shown are both printed in black. The first presents a scene of a woman seated in an open gazebo. It is slightly scalloped. The scene is placed over the entire surface of the dish. The second plate is not scalloped and the rim carries no printing.

The center scene shows a girl seated on a riverbank under the branches of a large willow tree. Next to her at left there is a large deep basket filled with tall covered bottles. She is gesturing a small dog or monkey which is climbing the bank at right. A stream divides the scene and at right across the water there is a pagoda. At extreme left there are a fence and some bushes. In the background at left, across the stream there are an island and another pagoda.

Jean Pillemont (1719-1808) was an important French artist. He created exquisite fantastic designs that peopled imaginative Chinese architecture and decor with small costumed figures. His work was very popular in England.

Marked (imp.) Adams, GMK. 18, 1800-64.

"CLEWS ORIENTAL"

Made by James and Ralph Clews

The rim of this plate is embossed with flowers and fruits. Flowers and leaves are printed over the embossing. The outer edge is trimmed with a band of small fleur-de-lis set beneath two narrow lines. The top of the well is also embossed with interlacing circles, and the design is printed over half of them. The well is covered with Oriental motifs of crane and fence, rock forms, and over-scaled dahlias and peony tree.

Marked (imp.) Clews Warranted Staffordshire, GMK. 919, 1818-34.

119

DAMASCUS

Made by William Adams and Sons

These three dishes bear the same design on their rims. The edge is outlined with a band of small triangles set above a white line. The reserves are framed by angular ribbons that end in squares under a floral pattern that separates the scenic areas. The scene in the reserves shows a horseman and a building with many towers, tents, and minarets. The background for the flowers and above the vignettes is covered with vertical zigzag dotted bars.

The saucer bears a design of a man holding a spear and driving a chariot pulled by a black horse and a white horse. Behind him at right there is a gazebo with fancy fringed roof and a tall tree. At left across the river, there are buildings, minarets, and three poplar trees. In the distance there are mountains. In the foreground there are some small flowers and leaves.

The large plate contains the scene of a horseman in the foreground who is pointing as he talks to two men who are seated on the ground. Behind them at the right there is a garden house with upturned roof and a very tall spire interspersed with onion shapes. There are palm trees and over-scaled bushes above and to the right of the structure. At left in the distance there are towers, domed buildings, and minarets set against mountain peaks. There are over-scaled flowers in the foreground and at left. The large plate is a later rendition of this pattern which has been attributed to Adams.

The cup plate shows the charioteer and at left there are bushes and a tall tree at right. At left across the river there are parts of a building and three poplars. In the background there are mountains. In the foreground there are many over-scaled leaves.

The cream pitcher is decorated with a different design on the rim and pedestal, but it does have a small area that shows the dotted zigzag lines on a stippled field, and the edges are outlined with the same small triangles above a white line. The chariot scene is the same as shown on the cup plate and saucer.

Marked W. Adams and Son (imp.), GMK. 22, 1819-64.

DAMASCUS (Cont'd.)

DELHI HINDOOSTAN

Made by Thomas and Benjamin Godwin

The edge of this eight sided platter is embossed. A narrow ribbon band outlines the octagonal shape as it follows the outer edge and passes under the molded floral handles. There are two pairs of cartouches on the rim. One facing pair shows a small boat on a river. It is passing domed buildings on the bank at right. The other pair presents two persons at left who stand near some dark rocks on the bank of a river. A domed temple is on the opposite shore. The vignettes are framed with foliated scrolls and with grapes and grape leaves on either side. The upper section of the rim is stippled. The lower part is covered with vertical curving lines and beads. A large bunch of grapes is placed over the lines in each corner and pale grape leaves divide the upper stippled part from the linear pattern. The vertical curving lines are the distinguishing feature of this pattern.

The entire well of the platter is printed with a scene inspired by India. An elephant with rider stands in the right middle ground. There are sheds and a large mosque at right behind the animal. At left in the distance there are other buildings. In the foreground a man sits on horseback. Another man with a pole stands in front of the horse. Two men are seated nearby. All wear turbans. They are in the shade of a tall lacy tree. Many bushes and rocks fill the extreme right foreground.

Marked T.&B.G., and "New Wharf" (imp.), GMK. 1734, 1809-34.

"EASTERN STREET SCENE"

Made by John and Richard Riley

There is a narrow band of diamonds around the edge of this gently scalloped plate. The rim is covered with a floral pattern of Sweet William and sprays of small orchids. Four shell-like scroll designs, consisting of ruffled triangular protuberances are placed between the alternating floral patterns.

In the central scene a large edifice is at right. It has apartments above an awning-shaped shop and is topped with a roofed open area, such as found in the hot countries in the Mideast. Other shops are at the street level next to the larger building. A square altar is at left in the background and a man stands before it making an offering to a seated image. Two tall posts rise from either side of the altar and are draped across the top with a ragged cloth. There are three figures inscribed on the side of the base of the altar. In the foreground there are three persons dressed in robes and tunics. There are ferns at left and flowers at right. An enormous flowering tree rises behind the altar and arches across the top of the scene. Vines dangle from its branches.

Marked Riley and "Semi China", GMK. 3329, 1808-28.

EQUESTRIAN VASE
Made by Joseph Clementson

This plate is slightly scalloped and the rim is covered with four scenic cartouches framed in an arabesque design which alternates with four triangular designs filled with a triangular scroll pattern set against netting. The scenic vignettes contain a large mosque in the center. In the foreground there are two men in tunics and pantaloons. One is seated, one stands. There are trees at right, shorter plants at left, a town in the distance. The spaces on the upper rim between the main designs are filled with four petaled flowerlets and the cavetto is covered with a wreath of leaves and berries.

The statue of the title is in the right foreground of the center scene and consists of Arabian horses on the pedestal, bowl and on the top of the basin. An allée of trees is at right, and at far right there is an urn on a pedestal. At left there is a platform and two robed figures sit on its edge. A man in a fez stands before them. A large Moorish castle is in the background and hills rise in the left distance.

Marked J.C. and Sons, like GMK. 910, 1839-64. (The other platter shown is titled "Alexandria". It presents the same horse fountain at right. The Islamic building is at left rear. The figures are omitted and over-scaled flowers are added to the left foreground.)

FAIRY VILLAS

Made by Maddock and Seddon

This is the original pattern which was afterwards made for many years by William Adams and Sons. The white scalloped edge of the plate is defined by a diaper pattern of beads and bars. The rim design consists of peonies that alternate with cartouches which contain bouquets on a point d'esprit background. The well is encircled by a wreath of tiny flower buds.

The center design shows a teahouse with stairs at right. There are tall trees behind it. At left there is a fancy porch with upcurved roof, and a figure holding a trident stands on the porch. In the background there is a river on which is placed a sailboat containing two figures. In the center background are trees and pagodas and in the foreground there are over-scaled flowers.

Marked M. and S., exact GMK. 2460, 1839-42.

INDIA PATTERN

Made by the Herculaneum Pottery Co.

The edge of this plate which is 4¼ inches diameter is covered with a scalloped pattern. The border of large flowers that appears on large dishes in this design has been cut in half, and the central scene covers the entire well. The specific pattern here is "View in the Fort of Madura". Two men ride in a howdah on an elephant as they approach a circular domed temple. There are three other persons dressed in white in the foreground. In the distance there is a river and across the water there are buildings and tall mountains surmounted with towers.

See Coysh Vol. 2, plate 38. 1809-20.

INDIA TEMPLE

Made by John and William Ridgway

This large scalloped plate has a white molded gadroon edge. The rim is patterned with four bouquets of stylized prunus set against a very dark ground. These alternate with four reserves, two of which contain a diamond diaper design with a floral symbol in the center, and two others that are filled with a fish scale pattern with a stylized floral reserve at top. Each reserve is framed on the side by foliated scrolls and a pair of small sprigs from each enters the well.

The central scene is surrounded by a row of delicate spearpoint and pictures a hexagonal three-story temple on a hill at right in the middle ground. Below it there is a small building with slanted roof, archways, and a semi-circular terrace. Two figures stand in the foreground on the bank of a stream. Each wears a pointed hat and each holds a pole. A large boat with folded sampan sails is at left. Behind the boat there is a promontory with trees. In the background there are other ships in the bay which is surrounded by sloping hills and high mountain peaks. Birds fly above the scene.

The cup plate is not scalloped, has no gadroon edge nor a rim pattern. The inner band of spearpoint was not used to surround the scenic transfer. Instead a bold wreath of arrowheads and points is placed around the edge of the plate. The same transfer as used on that of the dinner plate is used here and covers the entire cup plate.

Marked J.W.R. exact GMK. 3264, 1814-30.

INDIAN PAGODA

Made by Job and John Jackson

These three plates are all scalloped and a band of small bush-like patterns with oval beads at the base surrounds the white outer edges. The rim of the large plate is decorated with pairs of large scroll based scenes at four points. One pattern shows two tall pagodas and a little house set into hills on a seashore. The other pair contains a mountain peak topped with bushes and a small three-story building.

In the center a garden-like island at left has five buildings, four of which are towers or pagodas. A waterfall is shown in the foreground and at right there are bushes and trees and a lawn.

The cup plates are evidence of the different way transfers can be placed by different workers. One shows a small part of the scroll design from the border pattern, the other bears the complete scrolled flowers and besides carries most of the rim vignette. The other was decorated with an enlarged version of part of the rim scene. The bushy band around the outer rim is the distinguishing feature in this pattern.

Marked Jackson's, GMK. 2156, 1831-35.

INDIAN PAGODA (cont.)

JAPAN
Made by J. and M.P. Bell and Co.

This rounded oval well and tree platter has an outer edge design of zigzag lines and beads. Four fan-like medallions are placed at the corners. These are flanked by large leaves and small scrolls. Four horizontal sprays of Oriental stylized flowers (peonies, dahlias, and prunus) and leaves are placed between the fan shapes and a horizontal band of scrolls pointed in the center is placed above the flowers on a dark field.

In the center a large arch composed of beaded scrolls and enclosing a mosaic diaper design, encompasses a water scene containing a boat and rocks and pagodas at left. Over-scaled flowers are in the upper left of the arch, and a butterfly is over them. At right and joining the arch form, is a large dark urn decorated with a garden scene, featuring two men in robes. It is filled with over-scaled peony buds, leaves, and sprigs, and rests on dark rock forms. In the foreground there are large flowers with rock forms at right and lines which denote water. (Made in Scotland — but is of the same quality and type as Staffordshire.)

Marked Imperial, J. and M.P.B. and Co., GMK. 318, 1850-70.

JAPAN FLOWERS

Made by Ridgway, Morley, Wear and Co.

The rims of the plates shown are covered with a design of scenic cartouches, framed with scrolls and flanked by dahlias topped by a scallop shell. These alternate with a reserve filled with tiny sprigs on a stippled ground flanked by large double scallop shells that enclose a passion flower. The passion flowers are linked by a floral swag and scrolls and flowers descend into the well from the bottom of the shell designs. The scenic reserves each contain a different picture of a small garden house with two little figures in Oriental costume near lacy trees. Pairs of flowers and leaves are placed under the scenes.

A large urn filled with over-scaled flowers and tall branches is at left in the foreground of the central picture. At right a covered urn is set upon a small platform. A river runs diagonally across the scene and in the background there are towers and mountains. The cup plate shows different flowers and urn but they are placed in the same positions as above. The larger plate is scalloped; the cup plate is not.

Marked R.M.W. and Co., exact GMK. 3274, 1836-42.

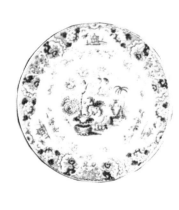

JAPANESE

Made by Ralph Hall and Son

The creamer shown bears the distinctive design on its side of a ricksha being pushed by a Chinese coolie who carries the handles over his shoulders. The vehicle is domed and draped and has two wheels. A woman is seated inside the contraption. There is an open gazebo behind an angled fence at left, a flowering tree at right and some water and pagodas in the background. The rim design is stippled and is strewn with flowers. There is a series of five U shaped ovals containing stylized flowers set next ,to a large spray of flowers on the lip. These ovals may alternate with another design on other items in the pattern. Deep triangular fringe, ending in trefoils and beads surrounds the upper collar.

Marked R. Hall and Sons, GMK. 1889, c. 1836.

JAPANESE

Maker unknown

The white edge of this unevenly scalloped plate is detailed with a band of printed beading. Six shield shapes framed by foliated scrolls and filled with a diamond diaper pattern, alternate with three festoons suspended from a scallop shell flanked by flowers and scrolls and with three pairs of flowers with dark leaves and sprigs. Above the pairs of flowers there are single stylized flowers flanked by scrolls and small sprays. The upper rim above the floral designs is filled with a worm track pattern. The bottom of the flowers enter the well and forms an uneven wreath. A large mosque situated on a river is at right in the central scene. A sailboat with scimitar prow is pulled up by the building. A gondola type boat is in the center foreground and at right there are over-scaled flowers. At left in the distance there are European type buildings with arched openings, tall trees, and mountains.

JAPONICA

Maker unknown

The saucer photographed is not scalloped, but both the cup plate and the child's toy plate are. The rim of the saucer is covered with small diamonds that give a point d'esprit effect. Six bouquets composed of peonies, forget-me-nots and daisies are set around the rim.

The child's plate bears the rim design of flowers but has no lace background. The saucer and the child's plate are decorated around the outer edge with small white dots on a stippled ground contained by scrolls which alternate with little flowers. The well of the saucer is encircled with a narrow row of rounded arches. The cup plate shown has no rim design at all.

All three items bear the same center scene, a baroque teahouse at left with a figure standing on its top steps. Another figure sits on the railing holding a pole. Both wear pointed broad brimmed hats. Behind the teahouse there is a flowering tree, and in the foreground there are over-scaled flowers. A sailboat is in the center of the stream. It has a covered shelter with a pagoda roof at the prow. A figure stands before the shelter and another person poles the boat. At right rear there is a house with upturned roof topped by a design that resembles a pineapple. Behind the building there are trees and a distant town. The boat is the distinguishing mark in this pattern. It appears in the bottom of the cup.

KAN-SU

Made by Thomas Walker

Both the plate and cup plate shown are fourteen-sided and the paneled rim bears a stippled pattern at the upper edge. Small leafy vines and flowers are placed over the stippling. The larger plate bears the complete rim design of a linked chain. Six large sections of the chain contain a scene of a European Gothic house, an arched bridge, and trees. The smaller connecting links contain three roses which are joined by the outer wreath of vines which entwines over the top of the scenic reserves. The lower rim background is covered with rows of concentric lines. The well is encircled by spearpoint.

On the cup plate only half of the rim design was used, and no spearpoint appears. The entire well of the cup plate is covered with the scenic central pattern. The complete picture appears on both examples and includes a large lakeside pagoda at right with curved roof and tall pointed decorative spire. A pair of tall trees, their trunks covered with flowers, are at left. There is a sailboat near the pagoda. In the foreground at right there are tropical bushes, and in the left background there are other buildings and mountains. Clouds are placed above the picture to complete the circular design.

Marked T. Walker, GMK. 3982, 1835-51.

135

KIN SHAN

Mark not located

A band of fleur-de-lis extends around the outer edge of this twelve-sided plate. The paneled rim is covered with wavy concentric lines, and a band of small mushroom-like beads encircles the well.

A pavilion is at left in the foreground in the central scene. Behind it there are tall trees. An arched bridge crosses a stream in the middle and links the pavilion to the right bank. Two people stand on the bridge near the pavilion. At right there is a large two-story structure which stands on a lawn high above the lake. There are bushes and poplars behind the building, and a pair of tall elms on the lakeside. In the foreground at right there is a flight of stone steps. In the background across the water there are a pagoda, tall trees, and mountain peaks.

Marked J. and V.

LANGE LIJSEN

Made by Spode

The title means "slender maiden" in Dutch, and the nickname for this pattern is Long Elizas. The pattern was taken by Spode from a Chinese design. The indented rim is covered with alternating designs of prunus trees in bloom flanked by low bushes, and scene showing a pair of Chinese girls looking at an arrangement of lotus blossoms in the center. There is a willow tree behind the girls and grass and bushes on either side. These design elements are separated by three swastikas and three chevron designs placed over a knot of double tassels. The well is encircled by a band of stylized lotus cups.

In the central scene a small boy hops or jumps as he approaches a fallen tree trunk and some bushes. A woman stands at right watching his performance. Behind them there is a bench at right, and a double arched bridge at left. A willow tree is at upper right. Its trunk arches to the left and its branches fall over the top of the picture like a curtain of rain.

Marked (imp.) Spode No. 28 GMK. 3648b, c. 1810-20.

MANHATTAN

Made by Ralph Stevenson

The rim of the scalloped platter shown is covered with a series of vertical arched designs. Trios of large flowers with dark leaves alternating with pairs of smaller blossoms are placed around the dish between the arches. A band of small dark beads is placed around the outer edge. The distinctive elements in the design consist of the diamond and loop at the top of each arch and the meeting of vertical lines in the well at a fleur-de-lis which forms small swags.

The central scene is framed with scrolls. There are several garden houses with upturned rooves on an island in the left middle ground of the scene. There is a winding river in the center of the picture, and a large boat with roofed shelter and upturned prow and stern carries five persons past the island. Another boat is at right. In the background there are islands with pagodas. A man with a parasol stands with a child on a grassy bank in the foreground. They are near a wide, curved, low bridge. Tall trees are at right, and large flowers and springs are placed at left and near the base of the bridge at right. The soup plate presents a different scene.

Marked R. Stevenson, GMK. 3707, 1832-35.

MANHATTAN (cont.)

MEDINA

Made by Cotton and Barlow, also made by Jacob Furnival and Co.

The rim of the large plate, made by Cotton and Barlow, is covered with concentric lines. Eight oval medallions are set into the background. Four contain a harbor scene with a large three masted boat at center and the other four which are smaller show a classic temple with a small dark sailboat at right. Sprays of flowers divide the vignettes and a vine of leaves connects the sprays around the top edge. The bottom of the rim design is contained by shallow scallops and flower forms and a second circle of a necklace of beads.

A two-tiered fountain of water falls into a large basin on a pedestal at right in the center scene. At extreme right there are tall trees. Several people are near the fountain in the foreground. At left there is a gazebo overlooking the river that divides the scene. A boat is placed just below the gazebo, and in the left background there is a temple with many minarets which probably represents the great mosque of Medina, the tomb of Mohammed. In the distance there are other buildings and Alpine peaks. Clouds complete the circular picture.

The cup plate, made by Jacob Furnival, is twelve-sided and the rim is paneled. The design is the same as that shown on the larger plate, but all figures with the exception of one person who is seated were omitted and so was the boat.

Marked as above (imp.), GMK. 1116, marked J.F. and C., GMK. 1643, 1845-70.

MEDINA
Made by Thomas Godwin

The rim of this scalloped plate is stippled. The outer edge is enhanced by small teardrops placed over a dark scalloped line that is beaded. Four oval vignettes flanked by dark side panels filled with rosettes and framed by foliated scrolls contain scenes of desert life. Each shows a different Bedouin tent, all have trees, and each contain costumed figures: some with guns, some with pipes, some seated, some standing. At the bottom of each vignette, there is a jewel form under three rosettes and five rays from each oval jewel enter the well. The reserves are separated by delicate branches of leaves and small flowers. At the bottom of each flowering stalk there is a group of six white stylized flowers and leaves. The rim designs are connected at the bottom with a double row of inverted scrolls with dotted centers, and beneath this, a lacy band from which delicate spearpoint extends to the center.

The central scene shows two men in Arab costume who stand in the foreground near a horse who is laden for a trip. Other people are sitting nearby at left under a canopy that forms a tent. A tall elm rises behind the tent. In the distance there are other temples, domed buildings, and minarets.

Marked T.G., exact GMK. 1731, 1834-54.

MEDINA

Made by William Ridgway

The lobed, eight-sided platter photographed carries a rim design of triangular foliated reserves filled with a diamond trellis design with half of a sun disc at the top and a small six petaled flower at bottom. These are separated by a pattern of large stylized bell flowers flanked with scrolls and accented by a swag of small flowers and leaves. The design differs on the various items of this pattern, but the platter photographed probably has most of the details of the original transfer.

Two men are on horseback on a riverbank near the center. In the foreground there are flowers, rocks, and bushes. On the ground are several jars and baskets of food and other supplies. Three tall palm trees rise at right, and two camels and a leader on foot are behind the trees. At left there are minaret towers, a square temple, tall trees, and garden walls. In the background there are other trees, domed buildings, peaked mountains, and clouds.

Marked W. Ridgway, GMK. 3300, 1830-54.

MOGUL

Made by George Miles and Charles James Mason

The rim of the platter photographed is covered with a wreath of stylized prunus, leaves, and small round fruits. The outer edge is decorated with a band of dark triangles and darts. A design of thick straight bars that resembles paling is placed around the cavetto.

In the center, the Mogul of the title sits in the shade of a parasol held by an attendant. Another gentlemen sits on a pillow below him. At left there is a table that supports a tall vase filled with flowers. A small jar placed on a round carpet is near the men. In the foreground there are stylized rocks, at right a stylized willow, and in the background at right, there is a house with upturned roof.

Marked Mason's Patent Ironstone China, GMK. 2530, c. 1813-29.

MOGUL SCENERY

Made by Thomas Mayer

These dishes all have scalloped edges, and the edges are defined by a wreath of heavy dark scrolls and small white five-petaled flowers. Swags of lace are festooned around the rim, and each swag encloses one or two flowers. These swags are the distinctive feature of this pattern. Small sprigs and flowers encircle the well.

The central scenes differ on the various items of this pattern. The scenes on the cup plate and the ladle are identical and show a man riding a camel past a domed building. The stand photographed shows a man at left adjusting the load on his camel while a man on horseback is at center.

The same scene appears on the side of the sauce tureen but the lid of the sauce tureen presents a zebra at front center. All have large flowers in the foreground and exotic trees at either sides of the scenes.

Marked T. Mayer, Stoke Upon Trent, GMK. 2569, 1826-35.

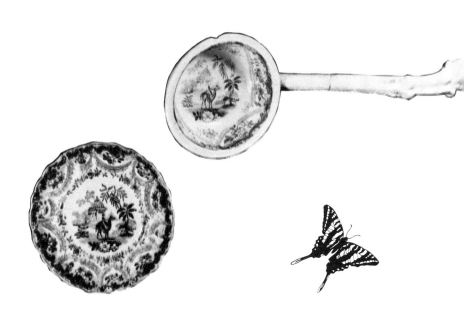

MOGUL SCENERY (cont.)

"MOSQUE"

Made by William Davenport

The rim on the lid of this soup tureen carries a design of fully open roses with leaves and buds. The upper rim is dark and stippled and is covered with a diamond diaper pattern. Arabesque designs and scrolls are placed between the roses and are part of the lower rim pattern of a lighter shade. A band of narrow running scallops outlines the outer edge of the plate and the bottom of the rim pattern.

In the center scene three black fishermen, dressed in white loincloths are in a skiff on a stream. A large mosque with dome and minarets is in the right background. At left there is a tall graceful tree rising from an island. In the background there are houses rising from another island. In the distance there are hills on which there are buildings. The largest hill at right is surmounted by another mosque.

Marked (imp.) Davenport and an anchor, GMK. 1181a, 1815-30.

NANKING

Made by Edward Challinor

Both the plate and cup plate shown are fourteen-sided and the paneled rims of both are covered with evenly spaced wavy lines that are separated by tiny dots. The dots are in vertical rows and give an effect of lacing. The rim pattern on both is contained at the upper edge of a row of white fleur-de-lis and beads placed against a dark band, and at the well by a wreath of arches whose sides terminate in fleur-de-lis. Small pointed lines are placed under the arches, and the combination of patterns forms a spearpoint design.

In the central scene of the larger plate, a tall elm rises from a base of bushes in the center foreground. There is a potted plant at its base and a man holding a pole over his shoulder stands at right on a nearby terrace. In the background at right there are a tall pagoda and mountain peaks. At left there are a two-storied house with flaring roof, part of a fence, and tall poplar trees.

The cup plate scene is dominated by a tall three-storied pavilion in the center background. Its base contains three square arches. A lake which covers the middle ground flows under the arches and there is a small sampan in the foreground which contains a single figure. A very tall tree rises from the left bank and other trees in the far distance complete the picture.

Marked E. Challinor, and "Ironstone", GMK. 835a, 1842-67.

NAPIER

Made by John and George Alcock

Both this cup plate and the dinner plate are unevenly scalloped and the outer edges are decorated with a combination of a geometric herringbone pattern, scrolls, and small stylized daisies in a band contained by double lines which echoes the scallops of the mold. Both plates have the same rim pattern: scenic pagoda vignettes containing willow trees and a boat at left alternating with the stylized Oriental pattern that denotes rocks combined with large flowers. The latter is flanked by scrolls and small tassels. The wells are encircled by a brocade band of geometric pattern inset with floral ovals.

The large plate contains a center scene which shows a woman holding a child by the hand and attended by a person who holds a parasol. A small willow tree is behind the servant. The group stands on a platform at right. At left there is a boat on the lake and a woman in the boat holds another child by the hand as he plays in the water with a fish net. An attendant in coolie hat poles the craft with one hand and holds a sunshade over the child with the other. In the distance there are two islands with pagodas and trees and on the nearest two persons stand on the bank. A tiny boat is near them. In the foreground there are rocks and leaves, and behind these there is an ornate fence.

The cup plate omits both groups of adults and children, omits the fence, and platform and shows only the willow trees at right, the islands, the two people standing on the island, the tiny boat at left, and some rocks in the foreground.

Marked J. and G. Alcock, and "Imperial Stone", GMK. 69a, 1839-46.

NING PO

Made by Mellor Venables and Co.

The outer edge of this fourteen-sided and paneled plate is detailed with a row of scalloped lines intersected by a narrow white line. The rim is stippled and twelve trios of white flowers, half placed around a triangle and half around a basket shape at the upper rim are placed over the stippled ground. Small dark sprigs emanate from each and form a wreath around the rim. A row of inverted half circles are linked by a narrow line around the bottom of the rim and these in turn are contained by a row of zigzag.

The central scene belies the Chinese name. Tall elms rise at the left. A chalet, tall spires and towers are in the right background. A stream of water bearing small sailboats is in the center. In the foreground there are two female figures in peasant costume. One kneels and holds a basket, the other stands and holds a bolt of cloth. There is another basket and some fruit near them. At right a woman with a fringed hat poles a boat that has a swan neck prow.

Marked as above with "Royal Patent" (imp.) GMK. 2646, 1834-51.

ORIENTAL

Made by William Ridgway

Both the cup plates and the saucer photographed show a rim covered with trailing branches and small flowers set over a stippled field. Small oval reserves filled with a vertical bouquet alternate with scenic vignettes that contain a domed building and tall palm trees. Both designs are framed with white flowers and branches. The top of the rim design is edged with a very small scallop and the bottom of the rim pattern is confined at the well by tiny fringe.

The scenes differ on most items on this pattern, but the cup plate with the odd ʹoversize rim pattern has a camel and rider in the foreground, trees and mountains in the background. The saucer has the same design, and all designs show a small domed temple structure at left. On the second cup plate the camel has been eliminated as have the trees at right and the mountains in the distance.

Marked W.R. and "Opaque China", GMK. 3301, 1830-34.

ORIENTAL (cont.)

ORIENTAL

Maker unknown

The edge of this soup plate is lobed and the slightly curved sides are outlined by a printed band of white beads, small diamonds, and dark scallops set over a narrow white string. The upper half of the rim is covered with slanting straight lines that form a chevron pattern set over a large stylized chrysanthemum and a simpler design that forms a linear pattern over smaller stylized dahlias. The chrysanthemums are flanked by stylized leaves and a lily design. The leaf patterns enter the upper well. The dahlias are flanked by lozenges which meet to form a design over a bell flower in the upper well.

A wreath of small scrolled lozenges encircles the central scene which is dominated by a very large fancy parasol in the center. In its shade there are three persons: a standing servant, a seated woman with a fan, and a seated youth with a top. They are placed on the steps of a porch. Behind them there is an open garden house. A river divides the scene and a small boat is at left. Across the stream there are towers. In the foreground at right there are over-scaled flowers.

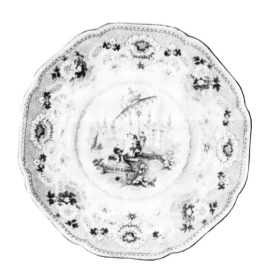

ORIENTAL FLOWER GARDEN

Made by Goodwin, Bridgwood, and Orton

Both this plate and the platter are unevenly scalloped and the white edge of each is gadrooned. A double band of printed scallops is next to the gadroon molding. The upper rim, which is stippled, is contained by baroque scallops that dip and form a reverse pointed C at four different points around the middle of the rim. Between these patterns there are double groups of flowers and these extend toward the center and enter the upper part of the well.

The central scene is circled by a band of small scallops and an inner band of beads. The scenes vary slightly, but over-scaled tall flowers known as peony trees are placed at the left on both dishes. They rise to the top of the picture from behind a fence structure which crosses the center. Other large flowers are placed in the foreground in front of the fence. At right there is an urn filled with flowers. It is placed on a pedestal with a scalloped apron. In the distance a river divides the scene. Two men stand on the right bank. There are pagodas in the background on the left bank and in the distance there are towers and mountains.

Marked G.B.O., GMK. 1739a, 1827-29.

ORIENTAL SCENERY

Made by John Hall and Sons

The first pattern shown is titled "Fakeer's Rock" in the Oriental series made by Hall. The cup plate has a border design confined by a rim of slanted leaf tips and consists of fruits and flowers, specifically grapes, pineapples, and a round fruit, a large rose, prunus, and Sweet William. The border descends into the well and is confined by a circle of small white scallops.

The central scene shows a far eastern type sailboat in the left foreground. Behind the boat there is a cliff hidden by trees. On its top there is a tall watchtower with pointed roof topped with a flagpole. In the distance there are mountains and trees. Large rounded white clouds complete the picture behind the dark tower.

Marked I. Hall and Sons, GMK. 1887.

The second pattern in this series is a large plate which is marked "Mahomedan Mosque and Tomb". This plate has the same band of stylized leaves that encircle the outer edge. The border contains the fruits described above.

In the center scene a rider on a camel crosses the scene toward the left. He is on a road that passes a large structure set upon a platform that contains three domed towers which is probably the tomb of the title. At extreme right on a high bank there is an object that resembles a lamppost, and at extreme left there is a tall lacy tree. Clouds and trees in the background complete the circular scene.

Marked I. Hall, GMK. 1885, 1814-32.

154

ORIENTAL SCENERY

Made by Thomas Mayer

Both the platter and the cup plate photographed are scalloped and the molded beaded edge was left white. A row of white pointed arched scallops set against a dark background and centered with a dark teardrop defines the outer edge. The upper rim is covered with a diaper design composed of diamonds and beads which is contained by large scrolls of sprays of large roses, peonies, and dahlias, flanked with very dark leaves, buds and forget-me-nots.

The central scene differs on the items on this pattern. The platter presents two boats rowed by oarsmen and containing warriors with shields and spears. The boat in the foreground bears a mask on its prow. A large Greco-Roman temple is at left and other temples are at right in the distance. Trees and flowers frame the scene on both sides of the platter. The cup plate shows part of a damaged temple at left and the war boat with masked prow approaching the steps of the temple. The identifying feature in this pattern is the outer rim decoration.

Marked T. Mayer, Stoke and an impressed eight-petaled rosette, GMK. 2569, c. 1826-35.

PALESTINE

Made by William Adams

These plates are scalloped and the edges are detailed with a row of pointed ovals and beads placed over a narrow white line. The rim background is stippled and is covered with a faint design of zigzag lines and dots. A ribbon design is used to outline scenic vignettes which are open at the well. The ribbon continues to a point on either side of the scenic vignettes and then rises to a point crowned by a pair of dahlias whose dark leaves fill the triangles thus created. Small rosettes are placed at each side of the bottom of the triangles, and a butterfly scroll center.

The scenic vignettes on the rims all carry the same picture of a man on a dark horse in the foreground. Another man in dark clothes stands near the horse at right. They are placed on a flower strewn bank of a river which crosses the picture. In the background one may discern a dome, minarets and a tent structure at left with a pointed roof.

The central scenes differ but all contain a tent-like gazebo with fancy roof set over a platform, also a river dividing the scene, with minarets, domes and mountains in the distance. All have figures in Persian costume. The largest plate shows many people including one on horseback, two women in the tent structure and two fishermen on a skiff on the river. The smaller plate and the cup plate each shows two persons near the tent. The cup plate has only three vignettes on the rim.

Marked Adams (imp.), GMK. 24, 1836-64.

PALESTINE (cont.)

PEKIN

Made by Enoch Wood

The fourteen-sided paneled rim of this plate is covered with a pattern of pale rustic fence pieces placed on a field of concentric narrow lines. Three rows of leafy sprigs are placed over the fence patterns. The outer edge is detailed by a band of white U shaped scallops on a dark field.

The rim design is contained at the well by a row of small scallops. A band of spearpoint, composed of a row of diamonds tipped with beads and pendant dots encircles the well. A man dressed in pantaloon, tunic and brimmed hat stands in the center of the scene. He holds a parasol in his left hand and points with his right. Near him there are two other persons; one is a lady who is seated in an elaborate wheelchair. Her attendant stands behind the chair. A lake is viewed beyond a rustic fence and there is an elaborate gazebo across the water. There are other buildings and bamboo trees in the distance. A tall elm and wide leafed plant are at extreme right. There are flowers and sprigs in the foreground. The pagoda and the fence are distinguishing features of this pattern.

Marked (imp.) E. Wood, and "White Enamel China", Burslem, GMK. 4248, c. 1835.

PERSIAN

Made by William Ridgway

This deep dish is scalloped, and the upper rim is covered with an all over design of sprigs and flowers which is contained by a ruffled and fringed scallop topped with small flowers. At three points the scallops form fans which enter the well and a bouquet of flowers and dark leaves is placed on top of these. Alternating with these are smaller fan shapes midway up the rim and a pair of garlands descend from them into the well and enclose a small marbelized field.

The central scenes differ in this pattern, and the rim of a large platter noted at a show was dominated by the fan and shell forms when seen elongated. The flower filled groups were placed in the corners of the octagonal platter and the floral field was very dominant and centered by a large fan on each side. The central scene shown here has two important elements: the large vase on a pedestal filled with stylized flowers at left and a boat with furled topsail and lowered triangular one at right. In the distance there are a temple, a town, and other buildings and hills. In the foreground there are the usual over-scaled flowers.

Marked W.R. and a beehive device, GMK. 3301, 1830-4.

SIAM

Made by Joseph Clementson

This twelve-sided dish has an embossed ridge around the paneled rim. Five unframed vignettes are set into a reticulated background around the rim. A band of spearpoint placed under two narrow lines contains the rim pattern at the upper well.

The central scene is divided by a body of water. Both banks are covered by domed temples and minarets. At left there are two palm trees and at right there are two elms. The banks in the foreground are covered with flowering vines. Tall mountains and clouds complete the picture. The distinguishing feature of this pattern are the domed scenic vignettes in the rim.

Marked J. Clementson and a Phoenix bird, GMK. 910, c. 1839-64.

SIMLA

Made by Thomas Walker

The design on the border of this plate consists of four shield shapes, framed with large foliated scrolls, which alternate with bouquets of dahlias, peonies and dark leaves. The outer dark edge is detailed with white scrolls. The center scene is of a towered pavilion at left. On its porch there stands a man holding a bird net. At right there are a tall bamboo tree and an overscaled peony tree set over a fret work structure. In the center foreground are two birds with curving tail feathers. There is a rock-form arch at left surmounted with flowers and some curved stone forms in the right foreground along with over-scaled flowers and leaves.

Marked T.W. see Godden page 734, 1845-51.

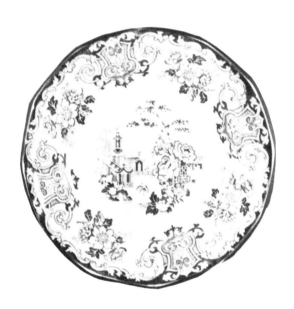

SINGAN

Maker unknown

The square scalloped dish photographed bears a butterfly pattern on the rim. The small half flowers with hooks and the small dark reserves are also distinguishing. A row of white dotted beads emphasizes the edge.

The willow scene in the center contains two men on the arched bridge at right. Another person is in the white pagoda doorway in the center. This design may be Spode's *Two Men Insect* pattern or *Ratcliffes of New Hall Works* as pictured in Little, Plate 48, which shows the peculiar half flower with hook inside the upper rim of the cup. This cup plate shows the same pattern and is imprinted in the same faint blue. The cup plate is marked G (imp.).

SINGANESE
Made by Ralph Hall and Co.

The outer edge of the larger fourteen-sided plate is detailed by a row of triangles crowned with beads and linked with oval beads surmounted by three tiny crosses. The paneled rim is covered with a sprig design. Five oval cartouches framed with irregular scallops are set around the rim. Each contains the same design of a rosette surrounded by sprigs. A group of five stylized dark flowers is placed between the oval reserves.

In the center scene a man in a tunic, trousers, and hat with a feather stands next to a woman who is seated on the grass. They are on a bank overlooking a body of water, which divides the scene. At left the bank is covered with over-scaled ferns, flowers, and two tall slender trees. At right there is a large square temple building with two tall fantastic towers. A small gazebo is attached to the large building and sits at the water's edge in the center of the scene. There are tall trees, large bushes, ferns and flowers surrounding the buildings. In the distance there is an island in the center of the river and there are towers and houses built on it. Alpine peaks in the background complete the scene.

The rim of the cup plate is not paneled and it is covered with only the upper half of the rim pattern used in this design, but even just a part of the pattern is distinguishing. The edge carries only a wreath of oval beads.

The central scene is different from that of the larger plate. It contains a standing figure dressed in tunic, pantaloons, and hat. He stands in the foreground near a small child who reaches for a pole held by the man. At right there are a coconut tree and other exotic tall flowering bushes. A stream divides the scene. At left there is a square stone temple surmounted by a tall pointed arch. In the distance one sees towers, buildings, and mountains.

Marked R.H. and Co., GMK. 1890a, 1841-9.

163

SINGANESE (cont.)

SIRIUS

Made by James and Thomas Edwards

Both the salad plate and the cup plate shown bear a printed triangle edging and the rims are covered with sprigs. Small stylized six petaled flowers are set around the rims.

The central scenes are the same, and may be supposed to represent a Syrian landscape. A couple dressed in Turkish garb are in the foreground. There is a tall flowering bush next to them at right. In the background at right there is a round building with conical roof. Other buildings and a tower appear against tall mountains in the background. A river divides the scene and a small sailboat is in the distance. At left a tall elm rises from a flowering and bushy bank. The cup plate is very like the large plate but the picture omits the tall elm at left.

Marked Edwards and "Porcelaine Opaque" and "Sevres" GMK. 1456, 1839-41.

SYRIAN

Maker unknown

This plate is gently and unevenly scalloped and the edge is detailed by a narrow band of pointed beads. The top part of the rim is dark. Four scenic vignettes are placed around the rim. These are framed with scrolls, small rosettes at top, and a pair of foliated scrolls at bottom and sides. Each contains a river scene with a sailboat at right that is passing in front of a tall roofed open pavilion tower in the central background. A small spray of flowers is in the foreground. The scenic patterns alternate with stippled reserves that contain a trio of large realistic flowers. The floral design is framed with the same design as the vignettes. The rim patterns are separated by a vertical pattern that resembles a lantern composed of scrolled hooks at top, a quatrefoil at center, and a pair of diamonds at the bottom. The rim design is contained at the well by a band of scallops and diamonds centered with a dot. Suspended from these is a wreath of hearts trimmed with lacy scrolls.

In the central scene a man seated on a camel is talking to another who holds the reins of a reclining camel at left. A bundle of wrapped items is in the foreground. Behind the figures there is a river and in the background there is a large round building that adjoins a tall tower topped with an onion shaped dome. Tall trees rise at either side of the scene, and in the distance there are little sailboats, trees, towers, and mountains.

Marked H.S.R.L.

TABLE AND FLOWERPOT

Made by George Miles and Charles James Mason

The rim pattern on this plate consists of five stylized flowers flanked by dark leaves placed over smaller blossoms and scrolls and five Indo-Chinese designs that resemble large spearheads. The latter are filled with a cellular diaper pattern and there is crosshatching in the areas above the flowers. The table of the title is at right and a small tray fruit is placed upon it. The flowerpot is a tall vase at left that is filled with peony trees and other flowers and leaves.

Marked Mason's Patent Ironstone (imp.), GMK. 2539, 1814-29.

TIPPECANOE

Made by John Wedge Wood

This is the same pattern as Singanese by Ralph Hall and Co. The only difference is the decorative band around the outer edge which consists of an outer row of five tiny straight lines over oval beads. A simple round mold was used here. Since Ralph Hall and Co. went out of business in 1849, perhaps Mr. Wood acquired the pattern after that and attached a different name to it. See Singanese.

Marked J. Wedgwood like GMK. 4276a, 1841-60.

VIEWS OF MESOPOTAMIA

Maker unknown

The white edge of this unevenly scalloped edge is embossed and the uppermost part of the rim, under the embossing, is very dark. The rest of the rim is covered with three Asiatic bird designs that alternate with a scrolled cartouche enclosing a scallop shell. The bird pattern consists of a pair of long-tailed crested pheasants who face each other as they perch on long foliated C scrolls which are flanked at the top with inverted cornucopia filled with flowers.

Four different sprays of flowers surround the central scene which is set in a rectangular frame of scrolls terminating in beads. A caravan is crossing the foreground of the desert scene pictured. Two camels and several men carrying spears are in the shade of a tall palm tree which rises at the left. In the background at right there is a large hexangle building with tall conical tower. There are domed buildings at left and other palm trees and hills in the distance. Mesopotamia comes from the Greek and means "Land between two rivers". The two rivers were the Tigris and the Euphrates. Mesopotamia is now Iraq.

PLATE III

"Columbia", Made by William Adams and Sons. 300 piece collection of William Stackhouse, Schnectady, New York.

Scenic Category

Scenic Category

In the early 1800s, with the advent of transfer printing, the potters were able to print pictures on inexpensive dishes. Before this time decoration was done by hand, the ware was costly and the production limited. Now plates could bear a scene of commemorative importance, such as those made to appeal to the pride of the citizens of the United States, or pictures of castles, mansions and abbeys dear to the English heart. Pastoral scenes, intended for the home market, and typical of their countryside contained rolling fields, domestic farm animals, groves of trees, ponds and brooks.

The figures in the foreground are usually attired in Medieval, Elizabethan, or Empire garb. Greyhounds are usually present at their feet as a sign of aristocray. Coursing (the sport of hunting hares with greyhounds, who pursue by sight) had been enjoyed by the wealthy since 1580. The addition of the costumed figures and the graceful dogs added a glamorous distinction to the designs.

It must always be kept in mind that although the names of real rivers and cities or countries were used as titles, the scenes were imaginary. The famous rivers and mountain ranges of Europe, and sites in America were freely depicted with foreground details of quaint villages and country cottages, or of great cities replete with spires and tall buildings. Most however contain dreamlike elements of tall graceful trees, a river or lake dividing the picture, an arched bridge, a gazebo, a castle or other aristocratic building or ruin, a stone platform with balustrade, wide steps to the water, and sometimes a statue or fountain, (or both.) These component could be arranged in different ways, but the results naturally bear a similarity.

The borders vary, some floral, some with reserves containing scenes, some are geometric. A few are uncomfortably alike, but most provide a dash of spice and save the patterns from monotony.

ABBEY

Made by Thomas Edwards

James and Thomas Edwards were in partnership from 1839-41. No mention is made in the various marks books as to when Thomas Edwards worked alone. This plate is twelve sided and the edge is detailed by a band of beaded scallops. The paneled rim is stippled and is decorated with a wreath of swags made with trios of small white flowers set on small dark leaves which are joined by sprigs. The cavetto is encircled by a wreath of dotted treillage contained by delicate white scrolls.

The abbey of the title can be seen at upper left in the central scene. It sits on a hill. There are six people on the grassy slope in the center. Tall trees rise at right. There are part of a wall and an arch in the lower middle ground. In the distance there are a lake, an island, and mountains. Vines and shrubs are placed on a grassy bank in the foreground.

Marked (imp.) T. Edwards and "Porcelain Opaque", c. 1841.

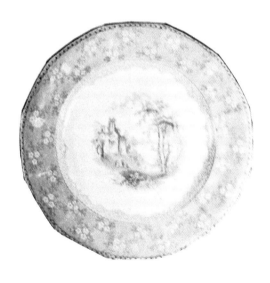

ABBEY

Made by Livesly Powell and Co.

The edge of this ten sided plate is decorated with a row of small fleur-de-lis joined with scallops. The same band is repeated around the well. The upper part of the rim is stippled and the stippling is contained by a wreath of white scrolls and leaves. Three framed oval cartouches containing a picture of a church building, an arched bridge over a central stream and trees on either side of the water are placed around the rim. The space between the vignettes is filled with narrow dotted concentric lines. A band of beads containing quatrefoils is placed beneath the lines and joins the bottom of the scenic reserves.

In the central scene four persons are in the foreground on the bank of a stream. Two women are seated on a rock. A man stands and points out the weed covered church ruins behind him to a standing child. The ruins are approached by an arched stone bridge at left. Tall trees are placed about the structure. There are other arches, towers, mountains, at left in the distance.

Marked L.P. and Co., GMK. 2386, 1851-66.

ABBEY RUINS

Made by Thomas Mayer

The three dishes photographed are unevenly scalloped, and the white outer edges of all are detailed with bands of tiny dark crosses and triangles. The stippled rims are decorated with four pairs of dahlias and large leaves which alternate with four patterns which contain a dark ewer, a scalloped figural medallion, a large ruffled flower, some fruits and sprigs. The cup plate shows two of each pair. These rim designs are each perched on a rectangular pointed bar surrounded by tiny flowers. In addition there is a smaller bar set in the well under each floral pair.

There are three deer in the foreground of the central scene of the platter. Two are lying amidst flowers and one stands near them. A tree rises at left. At right in the background there is the ruin of a large church, and at left in the distance there are trees and a ruin containing an arch.

The scene on the dinner plate shows a different ruin than the platter and it is placed at left. There are tall trees behind it. A stream divides the scene, and across the water one sees a bridge leading to town buildings. In the left distance there are Alpine peaks. In the foreground two cows stand in the water at right and three others stand in the foreground near some fallen columns. The cup plate shows three sheep at center left, a large ruined arch is behind them at right. A stream divides the scene, and other church ruins can be seen at left in the distance.

Marked T. Mayer, Longport, also (imp.) Mayer, GMK. 2568, 1836-38.

ABBEY RUINS (cont.)

ACROPOLIS

Maker unknown

The three dishes shown all bear the same edge trim of small hooked scrolls. The rim is decorated with a white brocade band filled with tiny flowers and C scrolls which is interrupted at six points by arches filled with cornucopia-shaped floral scrolls. Beneath the arches there are large vertical acanthus leaves which are the distinguishing feature of this pattern. The leaves end with a white rosette at the bottom and alternate with pairs of large white morning glories. The well is encircled by a row of white scrolls and a second band of small leaf forms.

The central scenes differ on these dishes, but all contain tall columns and temple ruins. Both of the round plates bear the same central pattern, but the scalloped plate bears a realistic version, and the plain plate has a stylized version of the same scene. The second plate, with the stylized version, is marked McK, and bears an ornate shield flanked with crowned animals, marked "Manufactory" on a ribbon incorporated into the mark. Below that is a round shield with a diagonal band marked McK. This was made by Kousnetzoff in Bronnitski, Russia after 1884. This plate is a late copy of the original pattern.

The fruit basket with its pierced sides is decorated like the scalloped plate, and the scene of columns, ruins, and mountains with small costumed figures in the foreground is realistic.

177

ACROPOLIS (cont.)

ADELAIDE'S BOWER

Maker unknown

This plate is deeply and evenly scalloped and the white outer edge is embossed and enhanced by a printed row of dark beads and a second row of white beads. The upper part of the rim is stippled. Two oval cartouches, containing flowers and scrolls flanking a tiny pair of swans, alternate with two cartouches containing a dark Japanese garden lantern at left, over-scaled flowers in the center, and a scene with a mountain stream and arched bridge and two small figures at right. The vignettes are separated by a garland of flowers, dark leaves, and sprigs surmounted by small reserves filled with a shell diaper pattern.

The central scene is dominated by three large columns at left, each topped with a different baroque finial. Two small figures in Chinese costume and coolie hats are seated on a platform at the bottom of the columns. Over-scaled flowers and dark scrolls fill the foreground and climb into the middle right. A Gothic (!) chapel with fancy roof is at the right rear. Tall lacy trees are placed behind the design and complete the circular picture.

Marked "Stone China".

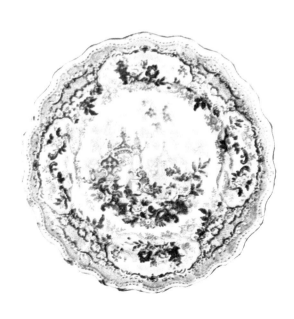

AILANTHUS

Made by C. & W.K. Harvey

This ten sided plate has a rim design of five scenic vignettes that are set without frames into a background of fine oval netting. Each scene is the same and shows a large tropical plant on either side of some flowers in the foreground, an open temple at right, an Eastern palace building and tower at left across the river. Tall peaks are in the background. The outer edge of the plate has a thin row of scalloped points, and the bottom of the rim design is contained by a very narrow white band, followed by a row of arches and triangles and beads that gives a lace effect.

In the center a very large urn is in the right foreground. Behind it there is a banana plant. There are several people in Persian costume in the center of the scene. Four are in the foreground near the urn, five others are in the middle standing on a platform overlooking a river. In the distance across the water there are minarets and domed buildings. At left there is a very tall tree, the ailanthus, with its air roots descending from a trunk. This tree was known to the Chinese as "The Tree of Heaven". Behind it there are some large reeds. There are flowers on the upper trunk and other blossoms appear on the tall palm like fronds at the top of the tree. The picture is circular, and is framed at top by the leaves and branches of a bushy tree that grows from behind banana fronds at left.

The Ailanthus, the "Tree of the Gods", is native to China. It bears small flowers which are yellow and light green and grow in clusters. Its leaves are food for certain silk worms.

Marked C. & W.K.H., GMK. 1968, 1835-53.

ALBANY

Made by John and Robert Godwin

The rim of this plate is twelve sided, slightly indented, and paneled. The uppermost part is very dark and the rest is covered with a wreath of grapes set between ovals formed by vines and enclosing single large grape leaves.

A chalet-type house is set at left in the central picture. Behind it at left and in the background there are tall slanted rooves of other buildings. A woman dressed in peasant garb and holding a child stands in the foreground. She is facing a man who is riding a pack laden mule. Another woman stands in the background at center. Tall trees arch over her head and white buildings can be seen in the distance.

Marked J. and R.G., GMK. 1726, 1834-66.

ALEPPO

Made by Clementson, Young, & Jameson

The outer edge of the rim on the plate shown is detailed by a row of small scrolls crowned with fleur-de-lis. Tiny flowers are placed on the outside and between the scrolls. The rim is paneled and is printed with vertical rows of triangular designs that resemble pine tree branches. A plain band contains the design at the bottom. A band of beads, scrolled arches, and pendant beads creates a spearpoint design around the cavetto.

The central scene on the dish shows classic ruins at right. In the foreground there are two boats on a stream that divides the picture. The larger boat contains a gondolier and three seated persons. A man waves to the group from the other boat. In the background there are a tall tree at left, Tuscan buildings, and a mountain peak. In the center background a bridge crosses the stream of water.

Aleppo is the second largest city in Syria and its importance dates back to the Hittites before 1000 B.C. A notable landmark is the great citadel dating from the 4th century B.C. It is situated on a hill overlooking the city. The building in the background may represent the citadel.

Marked as above and "Ironstone", GMK. 912, c. 1844.

ALLEGHANY

Made by Thomas Goodfellow

Both the dinner plate and the cup plate photographed are twelve sided, the rims are paneled, and the outer edges are decorated with rows of tiny leaves and stems. The rim design consists of five elongated reserves containing a lake scene with towered buildings in the distance and mountains and trees in the right foreground. These scenic vignettes alternate with a group of roses. The designs are framed by the wide links of a chain design connected with white quatrefoils. The bottom of the rim design is contained by a band of ovoid beads which is placed in the cavetto.

A river divides the central scene. There is a castle at water's edge at left and tall Alpine peaks rise behind the building. At right there is part of a terrace wall, an urn is set on the wall and a tall elm rises from behind the terrace balustrade. At left in the foreground there is a large white open urn on a pedestal. There are flowers and rocks on a slope beneath the urn. In the foreground there are three people, two men and a woman, who stand with a little dog on the bank of the river that divides the scene. On the cup plate the two men are omitted. The lady stands alone with her hand held out towards the dog.

Marked T. Goodfellow, G.M.K. 1738, 1828-59.

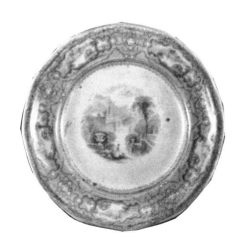

ANCIENT RUINS

Maker unknown

This tureen stand (tray) was printed in the same color as the pattern "Royal Sketches" shown in this category, and is marked with the same impressed mark. The dish is scalloped, the sides are cut to form an octagon and the edge is detailed by a narrow band of flat white scallops on a dark and medium dark ground. The upper part of the rim is filled with a vertical pattern of pleats of irregular lengths that give a lace effect. Small bouquets of flowers are placed over the lace. Swags of larger flowers and narrow ribbons are placed in each corner and pairs of larger flowers are on each of the four sides of the dish.

In the central scene a tall fountain rises from a basin and pedestal at left. At right a man stands on a platform in front of a ruin of a large arch surmounted by a statue. Gothic ruins can be seen in the right background. Behind the fountain there is a lake, and beyond the water one sees other buildings. There is a sailboat in the middle of the lake. There are flowers and bushes and tall lacy trees on either sides of the scene, and slabs, rocks, and over-scaled flowers in the foreground.

Marked N. (imp.)

ANDALUSIA

Made by William Adams and Sons

The edges of these plates were left white and were embossed with beads. The outer edges of both dishes are trimmed with a pattern that resembles small vertical leaves and little straight lines. Six oval cartouches, filled with diamond treillage centered with a large fan-like shell are placed against a very dark area at the top of the rim. Large realistic flowers with very dark leaves are placed beneath the ovals. The spaces between the above designs are divided. The upper half carries stylized flowers, notably a dark daisy at right next to a large white center blossom. These are placed against a stippled ground. The bottom half of the areas is encased in foliated scrolls that enter the well and form a Rococo triangle which is filled with a beaded ground. A wreath of triangles terminating in small tassels towards the rim, and containing rosettes encircles the central scene.

The first plate shows two people on horseback, one horse is white, one is dark. A woman, child, and small dog are standing in front of the horsemen and next to a tall gateway at right. A man stands next to the white horse at left, carries a spear over his shoulder and holds two greyhounds on leash. There are tall trees in the background and a gazebo with dome on a hill in the center distance. In the foreground there are stone steps, some shrubs, and at right two over-scaled flowers.

The second plate shows the noblemen at the hunt. A man stands near the riders and holds a spear, another restrains the dogs. In the distance there are trees and buildings. The gazebo with domed top is at right.

Marked (imp.) Adams, GMK. 18, 1800-64.

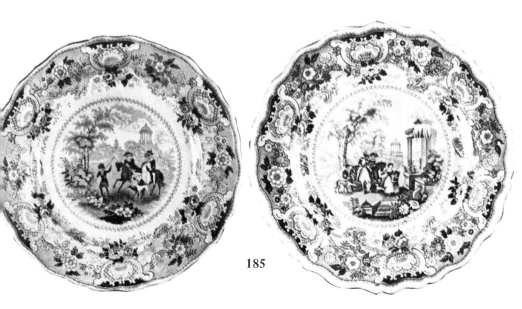

185

ANTIQUARIAN

Maker unknown

The unevenly scalloped edge of this plate is set off by a white molded beading. A dark line follows the scalloped outline and is decorated in turn by a band of little white scrolls that give a dentil effect. Small flowers are placed at six points in this line. The upper rim is covered with a floral diaper pattern. A row of foliated scallops connects six pairs of dahlias with very dark leaves which are placed in the center of the rim. There are small baskets of flowers suspended by chains under the dahlias and these enter the well. Swags of flowers are placed between the baskets and these garlands connect the ends of the scroll designs between the large flowers. The swags also enter the well.

In the foreground of the central scene there are a pair of resting deer. The larger one in the center has very large antlers. Over-scaled flowers are placed to the left and right. There is a ruined weed-over-grown Gothic tower at right. A tall elm rises from the ruined arches. In the background, across a stream, there is a large church. In the distance there are other buildings and trees.

ANTIQUITIES

Made by John Hall & Sons

The edge of this scalloped plate is decorated with a bold band of ovals, interspersed after each series of eight ovals with a rosette. The upper part of the rim is stippled and at three equidistant locations there are white stylized flowers set against a dark background which is contained by a wreath of scrolls. Three pairs of over-scaled roses and lilies with baroque scrolls at left, and pairs of small flowers and sprigs at right are placed around the rim. These are separated by a pair of medium-size roses placed over a long curving scroll and sprigs. The latter design is almost enclosed in a cartouche form except for a small opening at left.

The central scene, surrounded by a circle of beaded scallops, shows a sailboat at right in the foreground. A man stands fixing the sail and a woman is seated in the stern. At left there is a tall arch surmounted by statues and an extension from the arch which also is decorated with a statue.

A river divides the scene and at right there are tall trees rising from a rocky bank. In the distance there is a large double-domed building. In the foreground there are over-scaled flowers at left and some rocks and plants in the center.

Marked J. Hall & Sons, GMK. 1887, 1822-32.

ARABIAN
Made by Francis Dillon

Three plates are shown, a cup plate, saucer and dinner plate. These plates are unevenly scalloped and their outer edges are detailed with a printed band of small triangles containing a small dark vertical line and beads. The rims carry a design of four scenic vignettes which picture a temple with domed tower in the center, which is situated on an island in the background. There are tall trees behind the building. At left there is a sailboat and in the foreground there is a rowboat with two figures, one of whom is in the stern pulling at a fish net. There are tall mountains in the distance. Under each scene there is a wing-like form. Bouquets of flowers alternate with the reserves and are separated from them by curled diagonal, ribbon-like bands that end at the well with scrolls and are connected by a narrow band of small beads. The upper well bears a plain band and a row of white diamonds is placed next to this. A wreath of spearpoints is suspended from the diamonds. The spearpoint is shortened on the cup plate.

The scenes differ on the plates but the dinner plate and the cup plate each have an urn at right with trees behind it and flowers at its pedestal base. Each shows a stream dividing the scene and a temple on an island in the left background.

The larger plate shows towers and buildings on mountains behind the temple and a covered boat like a gondola in the middle ground. Both plates have over-scaled flowers in the right and left foreground.

The saucer shows a rider wearing a long, patterned skirt and plumed turban who is astride a noble black steed. In the background at right there is a gateway to a Moslem temple or palace. The saucer is not scalloped.

Marked F.D. "No. 7" and (imp.) Dillon, GMK. 1288, c. 1834-43.

188

ARABIAN (cont.)

ARCHIPELAGO

Made by John Ridgway & Co.

The plate shown is fourteen sided and the paneled rim is covered with a design of concentric lines filled with alternating white and dark, short lines. Five-petaled white flowers are placed midway around the rim. A band of double narrow lines, interrupted by crossed ovals and tiny matched scrolls, is placed around the upper well. Swags of small flowers are linked to the ovals.

The central scene is dominated by the boats seen in the foreground. A large sailboat with upswept, curved prow is at right. A rowboat carrying three figures is in the foreground and there is a smaller boat with sails behind the rowboat. Other vessels can be seen in the distance. At left in the background, past some rocky points and a tree, there is a church-like building with double towers. In the center distance there are other buildings.

Marked J.R. & Co., GMK. 3259, c. 1841-55.

ARDENNE

Made by Edward Challinor

The border on this saucer has a background of horizontal, concentric lines. The rim is divided at eight places by scrolled cartouches which contain alternating designs of dark and light floral garlands. A band of small spearpoint is placed around the bottom of the rim.

The center scene shows a large monument in the right foreground. A man, woman and boy are standing in the center next to the monument. Steps run down from the structure to a river which divides the scene. A man stands on the lowest step. There is a castle at left across the river. Tall trees are in the right background and clouds above complete the circular picture.

Marked E. Challinor, GMK. 835a, c. 1842-67.

ARCTIC SCENERY

Maker unknown

The rim of this scalloped plate is covered with alternating reserves which contain four different sprays of flowers that alternate with scenes of animals found in the tropics. The designs are separated by a band composed of rosettes and quatrefoils, and the same design is used to contain the rim pattern at the well. A second band in the well is stippled and a wreath of sprigs forms a deep arch pattern pointing towards the center. The outer edge of the rim is decorated with a row of rosettes.

In the central scene which fills the well two explorers are in the foreground. One is seated on the ice near a sledge laden with crates; the other man stands near him. In the middle distance at left some figures are working on a pair of tent-covered boats, that are set up on their keels. Other explorers can be seen on snowy peaks at left and near other sleds in the right distance.

Other plates in this series bear different tropic animals in the rim and different scenes in the center. Sir William Perry used sledges when he tried to reach the North Pole and this scene may commemorate his exploit.

ATHENS

Made by William Adams & Sons

These plates are fourteen sided and the rims are decorated with oblong vignettes which contain an Eastern scene of temples and domed towers and that are framed with fancy scrolls. A half-flower design in a dark field at the top of the rim separates the cartouches. The well is encircled by a thick row of arches and trefoils which effects a spearpoint wreath.

The central scene on the larger plate is dominated by a tall fountain mounted on a scrolled pedestal, and surmounted by a cupid holding a basin overhead. Behind the fountain there are tall, heavy trees. Two swans are placed in the water at center left and in the left background there are columned temples and some elm trees.

The cup plate design omits the fountain but contains all of the other elements. The swans are a distinguishing feature.

Marked W. Adams & Sons, GMK. 23, dated 1849.

BARONIAL HALLS

Made by Thomas, John and Joseph Mayer

The paneled rims of these fourteen-sided plates are covered with a network of loose diamonds and beads placed over a field of concentric, white lines. The outer edge of each is trimmed with a band of small dark arches topped by white quartrefoils. The lower edge is finished with a band of small white arches. A row of alternating long spears and double arches encircles the well on the cavetto.

A man, woman and child, dressed in Elizabethan garb, stand in the foreground of the center scene. Next to them at the left are two dogs, one dark and one light. Part of a stone wall and bushes are at far left and flowers and shrubs are placed across the foreground. The Baronial Hall of the title stands in the left center; its portucullis guarded by two soldiers with spears. At the right in the background there is a Gothic arch and tall trees.

The second plate presents the figures and two small, frolicking dogs in the center. In the background at right there is a tall Gothic castle, another Baronial Hall, with many banks of windows. The scenes differ on the various items in this pattern but all contain a castle and costumed figures.

Marked T.J. and J. Mayer, Longport, GMK. 2570, c. 1843-55.

BATALHA PORTUGAL

Maker unknown

This plate is gently indented in six spots around the rim and the edge is detailed by a band of white beads connected by small scallops. The rim is covered with a floral design. The same beaded design, as described above but in a smaller version, separates the rim design from the well picture.

A very large Gothic building, that resembles a religious seminary structure, covers the entire background of the center scene. There are trees on each side of the picture, and at left a shepherd watches over some white lambs. In the foreground there are six persons in different costumes. Four are seated, including a woman dressed in Portuguese fisherman's hat and shawl at left, and a child in a bonnet at right. A small white dog is next to the woman. There is a basket covered with a napkin on the ground near the seated figures in the center. Over-scaled flowers are placed across the foreground.

195

BATTERY & C, NEW YORK
Made by John and Job Jackson

A beaded, dark band outlines the white scalloped edge of this plate. The upper rim is stippled and is sprinkled with small flowers. It is contained at the edge by small scrolls. Six pairs of large flowers with very dark leaves form a wreath around the lower rim and the upper part of the well.

In the central scene a woman and child stand in the left foreground under the shade of a large tree. Two other persons stand in the center on the lawn of the Battery, the fort established at the base of Manhattan on the grounds of the old fortified area. A fence surrounds the park. A large pavilion, extending out over the Hudson River, which is in the background, is across the lawn. This is the "C" of the title; Larson on page 160 states that the view represents Castle Garden which was built on the Battery.

Marked Jackson's Warranted, GMK. 2156, c. 1831-35.

BELVOIR

Made by Joseph Heath

The deep dish photographed is fourteen-sided and the paneled rim is covered with concentric lines that peak at every one-half inch. This causes a vertical herringbone pattern effect. Pairs of branches, bearing oak leaves and acorns, are placed over the linear field. The branches cross at the outer edge and are tied at the center and resemble bowknots. They almost meet at the bottom and effect a swag design. The bottom of the rim design is confined by a narrow, dark, diamond beaded band in which small shields bearing a diagonal bar are set in twelve places above the well, and above a second row of spearpoint.

In the center of the scene in the well a rustic gazebo, shaded by very tall elms, is placed at right. It is connected to the bank in the foreground by a bridge over a narrow waterfall. At the entrance to the bridge a man, holding a fishing pole, stands talking to a man and woman; his dog is seated nearby. There are flowers and rocks in the foreground. In the distance at left there is a Gothic castle.

Marked J.H., GMK. 1933, c. 1845-53.

BLANTYRE

Made by John and George Alcock

The paneled rims of these twelve-sided plates are covered with narrow, concentric lines, and so are the collar and foot rim of the teapot shown. The concentric lines step upward every half inch. Short, deep swags of sprigs are placed over the linear background and these are topped with a single rosette. There is also a rosette at the bottom of each dip. (The cup plate displays the lower half of the rim pattern only.) Each dish has a running scallop composed of a dark and a light line at the bottom of the rim pattern. A net of pointed arch form is placed beneath the scallops and the spaces in the net are filled with small diamonds.

The central scene on the large plate shows a rustic pavilion at left. It is formed of arched, trellis work. A willow tree and an elm rise on the left bank in back of the pavilion. A small, rustic bridge crosses the brook at center. Three people, a woman holding a parasol, a seated man in tall hat, and a child, are at right on the grassy bank in the foreground. In the distance across the lake there are castles and trees.

The cup plate transfer omits the human figures and some of the trees.

The scene on the teapot contains the same elements as those on the large plate but shows many more castles in the background and in the distance at right.

Marked J. and G. Alcock, GMK. 68, c. 1839-46.

BLANTYRE (cont.)

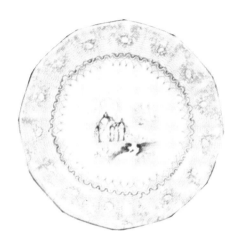

BLENHEIM

Probably made by Samuel Alcock

The rims of the plates photographed are covered with a pattern of sprigs and a large, curving branch of leaves. Unframed vignettes are set into the sprigs and contain a scene centered with a castle with a pointed tower which surmounts a hill. There are small white buildings at left, tall trees at right and mountains in the background. Bands of four loops are set under the scenic reserves and these connect with swags of rosettes placed under the leafy branches.

In the center scene there are many Alpine peaks, each topped with castles or towers. In the right foreground there is a large Gothic ruin of walls and a tower with ornated pointed rooves. At left there are two pine trees and a large boulder. Several rocks and shrubs are in the foreground and complete the scene.

On large plate a woman and boy, in peasant costume, stand near a donkey. There are steep rocks behind them at right and there is a lake in the background.

Marked Florentine China, with a beehive, see Godden page 18, c. 1830-59.

BOLOGNA

Made by William Adams & Sons

The rim of this plate is scalloped and is concave. The outer edge is detailed with a row of small beads. Concentric, wave-like lines are placed around the rim. Six reserves are set into this field. Three of them contain large flowers and dark leaves, and the alternating three show a scene of two men on the shore, one is pointing at a sailboat at right. In the center distance there is a temple with a pediment and attached domed towers. The reserves are framed by heavy C scrolls that resemble caterpillars. These scrolls also frame the back stamp on the reverse side of the dishes. A row of vertical keys descends into the well and frames the central scene. The entire border design is elaborate and distinctive.

The scenes differ on various sizes of the plates and on the hollow-ware in this pattern. The plate photographed shows a gondola containing three men and three women in the foreground, and it approaches a landing that has a balustrade terminating with an urn at left. In the background there are many city buildings and in the distance there are mountains. Laidecker stated there were no hollow pieces made in this pattern. Here is an example of a pitcher that has a scene similar to that described on the plate, the border is completely different, but it is back-stamped Bologna.

Marked (imp.) Adams, GMK. 18, c. 1830-40.

BOSPHORUS (THE)

Made by Ralph Hall & Co.

The edge of this plate is decorated with an outer band of triangles, narrow scalloped lines, and a deep wreath composed of dark rosettes with white centers and a tiny wreath of flowers placed under the outer band. Five trios of stylized flowers, ferns and sprigs alternate with five groups of wheat heads, tiny flowers and leaves around the rim. The bottom of both designs enter the well. The wheat design is distinctive.

The center scene shows a man in a turban who is punting a small ornate boat on a lake in front of a small temple that has a parasol roof. A lady sits in the boat near the curved, upturned stern. A large tassel linked to the craft by a narrow line is seen at right as it trails in the water. The high prow is carved with a dragon-head design and there is a tasseled canopy covering the front part of the boat. At left there is an urn full of flowers, steps leading down to the lake, part of a railing and tall trees. In the distance there are a sailboat, towers, trees and mountains. In the foreground there are small baroque scrolls at left and some flowers and ferns at center.

Marked R. Hall & Co., GMK. 1890, c. 1841-9.

BOSPHORUS

Made by Thomas, John and Joseph Mayer

The white edges of the unevenly scalloped plates are decorated with bands of white oval beads. Four scenic cartouches alternate with four floral reserves around the rim of the larger plate. The scenic cartouches show an Eastern sailboat at right, a temple in the center distance and a tall, leafy tree at left with shrubs in the foreground. The floral pattern consists of two large flowers set against a stippled ground. The reserves are separated by a vertical, scrolled band containing treillage and centered with a fleurette. A large stylized flower is placed at the bottom of the vertical design, it is flanked by a pair of smaller flowers and its leaves enter the well and cross the wreath of triangular pennants that surrounds the well.

In the foreground of the center scene on the larger plate there are two people on the river bank. They are both holding poles, one is seated, the other stands and waves at a very large boat with dark sails that is in the middle of the scene. A small skiff is near the large boat. At left there are tall trees and thick bushes. In the distance there are the domed buildings and minarets of Damascus.

The rim of the cup plate has only three scenic reserves but in all other respects the rim pattern duplicates the pattern shown on the larger plate. The central picture is different and eliminates the figures in the foreground. A large sailboat is at center and there are buildings and mountains in the distance.

Marked T.J. and J. Mayer, and "Longport", GMK. 2570, c. 1842-55.

BRIDGE OF LUCANO, ITALY (THE)

Made by Josiah Spode

The view of the four-arched bridge at Lucano, Italy, appears on the sides of the sauce tureen photographed. Behind the bridge there is a tall, round tower and three very large birds fly above the tower. In the distance there is a sloping hill. Trees are placed on both sides of the scene. In the foreground two cows graze on the river bank. The central scene appears on the bowl of the sauce ladle. The rim design can be seen on the lid and consists of strands of wheat ears, maple-type leaves, long leafy branches with blackberries and some small grapes with large white leaves and shadowy tendrils. This tureen is marked with the entire title on a ribbon across the base of a laurel wreath.

Marked with a printed crown in a laurel wreath, see Little, illustration #61; Coysh Book I #105, 1810-1815.

BRITISH LAKES
Maker unknown

The toddy plate (4-¾" diameter) shown has a white scalloped edge outlined by a white band flanked with small, dark beads. The upper part of the rim is stippled and the lower half is covered with large white flame-like leaves that are placed over triangular openings edged with small dark beading.

The central scene fills the well. There are two persons in the foreground, one stands with upraised arms, the other sits on the bank of a large stream that divides the picture. At right there are tall trees and in the middle ground there is a large white house. There are towers behind the structure. At left across the water there are other buildings. In the distance there are a large lake and tall mountains.

Laidecker attributes this pattern to Charles James Mason & Co., c. 1829-45. Marked only — & S.

205

BRITISH PALACES
Made by Ralph Stevenson

The edge of this scalloped cup plate is enhanced by a row of molded, white beads. A band of printed dark beads and finally a narrow black scallop outlines the outer edge. Except for the scenic medallion in the center the entire dish is covered with a lacy point d'esprit design. Large roses and dahlias flanked by very dark leaves form a dark wreath around the entire rim and most of the well.

The center medallion is framed by a scalloped outer line and a narrow stippled band inset with quatrefoils, small beads and a small white, double plume. A church is in the center background of the scene. A gazebo is at left of the large building. A stream is placed horizontally across the center of the picture. Tall trees rise on either side. The foreground is covered with dark grass and ferns.

The larger plate shown bears an American view and it is entitled "Erie Canal at Buffalo Lace Border". The center scenic medallion is framed with scrolls that form arches which are filled with rosettes. Six large, spearpoint designs extend from the frame into the lace border. The scene shows a canal boat being pulled to the canal bank by two men. Lake Erie is in the background. Laidecker (Pt II) states that this border pattern was used for both English and American Scenes and also for a scene entitled "View of the Ganges". He states one plate is titled Windsor Castle and subtitled British Palaces. The cup plate is titled "British Palaces".

See Godden page 596, 1810-35.

BRITISH SCENERY
Maker unknown

The edge of this slightly scalloped dish is outlined by a row of ovoid beads, topped with dark dots. The same design separates the rim pattern of roses and dark heavily veined three-sectioned leaves from the central scene. In the picture a very large multistoried stone windmill is in the left middle ground. A man stands on a circular balcony at the first level and pulls on a rope attached to a trap door opening behind the blades. There is a large, domed structure at the base of the mill. In the center a man stands beside a horse; he seems to be adjusting the shaft of a two-wheel cart drawn by a white horse. Tall trees rise at either side of the scene, flowers and sprigs are strewn across the foreground.

BRUSSELS
Made by John Wedge Wood

The edge of this twelve-sided plate is trimmed with a band of small foliated scrolls. A similar design is used at the well to contain the worm-track rim pattern which resembles oyster shapes. A woman stands on a platform in the foreground of the central scene. She faces a man who wears a hat and vest and is seated among some rocks and some over-scaled plants at left. At right there is a tall palm tree. A river divides the scene and there is a small island at the left. In the background at left there are domed buildings and some towers. In the distance there are other towers, buildings and mountains.

Marked J. Wedgwood and "Iron Stone", exact GMK. 4276a, c. 1841-60.

BYLAND ABBEY, YORKSHIRE
Maker unknown

The soup plate photographed is indented at eight points around the edge and the edge is detailed by a row of white, U-shaped narrow scallops. A wreath of flowers, roses, forget-me-nots and dark leaves with heavy white veins encircles and covers the rim.

A man and woman stand in the foreground of the central scene. He wears kilts, boots, a tam-o'-shanter and carries a shepherd's crook. She is dressed in a long gown, cape and wide brimmed hat. They are standing on the bank of a stream in which there are large dark rocks. The opposite steep bank is covered with pine brush.

Behind the pine branches there is a cottage at left with smoke rising from its chimney. In the center background stands the tall Gothic ruins of the Abbey surrounded by weeds and leafy growth; part of its entrance gate is at left and in the left distance there is another ruin of triple arches surrounded by trees. At right a tall pine arches over the top of the scene. Clouds complete the circular picture.

CALEDONIA

Made by William Adams

Each of the three plates shown is scalloped and the edges are outlined with small triangles, scallops and a plain narrow white line. Each presents the same rim pattern consisting of four scenic reserves separated by a pair of foliated white scrolls flanking a single realistic flower with dark leaves. Both rim designs are framed with small dark beads and the scenic areas are also framed with a white line, white quatrefoils and a circled rosette at the bottom. The scenes are all the same, and show a man dressed in kilts and carrying a rifle in his left hand; he stands on a mountain peak and waves his cap in the air with his right hand. Another Scotsman reclines on the slope nearby. At right there are mountains behind a meadow and a pair of deer are fleeing across the ground. Bushes at left complete the rim scenes. The background is stippled and enters the well as triangular points from which small beads and arrows connected with crosses form spearpoint around the well.

Caledonia is a name for Scotland and these plates show Scottish huntsmen in kilts, diced socks, plaid scarfs and other native costume accoutrements. They stand on hilltops surrounded by mountain peaks. The largest plate shows the hunter blowing a horn as deer flee in the background. The scene on the second plate shows him waving as he stands with his dog near the fallen body of a large deer. The cup plate resembles the border vignettes in that a man stands on a hill waving his hat, holding his gun while a large deer flees at left.

Caledonia was the Roman name for northern Britain and was used in poetry as a name to describe the Highlands.

Marked (imp.) Adams, GMK. 18, c. 1800-64.

CALEDONIA (cont.)

CALIFORNIA

Made by Podmore Walker & Co.

Both the cup plate and larger dish are twelve-sided and the paneled rims are covered with concentric narrow lines. Superimposed over these are five scenic vignettes that picture a mansion with a tower and flanked by trees, a balustrade and an urn at right. Circular floral medallions alternate with the scenic patterns.

The central picture, on both plates, shows a large castle with colonnade at right set against a backdrop of Alpine peaks and tall poplars. A lake is in the center and there are small boats in the distance. A tall elm rises at left from a flower strewn bank. In the foreground there is a terrace with stairs at right. A statue stands on a pedestal at the foot of the stair railing. There are two boats filled with people in the water below the statue.

The cup plate scene contains only a single boat and that is in the foreground.

Marked Wedgwood and "Pearl Stone China", exact GMK. 3080, c. 1849.

CAMBRIAN

Made by George Phillips

The rims of these plates are scalloped and the outer molded edges are white. A row of tiny white quatrefoils and beads, from which tiny crosses descend, outlines the molded edge. The rims are covered with a diaper pattern of small, white stylized flowers set against a stippled field. A wreath of large, sprawling sprays of lilies, leaves and forget-me-nots alternating with equally large cabbage roses and leaves surrounds the rim. A narrow band of scrolls and flowers contains the rim design at the well.

The center scenes differ on items of this pattern, the larger plate shows a large stone mansion and tower at right. Behind it are hills topped by a ruin. An arched bridge crosses a stream in the center; there are tall trees at right. In the foreground there is a road. A man leads his mule in the background and a woman and child, with Welsh hats, walk together on the road. Flowers and rocks are placed across the bottom of the scene.

The cup plate shows a house at right and there are tall trees behind it. There are mountains and buildings in the distance. A seated man talks to a woman at left and there are small flowers across the bottom of the scene.

The word Cambrian is a variation of Cumbria and comes from the Latin version of Cymry, which means Welshmen; therefore, Cambrian means pertaining to Wales.

Marked Phillips, GMK. 3010, c. 1834-48.

213

CANOVA

Made by Thomas Mayer

The dishes photographed are gently scalloped and the outer rim of each bears the same design of small triangles and a row of small beads. The rims carry scenic vignettes, which alternate with floral reserves, and are separated by slanting bands filled with rosettes. Each small scene shows a distinctive dark urn on a square base and some flowers at left. A small sailboat topped with a slanting furled sail is afloat at right. There are mountains and lacy trees in the background.

On the cup plates, and on the larger plates, a wreath of triangular pennants surrounds the well. Wreaths of tiny flowers are set beneath the pennants. The central scenes differ on each item; each shows a different urn, all set on pedestals. The larger plates and cup plates show a gondola on a stream in the background. The large plates show buildings across the water but the cup plates do not. All show the dark oval top of a tall tree at the upper center part of the circular scene.

Canova was made in great quantities. Notice that the four cup plates bear a different center pattern, some have a deep, big wreath around the well and some do not. None are back-stamped but two have an impressed rosette. One cup plate does not even have the odd tree pattern with white center that appears on most items in this pattern.

Marked T. Mayer Imp., and "Stoke" GMK. 2569, c. 1826-35. (An identical pattern on hand is marked G. Phillips, Longport, and marked like GMK. 3012, c. 1834-48.)

CANOVA (cont.)

CANOVIAN

Made by Ralph and James Clews

The edge of this unevenly scalloped plate was left white. The rim is decorated with six, oval reserves containing small bouquets of large flowers. These reserves are placed against a stippled, dark dotted background. Between each there is a pair of crossed plumes; these plumes are the distinguishing feature of this pattern. Tiny flowers encircle the reserves and swag under the plumes. The well is wreathed by a band of rosettes and a deep spearpoint design.

The central scenes differ on the various size plates in this pattern; the one on the first plate shows a standing man who holds a pole over his shoulder as he talks to a seated woman who holds a baby. In the right background there is a white statue of a woman kneeling before a dark urn. The statue is placed on a high rectangular base. At left a white, rounded urn sits on the top of a dark pedestal. There are plants at the base of both pedestals. In the distance, across a lake, there are buildings and towers of Tuscan architecture. Tall trees frame the scene on both sides and there are pieces of broken columns and small flowers in the foreground.

The second plate shows a tall column at right, flowers twine up its height. A statue of a sitting woman, which is placed on a large rectangular pedestal, is in the foreground and a kneeling girl and a standing boy, both in peasant garb, are near the pedestal. The cup plate picture is dominated by the very large dark covered urn on pedestal at left. A woman sits on the ground at center near an over-scaled flower. Both of these plates also present Tuscan buildings in the distance across a lake.

Marked R.&J. Clews, see Godden, p. 151, c. 1818-34.

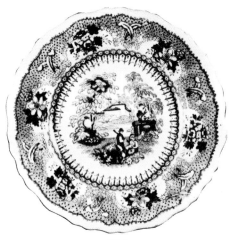

CANOVIAN (cont.)

CAROLINA

Made by Ralph Hall

The white edges of these deeply scalloped plates are enhanced by a very dark field and short fringe around the upper rim. This field is contained by foliated scrolls. The rim is covered with large reserves filled with white leaves, centered with round, grape-like fruit. The reserves are separated by narrow perpendicular lines topped by a scroll and a large fleurette. A pair of dark scrolls contains the linear pattern at the well. The linear pattern is repeated under the fruit-filled cartouches. A band of rosettes and diamonds encircles the upper well on the cavetto. Note that on the cup plate the linear pattern stands out and the well is heavily beaded. On the large plate very small beads are placed under the wreath.

The central scenes differ but each contains urns and birds. On the larger plate the urn is at left and a large bird sits on top of the urn and another perches on the pedestal base. They are plucking at a garland of jewel-like beads. There are foliated scrolls at extreme left, and flowers, rocks and coral forms in the foreground. Tall shade trees are behind the birds and the urn. At right there are two men and a woman rowing in a skiff and in the background there are classical buildings and an arched bridge. On the cup plate a woman is seated in the center of the scene, a man stands beside her. There is a towered building behind them. Overhead on over-scaled bird flies toward an urn set on a pedestal at right. There are flowers and stones at the base of the pedestal.

Marked R. Hall, GMK. 1888, c. 1822-41.

CARSTAIRS ON THE CLYDE

Made by Belle Vue Pottery

This plate is gently scalloped and the outer edge is decorated with a row of light beads on a dark ground, interrupted by twelve, small shield forms with dark centers. The upper part of the rim is stippled and small flowering branches are placed between the shields on the stippled ground. Three large peonies, flanked by very dark leaves and smaller blossoms, alternate around the lower rim and part of the well with sprays of small flowers and sprigs.

A large English castle is pictured in its park-like grounds in the background of the central scene. A man, woman and child stand on the lawn in the center and there are a pair of trees and some shrubs at right. In the foreground two deer are lying near small pine trees. A tall elm rises at left. There are over-scaled flowers in the foreground. Clouds complete the circular picture.

Marked "Belle Vue", GMK. 322, c. 1826-41.

CASHIOBURY, HERTFORDSHIRE
Made by Enoch Wood & Sons

The rim of this plate is indented slightly in eight places and a rope design is placed around the edge. The rim is covered with a stippled field. Large bunches of grapes and their leaves are placed around the rim and some forget-me-nots appear next to the grapes. A four-ply band, bound with crosses, contains the rim pattern at the well and morning-glories twine around the band in such a way that the blossoms appear on the rim.

A large country castle is seen in the background of the central picture. It is of Gothic architecture and has square towers and arched windows. The roof is castellated. The building sits in a park of trees and shady lawns. In the foreground two figures stand on a wide curving driveway at right. At left three cows stand in a small pond.

Laidecker reports that the views in these series were taken from "The Seats of Noblemen In England, Wales, Scotland and Ireland" by John Preston Neal, London, 1822. This is probably part of a series. (See Compton Vernay in this category.)

Marked (imp.) Wood, GMK. 4261, c. 1818-46.

CASSINO

Made by William Adams & Son

A series of concentric lines, which dip and form a scallop, encircle the rims of these plates. A dot is placed in each dip and a short straight line accents the upper arch of the scallop. The effect is that a series of vertical chevrons on a field of horizontal lines. The design is confined at the upper edge by a dark wreath of interlacing scallops and triangles, topped by fleur-de-lis and the well is contained by a large fleur-de-lis pattern in the cavetto.

In the central scene a man holding a pole stands near a woman who holds a small animal and a child who stands nearby on the grassy banks of a lake. Marble stairs rise at right and tall trees rise near the stairs behind an urn on a pedestal. In the background there are Gothic church buildings.

The cup plate shown is fourteen sided and the paneled rim bears the same design as the larger plate. The central scene is different and shows a group of people in the foreground. A tall tree and a pair of gate posts are at left, and there are church towers and a temple ruin in the background at right.

Marked (imp.) Adams, GMK. 18, c. 1800-64. (The large plate is a later rendition of the early pattern; it is marked George Jones and is like mark 2216. It would date c. 1854.)

CASTLE SCENERY

Made by Jacob Furnigal

The decoration on this plate is Moorish in effect. The rim contains five arched vignettes set against a reticulated background. The scenes in the reserves show a castle at right with many domed towers, a river divides the picture, and there is a large tree at left. There are mountain peaks in the background. A wreath of heavy spearpoint encircles the cavetto.

The central scene is framed by Moorish arches at the top. Tall columns rise from both sides of a platform on which there are two figures, one stands and one is kneeling. A dark urn is on the pavement near them. The scenes differ on the various items of this pattern. In the background there appears to be a lake and on the left bank there are many domed buildings.

Marked J.F., like mark 1643, c. 1845-70.

CATHEDRAL

Possibly made by Joseph Heath & Co.

The edge of this saucer is outlined by a small row of diamonds and next to that there is a circle of small beads. Three scrolled reserves on the rim show a bird perching in the center against a stippled background. Between the bird designs the upper rim is covered with a diaper design which is contained by a pair of scrolled arches. The arches are joined by a pair of large flowers, leaves and sprigs.

The well is encircled by a roll of small scallops and tiny triangles. In the center of the scene in the well there is a large, domed cathedral on the farther banks of a river. At right in the foreground there is a pedestal supporting an urn filled with over-scaled flowers. Very large flowers and leaves are in the center foreground. The bird designs in the border is the distinguishing detail of this pattern.

This is marked with an Impressed propeller, c. 1828-41.(It may have been made by Ralph Hall who used the same imp. mark c. 1822-49.)

CATSKILL MOSS

Made by William Ridgway & Sons

The paneled rim of this plate is covered with a mosaic design formed by small irregularly-shaped tile patterns, each centered with a small bead. Placed over this are eight identical sprays of seaweed-type, the moss of the title. The outer edge of the rim decoration is contained by a band of squared scallops, each centered with a tiny trefoil. The bottom of the rim design terminates in small straight sprigs.

The center view represents Meredith, New Hampshire. A man and woman are at right, he is seated on a rock. They are on a hill overlooking the town and lake. At left there are rocks, a wooden gate and three tall elms. In the distance the tree-covered foothills are placed in front of tall mountains that fill the background.

Marked C.C. (See Little, p. 151), c. 1831-48.

CHANTILLY I

Maker unknown

The edge of this scalloped plate is embossed with a double-ridge crossed with large leaves. The rim is covered with narrow concentric lines and a wreath of white scrolls and leaves is placed around the border. In the five spaces left on the upper rim by the curving scrolls there are trios of dark flowers with leaves. The well is encircled by squares containing five narrow lines and divided by spearpointed, vertical lines.

A fountain basin upheld by three cherubs who stand on a hexagonal tiered pedestal is at right in the foreground of the central scene. There is another large urn directly behind the basin and a smaller one, surrounded by flowers at its base, is at left. At right there is a balustrade, some bushes and a tall tree. A river divides the scene and a fountain jet rises from the river bank at left. Behind it there are tall trees and a Norman castle with many pointed towers. Clouds complete the circular scene.

"CHANTILLY II"

Maker unknown

This plate is unevenly scalloped and the upper part of the rim is stippled. Pairs of flowers composed of passion flowers and a large rose alternate with other pairs composed of a peony and dahlia. The flowers are separated by a scrolled arch design centered at top with an oval fleurette placed over a triangular scroll design with three beads pendant.

The center scene is remarkably like Chantilly I except that the position of the items in the transfers are reversed. A large urn is placed at left supported by three cherubs sitting on acanthus leaves; another urn is placed on a leafy tall pedestal in back of it and a small open urn surrounded by roses is set on the lawn at right. There are tall trees at left behind a balustrade. A river divides the scene. A fountain jet rises from behind a garden wall at right. Behind it there are tall bushes, trees and a large castle. Clouds complete the circular scene.

Marked "Iron Stone China". Possibly Ridgway, GMK. 2357.

CHATEAU

Made by John Edwards

The photographs of these plates show the bottom of a twelve-sided butter dish and a twelve-sided drainer which fits across the well. The rim of the dish is covered with narrow, concentric lines decorated with five oblong scrolled reserves, each containing a spray of flowers. The floral patterns are separated by a pair of large U-shapes formed of foliated scrolls. The bottom of the rim pattern is scalloped and a band of U-shaped arches encircles the well.

Both the drainer and the center scene on the dish show a large chateau at right center in the middle ground. At far right an elm rises from a rocky bank. A stream divides the scene and in the left background there are tall trees and the towers of another chateau. In the foreground a woman stands upon a high rock overlooking the scene and a man stands on the riverbank below her. The bank is covered with stones and bushes which cross the foreground.

Marked (imp.) J.E. and "Iron Stone", GMK. 1449, c. 1847-73.

CIALKA KAVAK
Maker unknown

The central picture shows a log house at center. In the foreground a woman carries a bucket in one hand and balances a stick and bundle over her shoulder with the other hand. Two women in peasant costume, similar to that on the foreground figure, stand near the log house. There are other wooden buildings under the ridge of a forested hill in the right background.

The distinctive rim design used in this series, which is a scriptural series according to Laidecker, consists of a row of small dark arches that is set around the edge of the rims. On the rim there are three tall, Greco-Roman incense braziers which alternate with three sprays of morning-glories, dahlias and poppies set upon a base of scrolls, flanked by long, large foliated scrolls whose tips touch the mask handles of the braziers. The border is distinctive. See Pera in this same category which dates this pattern to 1815.

CLAREMONT

Made by Barker & Son

The dinner plate, the cup plate and the pitcher photographed bear the same scene of three people on a flower-strewn bank of a stream. A woman stands near a man who is holding a fishing pole, and a seated woman who also holds a pole. A small, dark greyhound is with them at left. In the background, across the river, there is a two-story stone building with six, high multi-paned windows and two arched windows on the riverside. A statue is placed over the windows. Tall poplars and Alpine peaks are at right behind the villa. Tall towers surmounted with statues are in the background and there are other buildings and trees in the distance. At left there are tall elms with climbing vines climbing their trunks. A stone wall topped with two small towers enters the water just behind the trees.

The cup plate's picture eliminates the small dog and the small stone wall at left. It does not have the border of concentric lines that goes straight for ¾" then forms a scallop, contained at top and bottom by rows of fleur-de-lis. This border can be clearly seen on the collar of the pitcher. The cup plate has a plain white rim which was embossed with swags and bows and lozenges.

Marked B. & S., GMK. 256, 1850-60.

CLAREMONT (cont.)

CLYDE SCENERY

Made by Job and John Jackson

The scalloped edges of these plates are white, and a row of tiny mushroom shapes forms an edge around the rim pattern which contains four cartouches separated by a shield design flanked by flowers. In each scenic vignette there is a large dark sailboat at left, a dark cottage and large tree at right, and a rowboat in the foreground. There are other sailboats in the background. The rim design is contained by a circle of small diamonds and feathers, and the central scene is surrounded by a wide wreath composed of a triangular trio of flowers that alternates with a scroll design and then is contained by a row of beading.

The central scenes differ on each size dish on this pattern. The dinner plate photographed shows two small boats on the river Clyde. In the foreground there are three people on the bank which is covered with weeds and small white flowers. On the opposite shore in the background there are houses on either side of a wide road, a church and some trees. The second plate, which is a supper size, has a scene showing two young girls wearing aprons and headdresses, who stand with a little dog in a glade near a stream which flows through the center of the picture. There are five white swans in the river. In the distance the stream flows under a triple arched bridge and in the background there is a large castle. There are tall trees at right and flowers in the left foreground.

The first cup plate has the same rim pattern as the larger plates. The scene is different of course. It shows a sailboat on the river. In the background there are farm buildings and trees. The second cup plate bears the distinctive rim design of scenic cartouches containing a boat with dark sail, the dark rowboat, and the house which are separated with shield designs flanked by flowers. The wreath around the well is omitted in the second cup plate and the central scene covers the entire well and ascends to the rim. In the foreground there is a pair of cows, one dark and standing, the other animal white and lies in the shade at the base of a tall tree. In the background there are a manor house at left and a chapel at right. In the distance a forest covers the hills. There are white flowers in the foreground. The distinctive features in this pattern are the scenic cartouches in the rim and the heavy floral frame around the central scene.

Marked *Jackson's Warranted* and (imp.) rosette, GMK. 2156, 1831-35.

CLYDE SCENERY (cont.)

COBLENZ

This scalloped plate has a white edge decorated with a pattern of small straight lines. The upper half of the rim is stippled, and six large white flowers with dark leaves flanked by small white flowers and sprigs are placed under fragments of white lattice around the rim. Part of the sprigs and leaves enter the well and form an irregular wreath. In the center a large arched bridge crosses the scene at right. In the foreground there is a large body of water and a small boat approaches the flower strewn bank in the foreground. In the left distance there are city buildings. Coblenz is on the Rhine at the mouth of the Mosel River. This plate is one of a series of Rhine views.

COLOGNE

Made by John Alcock

Both the dinner plate and the cup plate photographed are twelve sided and the rims are paneled. The larger plate has a molded ridge at the edge and five large scroll designs encompassing a teardrop extend over the ridge to the edge. In between the large designs there are flat scrolls. The rim design of wormtrack type, placed over narrow concentric lines, is contained at the bottom by a dark line and small trios of leaves and stems intertwine over this line and drop into the well forming a pattern that resembles double circles.

At left in the foreground of the central scene on the dinner plate there are four people. Two ladies stand together, a man sits on the ground at their feet and another man stands next to them and is pointing to the right. There are tall elms at left. In the background at right across the river one sees a Gothic chapel. There is a castle behind it. There are tall trees at right, mountains in the distance, and shrubs in the foreground. The cup plate omits the top part of the rim design, and the two ladies and one man are omitted from the foreground, leaving just the one man standing and pointing towards the water.

Marked as above with "Cobridge", GMK. 67, 1853-61.

COLOGNE

Made by Ralph Stevenson and Son

The edges of these scalloped plates are detailed by a band of small crosses. The rims are indented so that the upper part puffs out and the decoration is applied so that the tops of the peacock feathers between the cartouches end in arches at the puffed area. Smaller arches and flowers are placed over the feathers. The vignettes contain a pair of large flowers, forget-me-nots, leaves and sprigs. The well is defined by two lacy wreaths. One is composed of a triple row of joined diamonds. The inner one is a large lace design.

The river scene in the well on the large plate contains Gothic buildings at right, in the middleground, and in the distance at right. At left there are tall trees whose roots cling to a steep grassy bank that is covered with bushes. At right there are tall trees and steep stony banks. Alpine peaks in the background and clouds above all complete the circular design. The second plate has the same elements as the first except that the buildings are at left and the trees are at right. The stream divides the scene as is usual in these patterns.

The rim design of the cup plates is the same as on the larger plates. The triple diamond dark band around the well is omitted but the oval lacy wreath is retained. The central picture is different from either plate shown above. The second cup plate shows a different scene and has no rim design with vignettes but both diamond wreaths are used as a rim pattern instead. The cup plates show a different river view with buildings on the left bank only. One cup plate is marked with an impressed anchor.

The second large plate is marked W. & C.. Ralph Stevenson and his son potted until 1835. Wood and Challinor must have secured this pattern after that as they worked from 1834-43.

Marked R.S. & S. GMK. 3706, 1832-35.

COLOGNE (cont.)

COLUMBIA

Made by William Adams and Sons

The twelve sided plates pictured here are paneled and the rims are covered with white foliated scrolls and small white flowers set against a background of concentric lines. Five groups of daisies and dark leaves are placed between the white flowers and are almost encircled by the fine scroll lines. The rim design is confined at the well by spearpoint.

A Gothic shrine which encloses a statue is in the middle of the central scene on the large plate. A woman holding a child by one hand and a parasol over her head with her other hand is standing with a man dressed in frock coat near the shrine. There are a small stone bridge and tall trees at left. In the distance there are buildings, mountain peaks, and a river. Terraced steps and flowering bushes are in the foreground. The cup plate shows a Gothic shrine at left also. One figure, a man, dressed in frock coat and white trousers, stands in the center of the scene. A river divides the background picture which contains a building at left across the stream and mountains in the distance. There are sprigs, bushes and flowers in the foreground.

Marked W. Adams and Sons, GMK. 22, c. 1850.

COLUMBIA

Made by John Wedge Wood

Both these plates are twelve sided and the paneled rims are covered with concentric lines which form a background for five scenic cartouches. Each scene shows a large castle with many towers in the background. At right there is a tall dark tree. In the spaces between the scenic reserves there are white flowers set over a shell pattern. The flowers are framed with an oval composed of scrolls and flanked with a trellis pattern. There are parts of scrolls, flowers, and leaves, around the outer edge and a circle of fleur-de-lis around the cavetto.

The patterns in the centers are about the same on both plates. Tall trees rise at right. A river divides the scene in the center. There is a small boat midstream. At left there are trees and a row of rounded bushes on top of a retaining wall. There are castle buildings in the left background and tall mountains in the distance. A moon (or sun) and clouds are overhead. In the foreground there is a flowered terrace. A balustrade is at left and a large urn is placed on a pedestal at the end of the balustrade. There are four persons on the terrace, a lady, two men, one of whom is pointing to the water, and a man who is seated. The cup plate shows only the lady and the man who is pointing.

Marked J. Wedgwood, and Ironstone, GMK. 4276a, c. 1848.

COLUMBIAN STAR

Made by John Ridgway

The distinctive border on this saucer is composed of a field of small stars on which larger stars are superimposed. A wreath of laurel winds around a rope band at the bottom of the rim design. A narrow row of laurel leaves outlines the outer edge. The center scene shows a log cabin with one window and a door. At the left is part of a fence. Two men stand in front of the building. There are tall trees at the right. A distant river scene with trees is at left, and in the foreground there are four tree stumps.

Marked Jn⁰, Ridgway, like GMK. 3255, 1830-41.

239

COMPTON VERNEY, WARWICKSHIRE

Made by Enoch Wood and Sons

The edge of the plate shown, lobed in eight places, is detailed with a narrow band of twisted cord. The background of the rim is stippled, and a wreath of grapes, grapeleaves, morning-glories, and forget-me-nots encircles it. A band around the upper well of four narrow white lines bound by crosses is entwined in several places by grape stems and dark leaves. The central picture presents a large country house in the background. There is an arched bridge at center and a lake in the foreground. A small boat with two figures in it is at center. There are tall trees at either side of the scene, and flowers, shrubs, and leaves in the foreground. This design is probably part of a scenic series, see Cashiobury (this category).

Marked (imp.) as above with "Burslem", GMK. 4257, 1818-46.

CONTINENTAL CATHEDRAL

Made by Thomas Shirley and Co.

The border design for this pattern appears around the collar of the pitcher shown. It is also placed on the top inside of the pitcher, and consists of shield shapes filled with diamond trellis which separate scenic vignettes that show a gazebo at left and church ruins at right. There are bouquets placed against a stippled ground set between the shields and these may alternate with the scenic designs on plate rims. A band of small diamonds encircles the outer edge.

The cathedral of the title appears in the background at right in the central scene. It is situated on a river which divides the picture. In the foreground three persons, two standing and one seated, are on the river bank. A balustrade is at right. A formal terrace with trees, columns, and ruins with a sphinx placed on a pedestal are at left. This pattern was made in Scotland but is of the same nature as Staffordshire.

Marked T.S. and Co. and "Warranted", GMK. 3522, 1840-57.

CORINTH

Made by James Edwards

The rim of this fourteen sided deep dish is detailed by a row of beads and zigzag. The rim is covered with an odd design that resembles crowded stalactites, all pointing outwards. Identical bouquets of five stylized daisies, leaves, and sprigs, are placed against the unique background.

The ruins of a columned building are at left center on the larger plate. A pair of tall elms, stony crags, and bushes are at extreme left. At right there is a steep grassy bank on which there is a pair of goats grazing under a tall tree. In the foreground there is a stone paved terrace and a flight of three steps that lead to an angled platform at left. A man and woman, dressed in Elizabethan court costume, stand at right conversing with a man who is seated on a remnant of a fallen column. The cup plate is almost a duplicate of the larger plate, except that the foreground figures are omitted.

Marked Jas. Edwards, (imp.) "Warranted", See Godden, pg. 230, 1842-51.

CORINTH

Made by George Phillips

The collar and the bottom of the pedestal of the sugar bowl shown are decorated by concentric lines, pointed and draped, so as to form swags. The outer edges are finished with a band of small pointed white leaves separated by ovals containing small sprigs.

The central river scene shows two large sailboats at right. A skiff is near the outer one which has a white curved prow. Two boards are placed from the skiff to the larger boat. There are small figures in the vessel. At right beyond the boats there are a columned temple and tall trees. In the center across the water there is a very large building with a long facade centered with a domed columned porch. Flanking pairs of stone steps lead to the porch. There are towers and buildings in the background. At left elms rise from a bank strewn with flowers, bushes and fragments of columns. Small flowers are strewn across the foreground against a dark stretch of water.

Marked G. Phillips, and "Longport", and "Ironstone", See Godden p. 492, 1834-48.

CORINTHIA

Made by Wedgwood and Co.

This company was formerly Podmore Walker and Co. There are six ovoid scenic cartouches framed with foliated scrolls on the rim of this plate. Each carries the same pattern of a twin towered building in the background, tall trees on either side, and a flight of steps with marble railing in the foreground and slanting up to the right. The background between the reserves is stippled. Bands of circles centered with quatrefoils enwreath both the top and bottom of the rim design. A narrow band is set next to this wreath. Both bands are interrupted by the cartouches on the bottom and the upper trim is interrupted by fleur-de-lis flanked by foliated scrolls. The well is encircled by a band of squares composed of double scrolled lines.

In the central scene a lady in court costume talks to two courtiers as they stand on the wide staircase of a terrace. Two small dogs are with them, and the lady pats one of them on the head. There are other people on the terrace behind them. A marble balustrade is at left and is topped by an urn. Tall trees rise at left and at right. There is a statue on a pedestal at right. In the background there is a large castle with square towers. Jagged clouds complete the circular picture. The little plate bears no border and has no well wreath. It omits one dog and one courtier and some of the people standing in the background.

Marked (imp.) as above, GMK. 4055, c. 1860.

CORINTHIAN

Maker unknown

The upper section of this scalloped plate is stippled and is very dark. Small scrolls are placed against the stippling. In three places around the rim there are very large full blown roses flanked by dark leaves, small flowers, and sprigs. These alternate with very dark flowers that resemble poinsettias placed equidistant around the lower rim and there is a pair of dahlias above the poinsettias.

A delicate chain of ovals and diamonds surrounds the central scene which shows a fishing boat being poled by a standing man. It moves across the stream towards a large ruined temple at left. Another person is seated in the boat and a third pulls up a net from the water. In the background two shepherds are driving their cattle across an arched bridge. There is a round multi-storied building with statues on the portico in the right background. In the distance there are other buildings, another small boat, and some mountains. In the foreground there are rocks, over-scaled flowers, and a tall tree which rises from the flowers at right.

CORSICA

Made by Wood and Challinor

The plate photographed is unevenly scalloped and the outer edge is detailed with a band of small bells and beads. Four fan shape cartouches are set around the rim. Two contain a scene of a dome-topped narrow temple and tall tower. The alternating pair contain a handled basket full of flowers. Lattice curves around the top of each reserve. There are six different patterns in rows between the cartouches. The upper rim is covered with small ovals, then there is a band of white C scrolls. Beneath these there are harlequin diamonds, then a wide scalloped band of oval rosettes and pairs of dark oblongs. Then follows a row of diamond drapery contained by a zigzag band, topped by white beads. Fine lines dotted with diamonds form a spearpoint beneath the zigzags. This border is distinctive.

In the center of the central scene a man and woman in court costume stand near a white urn on a pedestal at left. At right there are tall columned ruins. Beneath the pedestal at left there is a small flight of steps with a scroll railing. A tall elm rises behind the steps. In the background there are temple buildings and tall domed towers. White Alpine peaks appear in the distance.

Marked W. and Co., GMK. 4244, 1828-43.

CRYSTAL PALACE

Maker unknown (Possibly J. and M.P. Bell)

This octagon shaped platter bears a border of large grape leaves, grapes, and tendrils set against a stippled background. The Crystal Palace pictured in the center was built for the Great Exhibition of 1851 which Prince Albert, consort to Victoria, had planned as the first international exhibition to be held of the "Works of Industry of all Nations". The building was designed by Joseph Paxton, the celebrated designer of the great conservatory at Chatsworth. The Crystal Palace was a mammoth greenhouse that was erected in Hyde Park and proved to be a great attraction. After the exhibit was closed it was dismantled and moved to Sydenham. It was destroyed by fire in 1936. The cup plate shows a different view of the palace and the edge is trimmed with the lower part of the grape leaf rim pattern found on the platter.

C. 1851.

CYRENE

Made by William Adams and Sons

The rim of this plate is covered with a crisscross design of diagonal lines intercepted with square dotted crosses. There is a single bead in the center of each diamond formed by the lines. Five small oval scenic cartouches framed with angled borders are set around the rim. Each contain the same scene of a domed round building at right which adjoins a tower in the center. In the left background there is another tower. In the foreground there are dark pieces of fallen columns and some sprigs.

In the central scene a man is seated on a large rock which is surrounded by flowers and branches. He is dressed in short cape and long white trousers, and is facing a standing woman dressed in a long gown and part of a veil. A stream divides the picture, and the woman stands looking across the water towards some temple-like buildings and tall towers. There are other towers in the central distance. At right a pair of tall trees arch across the water. At their bases there are broken columns and other pieces of stone ruins.

Marked W. Adams and Sons, and "Stone China", GMK. 22, 1819-64.

DAMASCUS

Made by Enoch and Edward Wood

The edge of the plate shown is detailed by a band of quatrefoils. The rim is covered with sprigs, and eight dark rosettes which alternate with eight equal size groups of six small white starflowers are set around the rim. In the foreground of the central picture, two shepherds holding their crooks guard their goats. A woman sits near the men. She is perched on a high rock or a piece of a broken column. A stream divides this picture. At left there are two trees and some bushes. At right across the water there is a domed mosque-like structure and other buildings. There are over-scaled flowers in the foreground. In the distance there are mountain peaks.

Marked E. and E.W. and "Pearl China" Imp, GMK. 4264, 1818-46.

DELAWARE

Made by Charles Harvey

The upper rim of this twelve sided plate is decorated with a wreath of dahlias, peonies, forget-me-nots, dark leaves, and small white feathery scrolls. The rest of the rim is covered with a diamond design that is filled partially with a diaper pattern. Narrow concentric lines cover the background of the rim, and these contribute to the diaper pattern in the middle portion and fill the half diamonds on the lower rim. A band of small arches completes the lower rim pattern, and this is contained by a wreath of spearpoint that is placed around the cavetto.

The central scene is the usual romantic picture of a castle at right, a stream with an arched bridge in the center, and tall elms at left. At left there is also a high pedestal surmounted by an urn. This is at the end of a tall wall from which flowers are hanging. At right there is a curved staircase. The stairs lead to a lawn in the foreground on which four people are placed. There are two ladies in white skirts and two gentlemen in dark suits. Note the treatment of the sun or moon in the sky.

Marked (imp.) Harvey, with "Opaque Porcelain", GMK. 1967, 1835-53.

DELPHI

Made by William Adams and Sons

The white edge of this scenic platter is outlined by a band of dark beads. The rim is covered with a pattern of Grecian designs, large white foliated scrolls flanked by four trapezoid table-like figures which contain stylized flowers. There are also four large rosettes on the sides of the rim of the platter. These are crowned by a fan pattern filled with a diaper design. Another set of four designs, shield-shaped and flanked by dark foliated scrolls, is placed in the corners of the rim. The well is surrounded by a running scallop design placed above a series of beads.

In the central scene there are tall Gothic ruins at right in the middle ground. A river divides the scene, and on the left bank there are steps leading to the arch of a ruined temple. In the distance there are tall mountains. There are trees in the background and others at right and left. In the foreground there are three persons. Two stand, one sits at left reclining against a bank of over-scaled flowers. There is a bit of fencing at the right of the figures.

Marked Adams (imp.), GMK. 18, 1800-64.

DOMESTIC

Made by James Edwards

This plate is fourteen sided and the rim is covered with a trellis design consisting of diamonds that enclose small stylized flowers and shamrocks. The outer edge is decorated with small printed scallops and spearpoint. The bottom of the rim design is contained by a row of small fleur-de-lis.

In the central picture a man stands next to a tall tree at right. He is in a small fenced yard and in front of a cottage with a thatched roof. A woman sits by the open door of the house. Her spinning wheel is next to her. At left there is a covered well with winch and another large tree. In the background there is a river and three goats recline on its bank. In the distance there are mountains and some trees. The foreground shows a stretch of water and banks covered with large flowers and bushes.

Two cup plates are shown. One has no pattern on its paneled rim, the other has a rim pattern of sprigs. Both bear the same scene, identical to the larger plate with the omission of the well at left and the river scene at right. The cup plate with sprig border is marked with a tiny blue printed bell and perhaps was not made by Edwards but by J. and M.P. Bell. The cup plate shown in this book with the Webster Vase pattern has the same border and it was made by Bell.

Marked Jas. Edwards, See Godden, page 230, 1843-51.

DOMESTIC (cont.)

DORIA

Made by John Ridgway and Co.

    The rim of this twelve sided plate is paneled and is covered with a printing of narrow concentric lines that are formed in a vertical step pattern. The outer edge and the bottom of the rim is detailed by a row of heavy dark spearpoint. The scene in the center of the dish shows a large Tuscan mansion in the center. At right there are tall elms, poplars, bushes, and a balustrade. In the foreground at left there are three persons on a grassy bank of a river which divides the scene. Two small boats are on the water behind them. At far left there are very tall elms and part of a wall. In the distance there are a bridge, other buildings, and tall Alpine peaks.

    Marked as above, GMK. 3259b, 1841-55.

EASTERN SCENERY

Made by Enoch Wood and Sons

The rim of this eight sided lobed platter is covered with a design of five-petaled flowers with elongated leaves and clumps of forget-me-nots. A band of small dark triangles is placed around the outer edge. In the foreground of the central scene cattle stand in a stream which divides the picture. At right there are houses and trees. At left in the background there are the ruins of an Oriental temple. At extreme left other cattle graze under a pair of tall stylized trees. In the distance at upper right there are other buildings, towers, rocks and trees on what appears to be an island.

Marked E. Wood and Son, GMK. 4261, 1818-46.

ENGLISH CITIES – WELLS

Made by Enoch Wood and Sons

The gadrooned edges of these plates were left white as was true on all dishes marked "Celtic China" by Wood. There are many pattern elements on the rim. Three large, dark oval reserves framed with light foliated C scrolls and centered with two stylized flowers flanked by leaves alternate with three dark spade-shaped designs filled with white scrolls and flowers. Between these dark areas there are three large white realistic flowers with leaves placed next to an area filled with a diamond diaper pattern and a dark stylized daisy. The remaining spaces on the rim are filled with a vertical background of oblong beads contained by foliated scrolls; three are decorated with a diamond design and the other three contain a white flower near the top of the rim. A shadowy wreath of flowers, sprigs, and beads is placed at the bottom of the rim design in the cavetto.

The picture in the center is of the cathedral at Wells. It is encircled by a narrow band of spearpoint. In the foreground of the scene a man rides a white horse below the crest of a hill covered with grass and bushes. A tall tree rises at right. The imposing cathedral is seen across a tree lined river. Smaller buildings are placed on the opposite bank. There are hills and mountains behind the cathedral. The second plate shows the city buildings of Liverpool and bears the same rim design as the larger plate.

Marked E.W. and S. and "Celtic China", GMK. 4260, 1818-46.

255

ENGLISH VIEWS

Made by John Rogers & Son

The outer edge of this scalloped platter is gadrooned and was left white. A printed row of thick white small arches enhances the white edge. Very large flowers, roses of various types, with dark large leaves centered with a rose hip are placed around the rim. Small sprigs are printed on the stippled ground between the flowers.

The central scene shows three persons in the foreground. Two sit on boulders and one stands between them holding a fishing pole. A river flows past them in the background. Across the water cows graze in a meadow. Behind the cows there are imposing buildings, trees, and the slope of a mountain. Tall dark elms rise on either side of the picture. The distinguishing feature is the very dark leaves centered with the oval white rose hip in the border pattern.

Marked (imp.) Rogers, GMK. 3369, 1814-36.

EON

Made by George Wooliscroft

This is the famous windmill pattern. The plate is twelve sided and the edge is embossed. The rim carries four reserves. Two contain a windmill set in a river landscape. The others are a pastoral scene of men with farm animals and a cart. The panels are separated by a column composed of narrow white lines. White clovers twine around the columns and extend at right and left to the outer edge. The well is encircled by a spearpoint design. The windmill is dominant in the central scene and is at left. A stream divides the picture diagonally, and there are meadows, shrubs, and rocks on the left bank. Tall trees rise from the right bank. In the distance there are a tower and other buildings surrounded by a forest.

Marked G. Wooliscroft, GMK. 4308, 1851-64.

EPIRUS

Mark not located

Both the outer edge and the lower band at the bottom of the rim consist of fleur-de-lis and arrows that effect a spearpoint design. The rim is covered with narrow concentric lines that angle upwards. A statue of a man holding a shield is positioned on a tall pedestal at right in the central picture. A fallen tree lies beside the pedestal. In the foreground three persons, man, woman, and child, stand on a grassy lawn. Behind them there is a lake, and at left across the water poplars grow on a shrub covered bank. A tall elm rises at right, there are flowers and shrubs at its base. In the distance in the center of the scene there are a castle with towers, and tall mountain peaks.

Marked E.P. Troutbeck.

"EUROPA"

Made by John and Richard Riley

The edge of this plate is divided into eight gentle scallops and is detailed by a narrow band of interlocking triangles. The rim is covered with a wreath of wild roses, lilies and leaves against a dark background which is contained at the well by a ring of triangular floral designs set in a narrow band. In the foreground of the scene, which shows the countryside and the outskirts of a large town, there is a small procession. A woman is seated on a white bull. She is accompanied by three maidens. One leads the bull, the other two carry cymbals. A tall tree rises behind them. There is a lake or river at right. At left in the background white cattle graze in a large field. Coysh named this scene "Europa".

Marked Riley's Semi China, GMK. 3329, 1802-28.

EUROPEAN SCENERY

Made by Enoch Wood and Sons

These plates are gently scalloped and a row of tiny beads is placed around the edges. The upper rims are covered with a distinctive lacy draped design that falls in panels across the rim. Small white rosettes are placed at the top and appear to pin the swags in place. A wreath of morning-glories and dahlias with dark leaves encircles the lower part of the rim. On the cup plate only the upper part of the floral wreath appears but the lace swags and white rosettes remain.

The scenes differ on the various items. The larger plate shows two men in black capes face to face in the left foreground. At right there is a balustrade and in the right distance there are classic buildings. On the cup plate two men in a skiff approach a small house set on a rock at right.

Marked E.W. and S., GMK. 4260, 1818-46.

FLORENTINE

Made by Thomas, James, and John Mayer
Issued later by Liddle Elliot and Sons

Both the large plate and the scalloped cup plate bear the same border design. The outer edge is enhanced by a wreath of vines and oval beads. From this vine a spray of flowers falls towards the well. It is placed over a field of narrow lines and is framed by an oblong from which the flowers fall beneath the lower bar. The oblongs link six sided cartouches which contain a picture of a castle with eight narrow tall towers. The well is encircled by spearpoint at the bottom of the rim design.

A bridge with many arches crosses a river in the center of the scenic transfer. A castle is on a hilltop at left and tall trees rise from the right bank. In the foreground three people, a man, woman, and child, stand on a flower strewn bank. Another person is seated on the bank, and a small boat passes below him on the river. Mountains and clouds in the background complete the circular design. The cup plate has the same scenic center with the exception of the boat in the foreground. The woman and child are also omitted.

Marked T.J. and J. Mayer, GMK. 2570, c. 1843-55.

FLORENTINE

Made by Podmore Walker and Co.

Both the soup plate and the cup plate shown are scalloped. The rims are paneled and indented and the outer edges carry rows of printed beads. The rim design consists of four basket shapes, the lower part filled with a diamond treillage topped with bouquets, and the sides framed by large foliated scrolls. This basket design is distinctive. Between the scrolls there are pairs of large flowers. A half-flower is set above the pairs at the upper edge. These flowers are omitted on the cup plate. The pairs of flowers have very dark leaves that enter the well, and trail over the wreath of pennants and sprigs and vertical lines which surround the well.

There are three girls in the foreground of the central scene, two are seated at the base of a big pedestal at right that supports a large urn filled with over-scaled flowers. There are sprigs and shrubs at the base of the pedestal. The third girl stands at center and points towards the others. At left tall trees rise from behind part of a balustrade. There is a lake in the background and across the water there is a large building with open arches and a domed tower. The usual mountains are shown in the distance.

The scenes differ on the various items in this pattern. The cup plate also shows an urn on a pedestal at right. It too is filled with large flowers. There is part of a terrace in the center and a tall tree at left. A building with a very tall tower is in the distance. There are no figures in the scene.

Marked P.W. & Co., GMK. 3065, 1834-59.

FLORENTINE VILLAS

Made by Job and John Jackson

The scalloped edge of this plate is white. A row of dark oval beads is set on a dark scalloped line that follows the white edging. The indented rim is stippled and is encircled by a wreath composed of pairs of large roses and trios of smaller garden flowers set within baroque scrolls. A large stem covered with thorns curves up and to the left at the right edge of each rose. This is a distinctive feature to aid in identification of the pattern and is clearly seen on the cup plate. The floral wreath covers the rim and invades the upper part of the well.

Both plates show scenes of temples, placed at right on the larger plate and at left rear on the cup plate. Tall trees are at the right on the cup plate and at left on the luncheon dish. Both show a stream of water dividing the center of the scene. The larger dish shows two boats midstream. Each has a dark covered urn near the center.

Marked Jacksons' Warranted, GMK. 2156, 1831-5.

FOUNTAIN

Made by Enoch Wood and Sons

The edge of this scalloped platter is white and a row of white beads follows the curved lines. The upper part of the rim is stippled and a pattern of dots and dashes is placed over the stippling. Four oval cartouches, framed in small scrolls and containing a trefoil, alternate on the rim with four larger designs containing an elongated scallop shell with a fleur-de-lis at top against a dark ground. The second design is flanked by large foliated scrolls. The designs are joined by semi-curved lines and three large oblong beads. Small sprays are set under the rim pattern and enter the top of the well.

In the middle of the central scene a tall double-tiered fountain is set in a lake. In the background at right beyond some trees and bushes there is a tall cliff topped with trees. At left there are tall graceful trees, and in the left foreground there is part of a fallen column and some flowers. In the distance across the lake there are Alpine peaks.

Marked E. Wood and Sons, GMK. 4261, 1818-46.

FOUNTAIN SCENERY

Made by William Adams and Sons

These plates are irregularly scalloped and the edges are decorated with a row of printed beading interrupted by five coils and pairs of small rosettes. The upper part of the rim is dark. Triangular designs that curve to the right formed by C scrolls and filled with a vertical row of flowers create white lace-edged reserves that contain trios of large flowers, buds, and leaves. An irregular wreath of sprigs and tiny flowers outlines the shell-like lacy frame that surrounds the central scenes.

Each plate has a different picture, but both have a building with tower at right and a tall tree behind it. At left each shows a fanciful fountain emptying from urns set on pedestals covered with over-scaled flowers. The larger plate has a statue of a deer on the pedestal, the smaller one has a statue of a warrior and also presents a dark boat with fancy prow in the right middleground.

Marked (imp.) Adams, GMK. 18, 1800-64.

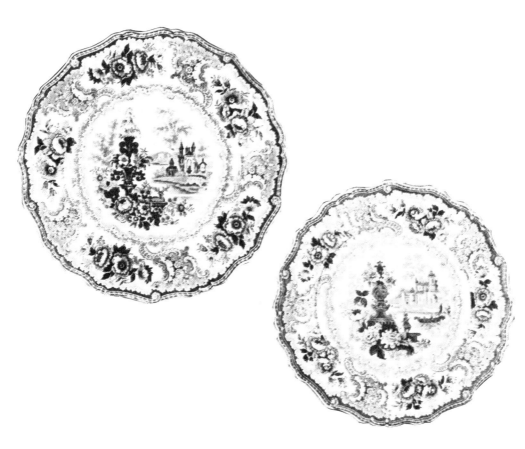

FRENCH SCENERY

Made by Herculaneum Pottery

The gadrooned edge of this unevenly scalloped plate was left white. The dark stippled field of the upper rim is contained at the edge by a printed row of small scallops and by large foliated scrolls with small flowers. The scrolls meet and form a baroque triangular pattern ending in small flowers in three places around the rim, and in three smaller triangles containing a pair of forget-me-nots. Three bouquets of large ruffled peonies with dark leaves alternate with three bouquets of dahlias in the arches formed by the scrolls.

A frame of scallops and dark beads is placed around the central scene which shows a tall fountain at left. It is surmounted by a statue of a kneeling boy with a water jar. Water gushes from the lion mask on the face of the plinth and falls into a circular basin on the ground. A girl stands near the fountain. Tall trees are placed on either side of it. A stream divides the picture and on the right bank there are a church, and a tall elm that curves over the scene. In the distance there are other buildings and mountains. In the foreground there is a dark bank and over-scaled flowers.

Marked with an imp. Liverbird, GMK. 2012, 1833-36.

FRIBURG

Made by William Davenport

This twelve sided plate has a rim covered with concentric narrow lines. The design that is superimposed on the lines is made up of ten sections divided by vertical bands. Five of the panels contain a small bouquet and others were left without pattern. The distinguishing feature is the white vine with flowers and tendrils curved around it that winds up and down, over and under the floral panels and into the middle of the plain ones. A row of spearpoint finishes the rim design in the cavetto.

The central scenes differ in this set. The particular one photographed has a fanciful narrow chalet at right. It is decorated with barge boards and crockets and a tall spire. At left there is a tall elm. A river winds through the middle of the scene. In the left background there are buildings, a tower, and some mountains.

Marked as above, (imp.) GMK. 1181a, 1844.

GARDEN SCENERY

Made by Thomas, John and Joseph Mayer

The larger dish in this pattern is fourteen sided and the rim is paneled. The cup plates are twelve sided and paneled. Whorls cover the rim and a small design of leaves with sprigs is placed over the whorls and gives a floral effect. The outer edge is detailed by a row of tiny quatrefoils, and the inner edge of the rim is scalloped and finished with spearpoint around the cavetto. Note that the large plate has three rows of flowers on the rim, the first cup plate two rows, and the second cup plate only one.

The soup plate pictures a rustic garden house at left in the scene. It has a thatched roof. There is a tall pine tree next to it and an elm behind it. A rustic fence is placed in back of the house at right. A man with a high hat, a woman with parasol and a child playing with a dog are in the foreground on a lawn which contains flowers and leaves at left. Behind the group there is a lake or river, a large Gothic castle at right and mountains and other buildings in the distance. The cup plates picture only the rustic fence and flowers and a willow tree at left. Each shows a different towered building in the background at right. There are no figures on either cup plate.

Marked T.J. and J. Mayer and Longport, GMK. 2570, 1843-55.

GEM

Maker unknown

The edge of this oval platter is decorated with a row of alternating dark and light small triangles set in a colored band with a white line inset and finished towards the rim with tiny dotted scallops. The rim is covered with groups of bellflowers hanging from pairs of budding stems. A feather and scroll design is placed to the right of the flowers. A beaded band flanked by the same little dotted scallops as above encircles the well, and the scrolls cross this. A wide band of rustic fencing with berries, leaves, and tendrils frames the central scene which shows a towering Gothic ruin at left center. In the right foreground there is a boat with double triangular sails. At left there are some bushes, flowers, and a piece of stone from the ruin. In the distance there are Alpine peaks. The sun (or moon) shines through clouds above the scene.

GEM (THE)

Made by Thomas, John, and Joseph Mayer

This pattern evidently is named for the medallions placed around the sprigged rim. *Three large scenic vignettes framed with pearls and stones and decorated with a pendant at the bottom alternate with three smaller medallions framed with beads and jewels. The designs are joined by a double chain centered with a diamond. A very dark plain band encircles the outer edge of the plate, and a row of spearpoint is placed around the bottom of the rim and enters the well.*

In the center picture a tall fountain rises from a basin at left. It is placed on top of a balustrade and there is a very large bushy tree behind it. Three small figures are placed below the steps of the terrace in the foreground. At right there are tall dark trees and a large columned building. A river divides the scene and in the distance there are small boats.

Marked T.J. and J. Mayer, GMK. 2570, 1843-55.

GENEVA

Made by Joseph Heath

The paneled rim of this twelve sided plate is covered with a background pattern of vertical lines. The outer edge is defined by a series of narrow scrolled bars containing slanted lines. Five heraldic heart-shaped patterns fashioned of foliated scrolls encircling a small diamond are placed around the rim. The spaces between these contains a trio of small white flowers surrounded by dark sprigs.

Tall elms frame both sides of the central scene. In the foreground there is a road in the center. A man carrying a stick is walking ahead of an aristocratic couple on horseback. The man is on a dark horse, the lady, with flowing veil and gown, is on a white steed. In the background across the lake there is a great white castle with crenellated towers. At right a curved low arched bridge continues the road to the castle, and in the background at left a tall arched bridge crosses the lake from the castle.

Marked J. Heath, GMK. 1993, 1845-53.

GENEVA

Made by John Wedge Wood

The rim of this twelve-sided plate is covered with narrow concentric lines. Superimposed over these are white foliated scrolls that arch and meet in a point to form double arches over a pair of rose sprays. The scrolls intertwine between the arches and form an M. A small rose is placed over the M. The bottom of the rim is encircled by a band of triangles in the cavetto.

In the central scene there is a large Gothic structure at right. A river divides the picture, and an arched bridge, surmounted by two statues, connects the building to the opposite tree-lined shore. In the distance there are other buildings and mountains. In the foreground at left there are wide stone steps. There is a covered urn on a pedestal at the foot of the stair railing which is draped with hanging flowers. In the foreground there is a small dark boat with high prow on the river. A man is punting it and two others are seated within as passengers.

Marked J. Wedgwood, GMK. 4276a, dated 1847.

GENEVESE

Made by James and Ralph Clews

The edge of this scalloped cup plate was left white, and a band of embossed beads enhances the outline. The upper rim is very dark and is contained by foliated scrolls. A design of roses and other flowers flanked by leaves alternate with a pattern of large roses flanked by long sprigs around the rim. A band of spearpoint that points toward the rim and a circle of beads next to it frames the central scene. In the center on this dish a chalet is at right. Tall trees are placed behind it. A stream is at left and there are some white buildings and mountains across the water in the background at left. Over-scaled flowers with dark leaves and a large C scroll are placed across the entire foreground.

Marked Clews Warranted Staffordshire, GMK. 918, 1818-34.

GENEVESE

Made by Minton

The rims of these plates, with the exception of one cup plate, are embossed with scrolls and fleur-de-lis. The dark outer edges are decorated with small scrolls and flowerlets. Large open roses and pairs of flowers surrounded by dark leaves and sprigs cover the rims. The distinguishing feature of the rim design is found in the curved scroll hung with four and five fat leaves, which can be noted at upper left in the pictures.

The scenes differ on the items of this pattern. Each cup plate pictures a small multi-storied building. In the middle distance there is a lake and other buildings can be seen at left. In the distance there are towering Alpine peaks. Tall lacy trees complete the background. In the foreground there are the usual over-scaled flowers and part of a C scroll. The large plates also show chalets, a lake in the center, and towers and mountain peaks in the distance. Tall lacy trees in the background. Two small figures are on the lawn near the building in the picture on the supper plate. Over-scaled flowers, sprigs, and parts of scrolls are placed across the foreground. The largest plate has a ring of diamonds and quatrefoils around the center scene.

Marked M and "Opaque" China, like GMK. 2685, 1822-36.

GENEVESE – Made by Minton (cont.)

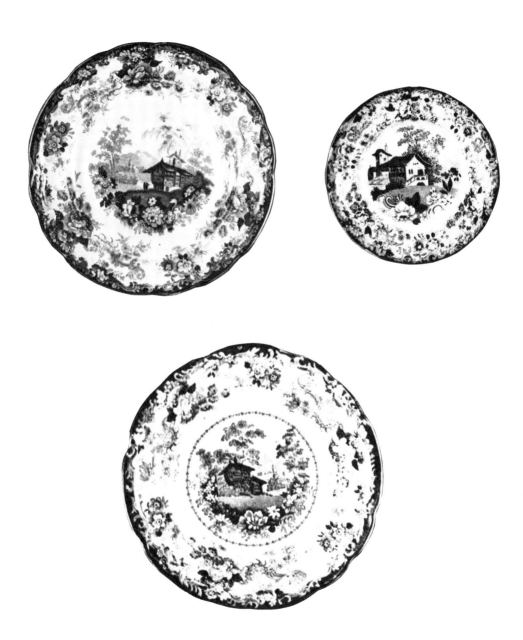

GENOA

Made by William Adams and Sons

This saucer is fourteen-sided. The edge is decorated with a dark narrow band of pointed scallops and beads and the paneled rim is covered with tiny dots that give a point d'esprit effect. A wreath of curved dark branches framed in white and set with small rosettes is placed over the dotted background. The rim design is contained by a scalloped line in the upper well and the cavetto is encircled by a row of snail-like scallops and short slanted tendrils.

In the central scene a facade of a ruined temple is set at right upon a hill. There is a slanted balustrade at the right of the edifice and tall poplars behind it. A waterfall cascades from a small hill below the temple and fills a pond in the right foreground. A river divides the scene. At center two figures stand on the bank near elm trees. Trees and buildings on the left across the river and mountains in the distance complete the scene.

Marked W. Adams and Sons, GMK. 22, 1819-64.

GENOA

Made by William Davenport

The background of the rim of this twelve-sided plate is covered with narrow concentric lines. Five horizontal cartouches, framed by curving lines and fleur-de-lis on each side, contain a scene of a large villa and church flanked by tall trees. The spaces between the vignettes are filled with a tiny diaper design that gives a brick effect and a swag of roses is placed across the top of the spaces and white leaf-like scrolls are at the bottom. Under both patterns there are scrolls flanking a leaf pendant and these form a wreath effect around the well.

The central scene is dominated by a white shrine at right which contains a statue in a niche. A fountain of water gushes from beneath the statue into a curved wide basin. Some people approach the fountain on horseback and two others are seated at left under tall trees. There are buildings, towers, and Alpine peaks in the distance. In the foreground there are pieces of fallen columns.

Marked Davenport, and an (imp.) anchor, GMK. 1181a, dated 1848.

GONDOLA

Probably made by William Davenport and Co.

Both the large plate and the toddy plate photographed are gently scalloped and the outer edges are detailed by a light band of beaded scallops contained by a dark row of triangular points. The larger plate has a rim design consisting of three large scenic reserves containing a picture of a statue of a man holding a horn aloft. The statue probably represents Neptune or Triton. It is placed on a rectangular pedestal and there are other figures at his feet. A city scene is placed behind the group. The reserves are set in baroque frames flanked by dark shields filled with white crosses and trimmed with foliated scrolls. Pairs of over-scaled flowers are placed between the cartouches. The upper third of the rim is stippled.

A double wreath of small scallops, beads, and fleur-de-lis interrupted by vertical dark fleur-de-lis at six points frames the central scene. On the dinner plate there are three large sailboats with upturned prows in the foreground. They are guided by boatmen with long oars. A city scene with columned buildings and towers is behind the boat. The transfer design on the toddy plate omits the wreath around the central scene and the boats differ in style from the larger plate. The distinguishing features of this design are the shield designs and the statue in the border.

Marked with an (imp.) anchor, GMK. 1181, c. 1840.

278

GOTHIC RUINS

Made by Charles Meigh

The white edge of this scalloped plate is detailed by a band of small white rosettes with dark centers. The stippled rim is trimmed with a wreath of Gothic scrolls and bell shapes composed of foliated scrolls. These alternate with an acanthus design. The bottom of the rim pattern is contained by a band of arches containing ovals and terminating in spearpoint. The ruins of a large church are at left center in the picture in the well. Tall arched towers and an empty rose window and Gothic pointed apertures extend from the center of the scene to the left. Tall trees rise at right. There are some rocks and bushes at left, and pieces of broken columns, flowers and leaves are at right in the foreground.

Marked C.M., GMK. 2614a, 1835-49.

GOTHIC SCENERY

Maker unknown

This plate is scalloped and the white outer edge is decorated with molded beading. The outer rim design is composed of white scrolls and small flowers set against a stippled dark background. Three different floral designs, each complete with sprigs and buds, are placed around the rim in six places. The first pattern is composed of seven-petaled flowers with a white petal center. The second is a large cabbage rose, sprays of ferns and forget-me-nots which enter the well in a clock like direction. The third flower pattern is a dahlia-type blossom set above a baroque foliated scroll from which flowers and ferns enter the well and

In the middle ground at left in the central scene there is a small tomb-like building with a tall arched entrance. A man and woman stand at the opening. A tall urn on a pedestal and some bushes are placed on the lawn in front of the structure. In the distance there are a towered domed building at right and tall mountains. Over-scaled flowers and leaves are placed across the foreground.

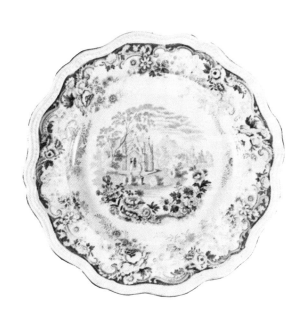

GRECIAN

Made by William Ridgway

The plate shown has an unevenly scalloped edge that is enhanced by a row of printed white beading on a dark background. The upper rim is covered with dainty flowers and leaves. There are six triangular scroll designs placed along the top edge. A row of chains and beads contains the floral designs. Beneath this there are is series of vertical arched divisions that contain stems and leaves that terminate in a wreath of poppies and smaller flowers.

A river divides the central scene. At left in the foreground a flight of steps descends to the water. A pair of stone lions stand guard on either side of the stairs. Three figures are at the top of the steps and a tall white statue of a woman holding an urn stands on a pedestal behind them at far left. Tall trees rise near the statue. An arched bridge crosses the stream in the background and leads to a palace at right. There are three gondolas on the water in the middleground, the largest is near the flight of stone steps.

Marked W.R., GMK. 3301, 1830-34.

GRECIAN

Maker unknown

The edge of this saucer is trimmed with a dark scalloped band enclosing beads. A diamond diaper pattern is placed around the rim. Three triangular scroll designs that flare at the top and which terminate at the bottom is a spray of small flowers alternate on the rim with a bouquet of a large rose, small flowers, dark leaves and buds. The rose buds enter the well as do the sprays below the triangular motifs. The top of the diaper field is contained by white scallops and the bottom by dark ones. A plain ribbon band connects the rim patterns at the bottom. Vertical bars of leaves crowned with rosettes surround the well.

The central picture, framed by a wreath of small triangles shows a statue of a woman holding a spear. She is placed on top of a columned temple at left. Large shrubs are next to the building at left. In the foreground a woman holding a jug stands behind a slanting balustrade and talks to another woman wearing a large hat. An elm rises at right. There are other buildings and tall trees in the background and shrubs in the foreground.

GRECIAN FONT

Made by William Adams and Sons

This edge of this saucer is outlined by small triangles and beads. The rim design is dominated by the semi-circular stylized floral designs. One set of three of these is embellished with scalloped rows of small flowers. These alternate with a drapery design which is skirt-like and composed of triangular lacy layers. Large acanthus leaves pointed toward the well and tipped with a bellflower that enters the well separate the semi-circular designs. These elements are placed against a stippled background.

A tall fountain topped by an urn gushes water into an oblong trough in the central scene. Three women are near the basin and one is filling a small dish. The other two are probably water sellers as they wear the fringed hats denoting that calling and each also carries two buckets. Lacy fernlike trees are behind the font, flowers and bushes are at right. There are over-scaled flowers in the foreground.

Marked (imp.) Adams, GMK. 18, 1800-64.

GRECIAN GARDENS

Made by Job and John Jackson

The rim design of this white-edged scalloped plate is distinguished by the lacy drapery bands that connect the floral groups and form an octagonal opening for the central scene. The outer edge of the rim is decorated with a row of tiny white shallow scallops, a dark band of triangles and a light band of arches containing a beaded heart. The floral groups, flanked by sprigs, cover the rim and tiny ferns enter the well under each bouquet.

A statue of Diana the huntress and her dog is placed on a pedestal at left. Tall trees rise behind her and there are flowers at left and in the foreground. A balustrade and some flowers are at right and in the distance at right across a lake there are a domed tall temple and columned buildings, trees and bushes.

Marked *Jackson's Warranted*, GMK. 2156, 1831-35.

GRECIAN SCENERY

Made by Edward and George Phillips

The white edges of these plates are scalloped. The upper parts of the rims are covered with a dark stippled field contained at the outer edges by a dark and light beaded line. Large foliated scrolls are placed beneath the stippling. Three pairs of large open roses, peonies, and leaves, flanked by sprays of daisies alternate on the rim with three pairs composed of a rose and a large dahlia set over a scroll and surrounded by sprigs and forget-me-nots. The well is encircled by a narrow wreath of oval beads separated by tiny diamonds and small crosses.

The central scene on the large plate shows fruits and flowers on the pedestal under a large urn in the left foreground. Two tall spikes of fruit clusters, leaves and roses rise from this base. At right a seated woman plays with a child and a little dog. At extreme left there is a high-prowed boat with tall sail. It is filled with standing men. In the distance across the river there is a circular tall fountain and there are many buildings on the banks of the waterway. The scene on the cup plate follows the pattern on the larger plate but shows a temple at right, and a different urn on top of the pedestal.

Marked E. and G. Phillips, GMK. 3009, 1822-34.

GRECIAN SCENERY

Maker unknown

The four pictures photographed of this pattern show the unevenly scalloped rims and dark beaded outer edges which are common to all size plates in this pattern. The upper rim is decorated with a design of foliated scrolls which is linked at three places near the edge with a scallop shell set under a pair of rosettes. Small sprigs are placed under the shells and the larger plates bear unframed vignettes around the rim each containing a scene of two small sailboats and differing Greco-Roman buildings and mountains. These are separated by floral bouquets, three placed under the scallop shell design and the other three under a pair of beaded scrolls.

The well on the largest plate is circled by a narrow band of U shapes. The central scenes differ, the one on the largest plate depicts a scene with a ruin at left and a large high-prowed boat in the center. The other plate shows a building with columned portico and high dome in the left background. A small sailboat is on a waterway nearby. Each plate shows people seated and standing in the foreground near fallen building stones, and each has tall trees and mountains. The cup plates contain identical central patterns and depict in the center scene two men standing near a pedestal base. They are on the bank of a river. A boat is midstream and there is a domed building at extreme right in the distance. Tall elm trees rise at left. The small dishes show only a very small part of the rim design.

Marked "Stone China".

GRECIAN SCENERY (cont.)

GRECIAN SCENERY

Made by Enoch Wood and Sons

    The distinctive white gadrooned scalloped edge used by Wood in his Celtic China series is enhanced by a row of printed scallops and trefoils placed on the upper rim of the plate shown. The entire plate is stippled. The rim design of wild roses, leaves, forget-me-nots, and a zinnia-type flower enters the well. A white circle composed of vertical beaded narrow bands separates the rim pattern from the central scene which contains a white temple-like mansion in the center. The windows of the uppermost level are illuminated. The building is surrounded by trees and bushes. In the foreground a courtier and lady stand on top of a hill that slopes downward to the castle. Their backs are to the viewer. There are two other couples on the slopes below.

    Marked E.W. and S. and "Celtic China", GMK. 4260, 1814-36.

"HARBOR SCENE"

Made by Josiah Wedgwood & Son

The border pattern for this design appears inside the upper part of the small cup photographed and consists of realistic white bellflowers and groups of white, wild roses separated by very dark leaves and forget-me-nots.

There are two large boats in the center of the scene on the body of the mug, one is white, one is dark. Both have sails and pennants and there are fishermen on both vessels. In the background there are towered buildings at left behind an arched bridge. At right in the distance there is a castle set above battlements on the river.

This is marked (imp.) Wedgwood, GMK. 4075, c. 1840-45.

289

"HERCULES FOUNTAIN"

Made by George Miles and Charles James Mason

The platter photographed is lobed and the edge is detailed with a band of twisted rope. Eight fan-shaped patterns, white and pleated at the top around a rosette, framed with dark beads and a double scallop band with four rosettes and leaves, are placed around the upper rim. Large peonies flanked by fern-like leaves, fronds and buds fill the rest of the rim. The well pattern is framed by small clusters of leaves set against a white scalloped background.

The central scene shows a large manor house at right behind some stylized trees. There are grassy lawns in the left background and two couples stroll thereon. The entrance to the lawn is flanked by white urns set on posts and a fence continues from the opening. There are spotted deer in a glade at right. The dominant design is the large fountain at center left. Winged griffons spout water into a pond and on top of a round urn there is a statue of Hercules killing the Hydra (the many headed beast). The statue is black against the sky in the background and a stream of white water falls from the dark figures.

Marked Mason's Warranted and "Semi China" GMK. 2546, 1818-29.

HOLLY

Maker unknown

This plate is gently scalloped and there is an embossed scalloped line near the outer edge. The concave rim is paneled and is covered with narrow, concentric lines. A wreath of holly leaves, berries and vines surrounds the rim. A white line contains the rim pattern and a wreath of furled leaves with tiny sprigs below them encircles the upper well. In the central scene a double-arched, stone bridge leads across a stream to a tall castle-like building at the right. At left there is a tall tree. In the foreground one sees part of a curving low wall and some fallen tree limbs.

Marked M.T. & Co. and "Ironstone China", see Athena for same mark, c. 1852.

HOLLYWELL COTTAGE, CAVAN

Made by John & Richard Riley

This pattern is distinguished by the rim design of over-scaled, foliated scrolls that embrace a diaper field of dark stylized rosettes set in diamond lattice. A shell form appears above the lattice. The scroll designs are separated by a trio of speckled lilies with buds. The white outer edge is enhanced by a wide printed band of beaded scallops. The rim is stippled below the border pattern and the stippling is separated from the center scene by a wreath of white beading.

In the central design three men are fishing from a long, flat, dark boat, in a river which crosses the middle of the scene. In the foreground there are rocks and bushes and tall trees at left. Across the water the "Cottage" is seen nestled in its park. Tall trees rise behind it. In the distance a church spire, topped by a cross is seen above the trees.

Marked Riley's, Semi China, and "Warranted", GMK. 3329, c. 1802-28.

HOLY BIBLE

Made by Job and John Jackson

The scalloped pointed edge of the large plates shown also appears on the cup plate. A band of white beads is placed against the outer edge of all three dishes. The rim design is distinguished by the baroque shield shapes filled with a net diaper pattern and framed with foliated scrolls. The shields alternate around the rim with open spaces containing a pair of large flowers, one white and with five petals and the other dark and multi-petaled. Large foliated scrolls and forget-me-nots are placed over the flowers against the stippled upper rim. All three plates bear the same lacy wreath of oval beads and deep spearpoint around the central scene.

The scenes differ on the various dishes of this pattern. On the largest plate the ruins of the city of Tadmor are shown. In the foreground a man leads his camel and another rides his beast on a path between tall, shaggy trees and a fallen column at right and column ruins at left. In the distance there are tall mountains with Alpine peaks. The plate is sub-titled "Tadmor in the Desert". Tadmor is an old name for Palmyra, which was destroyed when it rebelled against Roman rule.

The second plate is not sub-titled. It is marked only "Holy Bible". It shows two men, one on a camel and one on a horse, who are meeting on a road in the foreground. Behind them at left there is a palm tree and some columns. At right there is a tall, ruined, arch frame. The cup plate bears no back stamp. It carries a scene of temples and towers and mountains in the distance at left, tall palm trees at right, and shrubs and pieces of broken columns in the foreground. The distinctive elements in this pattern are the triangular, shield-shaped reserves filled with the diamond diaper pattern.

Marked Jackson's Warranted, GMK. 2156, c. 1831-5.

HOLY BIBLE (cont.)

HUDSON

Made by Thomas Edwards

The rim of the saucer shown is paneled and is covered with a basket-weave pattern consisting of concentric lines interspersed with small ovals bisected by a dark line. The effect is of hundreds of eyes. The top of the design is contained by a doubled scalloped line and beads. At the well a row of white, deep, small scallops filled with stippling and further decorated by a fleur-de-lis forms a wreath around the well.

In the center lake scene, there are two figures who hold fishing poles. The lady stands, the man is seated on the bank. Some large rocks are near him and there are others in the foreground. At right, a narrow flight of stone steps leads towards an oval doorway. In the distance there are towers and buildings. At left, a tall elm rises from behind a very steep bank. Across the water there is a classical building with a triangular pediment. In the distance there are other buildings and mountains.

Marked T.E., GMK. 1454, c. 1839-41.

ILLUSTRATIONS OF THE BIBLE

Made by Thomas Mayer

The concave rim of this unevenly scalloped plate is covered with a trellis pattern, enhanced with stylized, white flowers at the diamond intersections. In each diamond of the trellis there is a snowflake. The same eight-petaled white flowers are set around the outer rim against a dark stippled ground. Pairs of large flowers with very dark leaves are placed around the rim. The trellis pattern ends at the well with a band of rosettes but the slanting lines are continued and cross through a wreath made of octagonal beads inset with rosettes and terminate finally in a small beaded design around the well.

The backstamp reads "Tomb of Absalom, Village of Siloan the Brook Kedron". The tomb is at left on an elevation, the village is in the distance, the brook runs at right through a double arched bridge. There are four men in the foreground, two more stand below them at the base of a pair of tall palm trees, and still another person in white kneels at the tomb.

The backstamp on the bowl reads "Foot of Mount Sinai". The dish contains a picture of a goatherd with his flock of goats. He is seated at right holding his crook and drawing water from a small stream that crosses the scene. Two men in desert costume of burnoose and turban are behind the herdsman. They stand near a black horse. Small goats are placed against the hilly and rocky terrain of the scene and there are palm trees on a hill at left center. In the distance at right is Mount Sinai.

Marked T. Mayer and "Longport", GMK. 2568, c. 1836-38.

INDIAN TEMPLES

Maker unknown

This plate is unevenly scalloped and the outer edge is white. A row of small printed diamonds follows the scalloped outline. The rim bears three baroque cartouches, framed in scrolls and draped with small flowers. Each contains a distinctive picture of an open-air temple with peaked roof and attached arches. Between the vignettes there are sprays of large cabbage roses, dahlias, small flowers and leaves. The upper section of the rim is stippled.

A wreath of tiny spearpoint forms a frame around the central scene. This appears European and contains a castle with a rounded tower at right behind some leafy trees. At left center, there are very tall trees. At extreme left, one sees a boat with double sails. A river divides the scene horizontally in the middle ground. In the center there are two boats, one with a half-furled sail. In the foreground, there are two people seated and a man stands near them on a river bank. A boat with tall, triangular, dark mast is seen behind the figures. There are over-scaled flowers in the foreground. In the distance, across the water, one sees other buildings and hills.

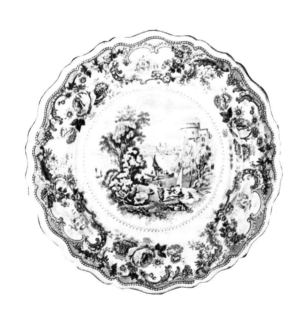

IONIC

Made by Clementson & Young

The very fine diamond diaper pattern shown on the collar of this pitcher is decorated with a wreath of oak leaves and small acorns. It is contained at the bottom by a narrow dark band of small diamonds, linked with half squares. Under this there is a light row of narrow arch forms that contain an oblong bar, which are linked with dark bars that are spearpointed.

The scene on the body of the pitcher is dominated by a large ruin with many arches at right. Across the river or bay, at left, there are tall elms and flowers. At extreme left, behind the trees, one sees other classic buildings and ruins. There are three people on the bank of the river in the foreground. A man and woman stand. Two greyhounds are near them. A woman is seated on the steps of a platform contained by a stone balustrade at the water's edge. There are arched openings at the extreme right in the foreground. A terrace is seen above the arches and there are tall trees, a lawn and a balustrade there. The identical scene was used on the outside of the small cup. This pattern is the same as Palmyra by Wood & Brownfield (this category).

Marked as above, GMK. 911, c. 1845-7.

ISOLA BELLA

Made by William Adams and Sons

The rims of the octagonal platter shown and of the fourteen-sided cup plate are covered with small sprigs. Eight starburst designs centered with three stylized flowers alternate around the rims with a trio of realistic blossoms. The pattern resembles inverted triangles.

In the center scene a man and woman are in the foreground. They are dressed in court costume. The man in doublet, cape and tights, leans on an urn placed at the end of a balustrade. The woman faces him and is patting a greyhound. There is a tall vase on a tripod at right. Roses climb the wall at right and tall elms rise from behind the vase. At left there is a tiered tall fountain surrounded by roses and other plants. A large formal building is at left and is connected to a chapel with tall columned tower. Both structures are surmounted with urns. There is a lake in the background and other buildings, trees, and mountains can be seen across the water. The cup plate pictures a woman wearing a shawl who stands near a tall fountain. At extreme right there is a statue on a pedestal and a towering elm. At left there is a small temple and behind that a large building with domed tower.

Marked W. Adams and Sons, and "Stone China", GMK. 22, 1819-64.

ITALIA

Made by Thomas Furnival & Co.

The edge of the twelve-sided plate shown is decorated with a band of dark, vertical ovals. The upper part of the rim is printed with a wreath of morning-glories and leaves that twine over a rod. The rest of the rim is covered with a diamond diaper pattern that terminates in a wreath of tiny, spearpoint around the cavetto.

In the foreground of the center scene, a man fishes from the bank of a stream that divides the picture. A man lies on a rocky bank behind him. A woman carrying a net over her shoulder stands and holds a child who pats a dog. Behind the figures there are four white sheep. There are sailboats in the water. An arched bridge crosses at mid-way in the scene. At right, there are tall trees and bushes. At left, there are a castle and round temple on a hill. In the distance there are mountains. In the foreground, there are the usual flowers and rocks and a small pond.

Marked T.F. & Co., GMK. 1645, c. 1844-46.

ITALIAN BUILDINGS
Made by Ralph Hall

Both the cup plate and supper plate photographed are gently scalloped and the rims are indented. The edge of the cup plate was left white, that of the larger plate was not. A printed scalloped band composed of small white V shapes interrupted by pairs of half flowers at three points outlines the edge of the plates. Three shield designs are placed under the half flowers. They alternate with a trio of large flowers which is flanked on the right by a half of a large shell pattern. Other small flowers and sprigs are placed between the main designs. The upper rim is stippled and there are shaded vertical lines in the middle section of the rim.

The central scene on both plates is framed by a circle of spearpoint. The scenes differ on the plates. The cup plate shows a lady wearing a large hat, holding flowers, and standing near an urn at left. A basket is at her feet. Behind her there is a river with a small sailboat. In the distance there are classic buildings at right. The larger plate adds a kneeling woman near the basket, a vase at center, different domed buildings, and Alpine peaks in the background. Both dishes show large flowers in the foreground. The distinctive detail in this design is the shaded rim design. This is like "Italian Villas" by Heath.

Marked R. Hall, GMK. 1888, 1822-41.

ITALIAN FLOWER GARDEN

Made by John and William Ridgway

The unusual mold used for this pattern produced a scalloped plate with twelve embossed flowers around the edge. A printed pattern of triangles over narrow white beads accentuates the white flowers. The upper part of the rim is stippled and is contained by foliated scrolls. Four large wild roses alternate with three tea roses around the rest of the rim. Both floral patterns are trimmed with sprigs and buds. A reverse row of triangles frames the well scene.

A Rococo pattern of large flowers, trellis, and scrolls is placed across the foreground in the central scene. One tall branch of prunus rises from the floral base and curves over the top of the scene. At left in the background there is a garden lantern of baluster shape. In the distance at right, and beyond a lake, there is a domed gazebo with lattice walls.

Marked J.W.R., GMK. 3260, 1814-30.

ITALIAN LAKES

Made by J. and M.P. Bell and Co.

The edge of this slightly scalloped plate is trimmed with a row of quatrefoil and triangles, placed next to a white band. Four cartouches flanked by baroque scrolls are placed against a background of mosaic lines, grape leaves, and bubbles. Two of the cartouches contain a scene of two seated boys and two dancing girls in a garden setting. The other two show a pair of Cupids; one pulls a mythical beast laden with grapes and the other rides its back. A band of scrolls placed above tassled rosettes encircles the upper well.

In the middle of the central scene a girl dances with a tambourine. Four persons are seated on the ground around her and one is playing a guitar. At right steps lead to a formal villa with a temple-like entrance. Tall trees rise near the steps. The lake of the title divides the scene, and across the water there are buildings, towers, trees, and tall mountains surmounted by other buildings. In the foreground there are small flowers.

Marked J. and M.P.B. & Co., GMK. 318, 1850-70.

ITALIAN SCENERY

Made by John Meir & Son

The edges of these dishes are decorated with a band of diamonds which enclose beads. Four scenic vignettes, framed with lily buds, leaves and scrolls, are placed against the stippled rim. Each contains a different bucolic scene that includes two figures, a cottage and trees. The reserves are separated by a very large, wild rose flanked by a pair of small white flowers with dark leaves at left and dark leaves and a single, dark blossom at right.

In the foreground of the central scene on the platter, a man on horseback is pointing to the right. A man stands near him at left and he has a gun over his shoulder. They are placed on a rocky bank of a river which flows through the middle of the scene. There are flowers and reeds in the foreground and tall bushy trees at right. In the background, there are the buildings and towers of a city placed on a hill which rises above the river. There are mountains behind the city. On the left bank there are trees on a promontory and two people stand near the water. A boat containing three persons is behind them.

The central scene on the dinner plate shows a woman dressed in white who is seated at right on a boulder. A cow stands, with a goat, on the stony bank of the foreground and another smaller goat is near the woman. Tall trees and bushes rise at right. There are over-scaled leafy plants in the foreground. A river divides the scene diagonally. A rowboat, containing a man who rows and one who stands holding a pole approaches the right shore. In the background, there is a castle at left, an arched bridge in the middle, and tall mountains in the distance. A few trees and part of a fence can be seen at the left.

Marked I.M. & S., GMK. 2634, c. 1837-97.

ITALIAN SCENERY (cont.)

ITALIAN VILLAS

Made by Joseph Heath & Co.

These plates are unevenly scalloped and the white rolled edges are contained by a narrow printed line and a band of printed white beads. Three distinctive, wide dark reserves, flanked by foliated scrolls, are placed over a large dahlia with dark leaves, flanked by single small flowers. These alternate around the upper rim with three smaller, but equally distinctively triangular dark areas in which there is a white V which are placed over a large, open rose and a large daisy. Shadowy small flowers are placed in the background of the rim and in the upper well. A roll of scallops and small spearpoint separate the rim pattern from the central scene.

The pictures differ on. the various items in this pattern, but each of the plates shown contains a fancy covered urn at right. Each urn has a row of white beads around the body. There are tall trees at left in both scenes and over-scaled flowers in the foreground and at right. Both show a lake in the background and imposing buildings on the far shore. Each has shadowy trees placed behind the urns. There are two figures with large, dark plummed hats in each scene. One shows two women, one of whom draws water from a fountain basin set beneath the urn; the other sits nearby facing the background. The second view presents a woman with a tall vase that she has placed on the edge of a pedestal near the urn. She holds the vase with one hand, and with the other hand, offers a bouquet to a man who is seated at left center.

Marked J.H. & Co., and (imp.) propeller mark, GMK. 1194a, c. 1838-41.

ITALY

Made by Edge Malkin & Co.

This toy plate is covered with a scenic pattern which shows a woman riding a donkey on the road in the foreground. A man with a long stick walks beside her. At right there is an obelisk and a tall elm tree. In the background at left there are large formal buildings of Tuscan architecture. Two men are pushing a pushcart on the road in the middle ground. There are towers, white buildings and mountains in the background.

Marked E.M. & Co., GMK. 1341, c. 1871-80.

ITALY

Made by Charles Meigh & Son

The rim of this plate is covered with four horizontal scenic reserves containing identical pictures of a river scene with buildings on both sides of the water, and a man, woman and dog standing at left near a tall tree and some bushes. The reserves are separated by a heart-shaped design filled with roses and flanked by large foliated scrolls which terminate in the top of the well. There is a band of running scrolls beneath the reserves and another of ovular beads below that. There is also a second band of tiny beads placed over a narrow band which runs beneath the designs of white scallops and dots and forms a cross design around the well.

In the foreground of the central scene, a man with his dog stands facing two women who are on a stone platform overlooking a river. At left there is a tall square column topped by an urn and a building that resembles a shrine with an oval niche. A tall tree rises in the center of the scene and there are other trees at left. At right across the water there are classic buildings. One is surmounted with three statutes. There are trees and mountains in the distance.

Marked C.M. & Son, like GMK. 2620, c. 1851-61.

IVANHOE

Made by Podmore Walker & Co.

These plates are twelve sided and their rims are covered with narrow, concentric lines that peak every one-half inch and the pattern formed by this creates a vertical division line. The outer edges and the well edges of the rims are decorated with bands of scrolled triangles which give a scalloped effect in the well.

The center scene on the larger plate shows a gazebo at right. It has a fancy, rustic trellised roof. Behind it there are tall chimney-like ruins. In the foreground at center left there are a man, woman and child on a bank overlooking a lake and small waterfall. A tall graceful elm rises from the left bank.

In the distance, one sees a castle, a tower on a mountain peak, and a bridge across the lake.

The cup plate has an identical rim design, which is the distinguishing feature of this pattern. The gazebo appears at right with the ruins behind it. The single figure of a woman is placed on the left bank under the elm. The background details have been omitted.

Marked P.W. & Co., and (imp.), "Pearl Stone Ware", GMK. 3067, c. 1834-59.

JENNY LIND

Made by Charles Meigh & Son

These plates are twelve sided and the paneled rims are stippled at the top. A wreath of leaves and berries set on a vine with tendrils was placed between the stippling and a fine net ground that covers the rest of the rim. Four scenic vignettes appear on the rim; they are unframed. Each contains the same scene of a Greek temple in the center with tall trees at either side.

The central scene shows a group of five people standing on a lawn in the foreground. One of the men in the center of the group is looking through a telescope at a castle across the lake. Tall elms rise at left and there are smaller trees at right and mountains in the distance. The number of people set in the scene varies on the different items in this pattern. The cup plate shows only two people, the man with the telescope and a seated lady.

Marked C.M. & S., GMK. 2620, c. 1851-61.

JESSAMINE
Made by James & Ralph Clews

A wreath of jasmine and passion flowers, leaves and vines, encircles the rim of the saucer photographed. Dark foliated scrolls, centered with fleur-de-lis are placed in six points around the upper rim. The edge of the dish is decorated with a narrow, printed scalloped design. The bottom of the rim pattern is contained by a double row of curved diamonds linked with fleur-de-lis that gives a lace effect and which terminates in the well to form spearpoint.

In the center scene there are a three story Gothic tower and chapel at left. In the foreground at right, a large deer with tall antlers stands amidst shrubs, an over-scaled jasmine blossom is at its feet. There are some other flowers and some boulders in the left and center foreground. Tall trees are placed behind the tower, and at its right and left, and form a circular effect for the scene.

Marked R. & J. Clews, see Godden, p. 151, c. 1818-34.

JUVENILE AMUSEMENT

Maker unknown

The border pattern on the sugar bowl and on its lid consists of an outer edging of white ovals, a stippled background on the upper rim, and a pattern of rectangular shapes topped with slanting sides (like a house with roof) which are filled with diamond trellis and flanked with large leaves and sprigs. Each is set upon a foliated scroll base. Scrolls form pointed arches between the above pattern. A peacock, with wings folded, is standing among some sprigs in each arch.

The oval panels on the sides of the vessel are framed in stars and beads and show a standing girl holding a bouquet and a boy kneeling nearby. They are at left, and the girl is holding out food to a peacock with its tail unfurled at right. Behind the bird there is a wall and on top of the wall there is a bird cage with an open door. A small bird sits on its roof. In the background there are bushes and towers. Groups of large fruits are on either side of the oval scenes.

KLUMN

Made by Wood & Challinor

The gently scalloped white edge of this plate is trimmed with a small, deep row of scallops containing rosettes. Foliated scrolls placed around the upper rim are interrupted by four large, inverted spade designs set over C scrolls, that are on top of a vase form flanked by tripods topped with rosettes. These large triangular designs are separated by floral patterns of leaves, sprigs and a large thistle. A small dark shield is placed over the thistle at the top of the rim. The entire rim is stippled. The space between the rim design and the center medallion is filled with a wreath of realistic flowers.

The scene in the center depicts a large castle set on a mountain in the middle of the picture. A high round tower dominates the scene. A bridge leads to the castle at right and at left there is a tall elm. In the foreground, two standing women, one with a basket on her head, and a seated man wearing a backpack, are facing the castle scene. There are large flowers and sprigs in the foreground of the scene and at right. There are a lake and mountains in the background. Clouds complete the circular scene.

Marked W. & C., GMK. 4244, c. 1834-43.

LANDSCAPE

W.R. Midwinter

This is a late rendition of an old pattern which has been noted in dark red and also in very dark green. The edge is unevenly scalloped and the bold rim pattern consists of paisley-like scrolls filled with white swirls that alternate with white stylized flowers with pinwheel stamen centers. Both designs are flanked by foliated scrolls and trios of small flowers with leaves. A white zigzag line separates the rim pattern from the well picture.

A man and woman stand together in the foreground in the central scene. Another man is seated on the ground in front of the pair. Behind them, at at left, there is a large, open, round, covered, columned garden house with ornate roof and finial. At left, there is an archway and a wall and a man and woman can be seen behind the arch. Tall trees rise from behind the wall. At right, a triple-arched bridge crosses a stream. A man driving a cow is at the bridge approach. In the distance there are hills, stylized trees, houses and clouds.

Marked as above, See Godden, p. 436, c. 1910.

LAUSANNE VILLA

Maker unknown

The white edge of this scalloped plate is embossed with beading. A narrow line of printed beads is set at the top of the rim pattern. Six shield designs, filled with a diamond diaper design and crowned by a scroll reserve containing the same diaper pattern are placed around the rim. There is a shell set into the upper diaper pattern. These designs separate the pattern of large flowers flanked by scrolls and smaller blossoms and three floral festoons that are suspended from a scroll design at the top. Above the two floral designs, the upper rim is printed with a fine diamond net.

A wreath of small buds surrounds the central scene of a church-like structure at right which is set upon the rocky bank of a river. A slanted double-arched bridge crosses the water and at left there is a tall bushy tree and a flower strewn bank. In the background, there is a rocky promontory and in the distance there are mountains. The foreground is covered with over-scaled flowers and sprigs.

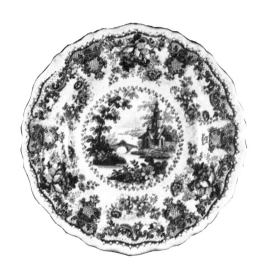

LOMBARDY

Made by Joseph Heath & Co.

The edge of this fourteen sided plate is detailed by a row of quatrefoils set over a dark scalloped line. The rim is covered with mossy sprigs and trios of stylized flowers flanked by small sprays are set into the moss. In the center scene in the foreground, there is a pair of gondolas. One has a light prow, the other a dark one, and each bears two figures. At left, behind the landing, which is flanked by an urn on one side and a statue of a lion on a pedestal on the other, there are towers and tall poplar trees. At right, across the stream, there are three small boats. Towers, buildings, and Alpine peaks are in the background. Note the overhead rays of light from the sun (or moon) streaming from behind billowing clouds.

Marked J. Heath & Co., and an (imp.) propeller, GMK. 1994, 1828-41.

LORRAINE

William Adams & Sons

The outer edges of these three plates are decorated with a band of large and small diamonds that produce a plaid effect. The rest of the rims are covered with a wreath of lilies, small flowers, leaves, sprigs, buds and scrolls. This is placed over a dark stippled ground at the top of the rim and crosses the plain part of the lower rim and invades the well.

The scene in the center on the largest plate is bucolic. Three cows are placed at left on a river bank under the branches of a tall curving elm. At right across the water, there is a chalet with a roof slanting over its balconies and porches. Behind the house one sees a tower topped with a cross, and rooves, tall poplars and other trees. In the middle distance there are buildings and mountains. In the foreground there are small branches of flowers. The dark cup plate shows the border clearly. The herd of animals has been reduced to a single cow on the left bank. Otherwise the scene is the same as on the larger examples. The flow blue cup plate shown illustrates how the transfer can seem so different when placed in a flowing color. The border pattern is the same and the outer edge of diamond plaid is the same. The only thing that is different on the second cup plate is that the building across the stream is a much more fanciful chalet.

Marked W. Adams and "Ironstone", GMK. 26, c. 1850.

LORRAINE (cont.)

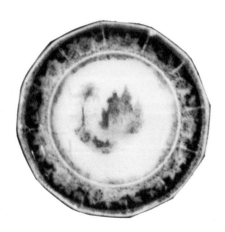

LOZERE
Made by Edward Challinor

Both of these plates are twelve sided and paneled but the edge of the cup plate does not show the angles as clearly as the salad plate. The rims are identical and bear a background of narrow, concentric lines. Oblong cartouches formed by scrolls and containing a scene of a castle with towers flanked by tall dark trees are placed in four places around the rim. The reserves are separated by a shield design filled with a diamond diaper pattern and topped by a pair of scrolls terminating in leaves and centered with a white fleur-de-lis. The well is encircled by a band of diamonds and pendant quatrefoils which gives a spearpoint effect. The central scene differs on these plates but the scene on the bread plate also appears on dinner plates in the pattern. Two women wearing shawls stand in a formal garden near a semi-circular stone bench in the foreground. There is a cherub supported fountain and basin at right. Behind the figures, one sees a lake or stream crossed by an arched bridge. In the distance at right, there is a turreted castle. Tall elms rise at left. The cup plate design omits the figures, the fountain and the arched bridge. The semi-circular stone bench is retained and is probably one of the distinguishing features of the pattern.

Marked E. Challinor and "Ironstone", GMK. 835A, c. 1842-67.

LUCERNE

Made by Joseph Clementson

The inner rim of the waste bowl photographed has a rim design composed of an abstract seaweed pattern set with conch shells and a flower in six places. The upper edge, both inside and out, is detailed by a band of scallops separated by bars and centered with beads. The inner edge of the rim design carries a lacy hanging border of tasseled squares containing a bead and a sprig topped with a double scroll.

The picture on both sides of the vessel are the same and depicts a Swiss scene. In the foreground a peasant woman stands holding a pole. A man is seated on the grass near her. He leans against a pile of rocks at left. There are flowers, a fence and pine trees at right. Behind the figures one sees a waterfall. A rustic bridge crosses over the falls in the center of the scene. At right there is a mill. Its wheel is near the entrance to the bridge. In the distance one can see the buildings of a town set against Alpine peaks.

Marked J.C., GMK. 910, c. 1839-64.

LUCERNE

Made by J.W. Parkhurst & Co.

There are four scenic cartouches framed with foliated scrolls on the rim of this dish. Each contains the same picture of a church at right, some bushes next to it, and a lake and tall trees at left. The space between the reserves is filled with a wavy, diaper pattern of diamonds. Scrolls from the cartouche frames meet under the diaper design. A vine runs around the edge and grape leaves and tendrils descend from this into the diaper pattern. A white band from which fleur-de-lis are suspended surrounds the upper well.

In the central scene there is a large chalet on a hill at left. Poplar trees can be seen behind the house. A road winds past the edifice and three tall trees rise near the road in the middle of the scene. There are flowers on the sloping bank of the lawn that rises to meet the road. Below the road one sees the Lake Lucerne of the title. There are towered buildings along the right shore, and part of a mountain slope in the distance. This pattern may appear under the W. Ridgway mark as Parkhurst succeeded Ridgway.

Marked J.W.P. & Co., GMK. 2954, c. 1852-80.

MALTESE
Made by William Brownfield

The rim of this plate is covered with an egg crate diaper pattern and seven groups of three white flowers with dark centers connected by lacy foliated scrolls at the top surround the rim. Tiny quatrefoils appear above the scrolls. The bottom of the rim design is contained by scallops. Straight lines descend from these to a white, wavy band, topped by trefoils. This is trimmed with trios of bud shapes which are placed in the well.

In the center a man and woman stand in the foreground. He is pointing to a statue of a Roman Emperor on a pedestal at left. There is a large covered urn at right. Behind the couple there is a river. A foot-bridge in the background connects a leafy bank at left which is surmounted by a double-storied gazebo to an island with a trellised arch, steps and a four-story church-like building with a gazebo at the right. In the background there are other buildings.

Marked W.B., GMK. 660, c. 1850-91.

"MANOR HOUSE"

Made by William Adams

The edge of this cup plate is decorated with a wide, scalloped band. Each scallop contains either a quatrefoil or a rosette. The transfer covers the entire surface of the dish. Trees arch up from either side of the scene and flowers and grassy shrubs are placed in a semi circle in the foreground. In the background and in the center of the scene a mansion sits on a hill overlooking a lake.

Marked (imp.) Adams, GMK. 18, c. 1800-64.

MANSION

Maker unknown

This deep dish is twelve sided. The upper part of the paneled rim is covered with a design of foliated scrolls placed over a striated field. At six points the scrolls terminate in a large fleur-de-lis design that points towards the well. A small stylized flower is placed above the fleur-de-lis and midway between the scrolls there is a white triangular design. Groups of realistic flowers are placed in the arched reserves created by the scrolls and fleur-de-lis.

In the center of the well of the larger dish the circular picture presents a large encrusted urn at left. There are flowers on the ground behind it and flowers and sprigs in the foreground. At right in the center distance, there is a large building which has pillars and is domed. It sits on a river bank. There are a pine tree and some stone blocks at extreme right. In the distance one sees mountains.

The cup plate bears almost the same rim design but that on the larger plate is printed with much greater detail. The distinguishing feature of the rim pattern is the spade shape design of the fleur-de-lis and the double foliated scrolls flanking it. The central scene is different on the cup plate and on it a small, two-handled urn is in the foreground on a stone platform which has steps at right. A tall elm is at extreme right and there are a castle-like building, a river and mountains in the background.

MANTUA
Made by Read & Clemenson

The pedestalled cake plate in the photograph is 11¾" diameter. The edge is slightly scalloped. Six scenic cartouches framed with foliated scrolls, are placed in a border field of stylized eight-petalled rosettes. Each cartouche contains a different picture of Italian villas and towered buildings. The well is encircled by a narrow row of lace from which small sprays and arrowheads descend towards the center and form a fancy spearpoint design interrupted by triangular shell designs at the bottom of the cartouches.

The center scene shows a gazebo at left. It is arched and capped with a domed roof. At right there is a small statue of a woman. In the middle ground there is an arched bridge over a stream and a boat is placed on the water in the foreground. A costumed man stands at the helm and two women are seated behind him. In the distance there are tall elms and a castle-like building.

The cup plate is scalloped. There are four cartouches on the flowered field but otherwise the border treatment is the same as that on the big plate. The central scene, however, shows a different type gazebo left and tall trees behind it. There is a stream of water in the center of the picture but the bridge, statue, boat and background buildings have been omitted. There are flowers in the foreground in the place of the boat.

Marked R. & C. and "Stoneware", GMK. 3212, c. 1833-35.

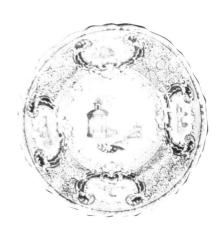

MARCELLA

Made by William Ridgway & Co.

A row of tiny, oval beads is placed around the white outside edge of the saucer photographed. On the rim there are three scenic cartouches framed by little flowers. These contain a classic domed building, an arched bridge and a tower at the right. The vignettes alternate with key-hole shaped cartouches containing a flower and sprigs framed with three little flowers. The background of the rim is filled with tiny branches. The bottom of the rim design is contained by a narrow, dark scalloped line.

In the center scene on the saucer there is a double-storied domed building and tower with a sphere placed on its spire. It rests on a platform and base composed of baroque scrolls and flowers. A figure is seated on the steps of the platform and another figure stands near him. At left there are tall, leafy trees and in the distance across a lake there are classic temple buildings.

In the bottom of the cup the domed building is shown at left; the arched bridge is present. These are details from the rim pattern (not shown). The scene on the cup plate shows a small, square domed building at left. Behind it there are other buildings and minarets. In the foreground, there is a branch of over-scaled leaves.

Marked W.R. & Co., GMK. 3303, c. 1834-54.

MARINO

Made by George Phillips, Thomas Phillips & Thomas Godwin

The large plate shown is twelve-sided and the paneled rim is covered with a worm track design. The cup plate described bears the same shape and rim design. The outer edges are detailed with a row of small beads and the bottom of the rim design is contained by a band of larger beads from which delicate spearpoint enters the well.

The larger plate presents a picture of an urn with a scalloped top at left. It sits upon a pedestal and in front of it in the foreground a large bouquet almost covers another urn whose outline can be seen at center. Part of a small rustic fence extends from the dark lower urn across the center of the foreground. At right across a stream, in the middle ground, there is a Gothic structure with many towers. A wide flight of steps leads from it down towards the water and a gondola is anchored near the steps. At left tall trees arch across the scene. There are clouds and Alpine peaks in the background. The plate is back-stamped G. Phillips and Longport, like GMK. 3012, 1834-38.

The cup plate presents a scene different from the one described above; there is a dark urn and tall tree at right, the buildings are at left rear and the gondola is in midstream.

Two different back-stamps have been located. One mark is that of T. Phillips & Son, GMK. 3016a, 1845-6. The other is marked Thos. Godwin, Burslem and "Stone China", GMK. 1730, 1834-54.
1834-54.

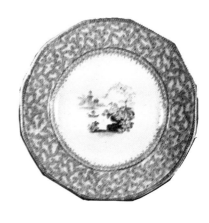

MARMORA

Made by William Ridway & Co.

The distinctive rim design composed of vertical trellis dividers, topped by a fan composed of trellis work, and flanked by flowers, is clearly seen in these photographs. The vertical bars separate scenic reserves framed on three sides with small flowers. Each scene is different but all show a boat on a stream, trees, temples and other buildings. The well is enwreathed on the cavetto with small flowers, which serve to connect the bottom of the vertical rim patterns and to complete the framing of the scenic vignettes.

The plates present different views but each has graceful trees at left which rise from a grassy bank. A river divides the scene and there are temple buildings and minaret towers at right. There is a small boat in each scene and there are two people, one standing and one seated on the rocks in the foreground of both plates.

Marked W.R. & Co., GMK. 3302, c. 1830-54.

MARSEILLAISE

Possibly made by Lewis Woolf

The edge of this platter is gently scalloped and the rim is covered with a repetitive design of pairs of dahlias with buds and leaves that are set in ovals created by interweaving white foliated scrolls and a dark stippled band centered with very dark beads. A row of small dotted circles and tiny triangles contains the rim design at the well.

The central scene shows a country house at left, complete with dove-côte tower and a pair of woven beehives on a stand near the front door. Tall trees rise behind the dwelling which is situated to overlook a large body of water, which fills the center of the scene. There are towers, other buildings and trees across the water on the right. In the foreground there is a group of five persons. A standing man is peering through a telescope at the dove-cote. A couple stand and face him. A man is seated on the ground at left and a woman sits in a rustic chair at right. Behind her there are tall elms and bushes. In the extreme right foreground there are some rocks and branches of heart-shaped leaves.

Marked L.W., see Godden, p. 726, c. 1856-70.

MARYLAND

Probably made by Samuel Alcock

The rim of this plate is covered with double scrolls in a Gothic pattern that terminates in a fleur-de-lis at the bottom of an oval. This forms a scalloped effect around the well. Inset into the rim scroll design are six oval reserves framed with baroque foliated scrolls. Each of these contains a tiny spray of flowers. Alternating with the floral reserves are six smaller designs which are open in the center.

A pair of tall trees rises from the center of the scene in the well. Behind them one sees a river and mountains in the distance. At extreme left there are the ruins of a large, many columned temple. In the foreground there is a pedestal topped with a white urn filled with flowers. Other flowers are placed around the base. A terrace with railing around it, and three wide steps leading to the platform, is placed across the middle of the scene. Behind the railing there are three figures on the river bank. A temple surmounts a hill at right in the distance.

Marked "Florentine China" with a beehive, see Godden, p. 28, c. 1830-59.

MAUSOLEUM

Maker unknown

The edge of the plate photographed is unevenly scalloped and is enhanced by a band of round beads and by an inner wreath of small leaves that fall against a stippled ground. The rim is divided into five rectangular scrolled cartouches, each containing a pair of flowers with dark leaves and sprigs. The cartouches are joined by foliated scrolls and the patterns are contained at the base of the rim by a row of short beaded lines and diamonds that gives a spearpoint effect.

A tall, round domed and columnated tower, surrounded by shorter buildings, is on an island at left in the center scene. Behind it there are tall willow b̶r̶a̶n̶c̶h̶e̶s and other trees. At right there is a tall arching tree on the̶ ̶o̶p̶p̶o̶s̶i̶t̶e̶ bank of a river which divides the scene. In the fore̶g̶r̶o̶u̶n̶d̶ a small boat. Two people are seated in it and one stan̶d̶i̶n̶g̶. In the distance there are other towered buildings, t̶r̶e̶e̶s̶ ̶a̶n̶d̶ peaks.

MAZARA

Made by John Meir & Son

The paneled rim of this twelve-sided plate is covered with a design of scalloped concentric lines that dip to a point and then curve upward to a second point. This gives an effect of dividing lines at the turning points. The edge is decorated with a band of small scrolls and fleur-de-lis, and the pattern is contained at the bottom of the rim by a dark line. A wreath of scroll-like branches is placed around the upper part of the well.

In the central scene a man is at left and stands near a wall. At center in the foreground there are rocks and a pair of trees rise behind them. At right there is a small villa of Tuscan architecture. At left in the distance there are a river and towered buildings.

Marked J. Meir & Son, GMK. 2636, c. 1837-97. (Note: This plate is dated 1874.)

MEDICI

Made by Mellor, Venables & Co.

The rim of the twelve-sided plate shown is covered with narrow concentric lines. A pattern of scrolls forms five oval reserves around the rim. Each reserve contains a covered urn with double curved handles which is placed in front of some branches. The scrolls intertwine between the reserves and terminate in trefoils. The rim pattern is contained at the well with a pattern of small pointed arches containing little beads.

In the center scene a large urn decorated with dancing figures is set on a stone parapet at left. Flowing vines, a slanted balustrade and tall trees are behind the urn. A stream divides the picture and at right there is a stone railing surmounted by two statues. A tall elm grows behind the railing. In the distance at right there are the towers of a castle and a large dark triumphal arch.

Marked M.V. & Co., and (imp.) "Iron Stone", (It is dated 1847.) GMK. 2645, c. 1834-51.

MESINA

Made by Wood & Challinor

The rim of this plate is covered with sprigs and a wreath consisting of a trio of stylized astors and leaves set on a very fine line, encircles it. A band of beads and spearpoint, set in scallops, is placed around the outer edge. A man and woman in court costume stand on a grassy bank near a rectangular stone pedestal in the foreground of the center scene. Two tall trees rise at left from a base of over-scaled flowers. A river divides the scene and at right and across the water, there is a church-like building with stone arches, Gothic pointed windows and spires crowned with ornaments. Some trees are placed behind the structure. In the distance there are other buildings and towers and tall mountain peaks.

Marked W. & C., and "Opaque China", GMK. 4244, c. 1828-43.

MILAN

Possibly made by South Wales Pottery

In the central scene two standing men, and a seated woman, are placed at right on a very steep, grassy river bank. Trailing vines drop towards the water from the bank, and also from the left river bank. There are tall elms on the right bank, and in the right background one sees a towered building. At left in the middle ground there is a very large castle with twin towers and wide steps that lead down to the river. There are two small sailboats in the middle of the stream. Tall mountains in the background at left and city buildings in the distance complete the picture.

The rim of this twelve-sided soup plate is covered with narrow, concentric lines. Twelve bars separate the alternating patterns of a large rose with dark leaves and a drooping bough laden with small round fruit and light leaves. The patterns are framed by oval garlands of leaves that intertwine over the bars. The well is encircled by a pattern of scallops, each containing a hairpin design.

Marked S.W.P., GMK. 3628, c. 1839-58.

MILANESE

Maker unknown

The edge of this scalloped plate was left white and a small band of triangles, interrupted by circular designs framed in small beads, follows the scalloped outline. Three large sprays of flowers, each different from the other, are placed around the rim and enter the well. These are separated by a pair of flowers and sprigs.

The central scene, framed by a circle of small dotted beads trimmed at six points with large spearpoints, contains a big sailboat in the center. It holds four figures, one of whom is seated in the stern under a fancy fringed sun shade. In the distance across the water there are trees, a tower and some smaller buildings. The foreground is covered with over-scaled flowers.

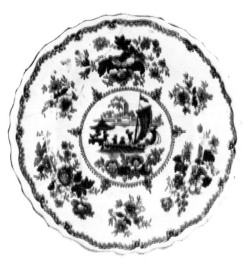

MILANESE PAVILIONS

Made by Joseph Heath & Co.

The edge of the unevenly scalloped plate photographed is detailed with a row of tiny, five-petalled flowers. The rim design consists of three oblong reserves containing round fruits, leaves and sprigs which alternate with three similar reserves containing a pair of large dahlias, buds and leaves. The designs are separated by distinctive, triangular foliate designs containing three stylized white flowers. The rim design is contained at the well by a string of small quatrefoils and stylized flowers. From this wreath a row of spearpoint descends across the cavetto and into the well.

The scene in the center of the dish shows a standing man and woman dressed in court costume. A wolf hound is at left. In the foreground on the lawn there are flowers and stones. A balustrade leads from the couple to an urn at right. There is a large arch surmounted by a statue in the right middle ground behind the urn. At left there is a stream and across the water one sees a castle-like building. Tall trees in the center complete the circular scene.

Marked J.H. & Co. with (imp.) propeller, GMK. 1994a, c. 1828-41.

MILANESE SCENERY

Maker unknown

The rims of these unevenly scalloped plates are indented and are paneled in four small panels over the four large foliate heraldic scroll designs that appear on the rim. Between these designs there are sprays, and in the center of each spray, on four sides of the rim are pairs of very dark small leaves. On the larger plate the upper part of the rim is stippled and is trimmed at the outer edge by a band of dark triangles and a row of white beads. The cup plate has no stippling on its rim. Its outer edge is enhanced with a row of white beads and dark triangles and beneath that there is a row of laurel leaves that connect the large designs to the small dark leaves. On both plates large bouquets of dahlias are placed under the arches on four sides of the plate. These bouquets cross the upper well and are joined by a pattern of lace which forms a frame around the central medallion.

On the large plate a man, woman, and seated child are in the right foreground near an arch. In the center of the plate there is a large white church-like structure with many spires. In the left foreground there are pieces of broken columns, over-scaled flowers, and bushy plants. The cup plate presents a different scene. It shows two girls in the foreground at left, a footbridge across a brook at right, white towers in the left background, and a tall lacy tree in the right background.

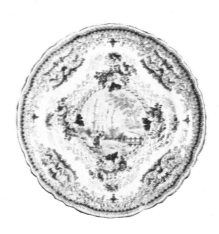

MILANESE VILLAS

Made by Francis Dillon

This plate is scalloped and the rim is covered with small sprays of flowers. Six shield designs flanked by foliated scrolls and centered with a fleurette are placed around the rim. Flowers placed on a pair of pine branches descend from the shields into the well. Realistic small bouquets are placed between the pine boughs on the lower rim and a string of dentils separates the bouquets from the upper rim floral field. The pine branches are the distinguishing feature of the rim design.

In the center scene two women and a man are seated on a bench in the foreground. Each is playing a lute, and a music stand complete with music score is next to the man. In the background part of a balustrade is at left, a classic temple is in the left middle ground which overlooks a lake. In the distance there are other buildings including a domed tower and mountain peaks. Tall elms rise on each side of the scene.

Marked imp. Dillon and also F.D., GMKs. 1288 1n3 1288a, 1834-40.

MISSOURI

Made by Barker & Son, and by Cork, Edge, & Malkin

We show two plates in this pattern. Barker & Co. made the design from 1850-1860 and then went out of business. Cork, Edge, & Malkin must have acquired the pattern at that time. The older plate is ten-sided and the rim is paneled, the newer plate is not. Each has the same rim design of horizontal scroll cartouches that are not easily discerned. They are filled with an abstract wormtrack design on a light stippled ground. Small faint bars separate the cartouches. There is a fleur-de-lis at the bottom of the bar and a jeweled oval at the upper rim. The rim pattern is contained by a band of small quatrefoils edged in white at the top and a row of spearpoint composed of short and long fleur-de-lis at the well.

The central scenes are the same, and contain a couple in Elizabethan clothes. They are with a pair of greyhounds on a terrace in the foreground. There are stairs and a stone railing at right and part of a small balustrade at left. Tall elms rise on either side of the scene. A river divides the picture. In the left background there are castles and in the distance there are other buildings and Alpine peaks.

Marked B. & S., GMK. 256, 1850-60 and C.E. & M., GMK. 1101, 1860-71.

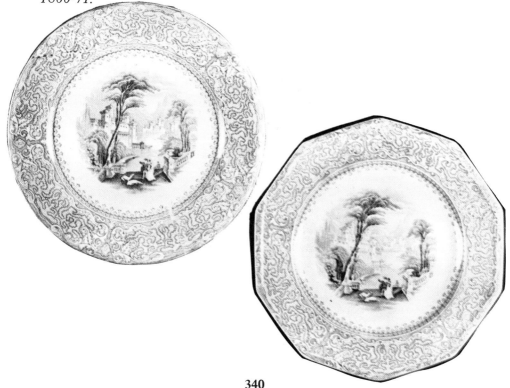

MONASTERY

Maker unknown

The white edge of the plate photographed is unevenly scalloped. A narrow band of scalloped beads is placed under the white edge. Three scenic reserves are placed on the rim. Each contains an identical scene of a river with a tall sailboat at left and a large dark rock at right. The prow of a boat with sail folded can also be seen at right. There are buildings in the background. The reserves are framed at top and bottom with small flowers and are divided by curtained draperies flanking a lacy swag. The lacy designs are crowned with flowers and the background is stippled. A delicate wreath of scrolls and diamonds encircles the well.

The ruin of a Gothic building, flanked by tall elms, is in the middle of the central scene. In the distance at left there are other ruins. A man on horseback at left is passing some trees and in the center under the brow of gently sloping fields two cows drink from a lake. In the foreground there are some classical ornamental pieces of ruined pillars, some ferns, flowers, and leaves.

MONOPTERIS

Made by John Rogers and Son

    This toy plate (4¾ inch diameter) is gently scalloped and its outer edge is dark and below the edge there is a band of ovals and triangles. The scene covers the entire dish and is dominated by the large domed ruins in the background. In the foreground a walking man drives an ox on a road past the ruins. Another man walks beside him. A large flowering tree overhangs the scene at left and continues across the top of the picture. There are a dark tree at right and over-scaled flowers in the foreground. This same scene appears on the adult size dishes in this pattern.

    Marked (imp.) Rogers, GMK. 3369, 1814-36.

MONTAGNE

Maker unknown

The rim of the plate shown is covered with a baroque design of flowers and treillage. The outer edge is detailed by a very dark band of beads. Flowers and sprigs from the rim design enter the upper well and form an irregular wreath around the central scene.

The Montagne (Mountain) of the title appears as part of steep Alpine peaks in the background. A river flows from left to right across the scene, and a castle is nestled among the trees on the right bank. Two men are in the foreground. One stands and points towards the mountains. He is dressed in cavalier clothes and carries a portfolio in his hand. The other one is seated, facing the scene. He carries a drum-like knapsack and holds a thick cane. Tall trees, bushes, and over-scaled flowers are at left behind the standing man, and there are rocks, bushes, and flowers in the foreground.

MONTILLA

Made by Davenport

The rim of this twelve-sided plate is covered with concentric narrow lines. Five pairs of flowers (a rose and a carnation) are placed around the rim and are separated by foliated scrolls that form large C curves between them. The scrolls are continuous around the upper part of the rim. The rim pattern is contained at the well by a band of squares filled with crosses separated by vertical bars that end in dotted points toward the center. Small scrolls that give a spearpoint effect are placed under each square.

A stream divides the central scene. On the right bank there is a baroque temple surmounted by an onion dome and spire in the shape of a cross. A statue can be seen in a Gothic niche midway in the building. Trees and bushes are placed near the structure. At left there are stones and bushes in the foreground. Tall trees with gnarled surface roots rise from the bank, and in the distance at left there are other buildings and mountains.

Marked as above, GMK. 1181a, 1820-60.

MOSELLE

Made by John and George Alcock

The lid of the teapot photographed shows a border design which appears as the background on the rim of the dishes in this pattern. A wreath of small flowers linking larger ones is placed against the plaid background and a row of delicate spearpoint enters the body from the rim design. A small scrolled arch form is placed over the smaller flowers.

The river scene on the body of the vessel shows a church with tall spires at right, another tower, and an oblong building with a shell-like roof. At left there are tall elms. A bridge crosses a river in the center of the scene and in the distance there are other buildings and mountains. In the foreground a man and woman dressed in peasant clothes stand on a grassy bank. He is holding a large deep basket. A skiff is pulled up to the shore behind them. The distinguishing feature is the diamond plaid background. It also appears on the handle of the teapot and quatrefoils can be noted at the intersection of the diamonds.

The plate shows the border design of diamond plaid inset with scenic cartouches. Each river scene shows a small boat in the left foreground, a castle in the center rear, and a dark bank and tree at right. Three slender reserves, flanked with a double line of scrolls, and filled with a vertical spray of flowers, are placed between the vignettes. The scene is different from that on the teapot, and includes a pine tree at right, tall elms at left, a tall towered building in the right rear, a river with an arched bridge, and a mansion on the right bank. In the foreground there are a seated man and a standing woman who holds a fishing pole.

Marked J. and G. Alcock, and "Cobridge", GMK. 68, 1839-46.

MOSELLE

Made by Ralph Hall and Co.

The rim of the saucer photographed is covered with a dark stippled field. Printed over this are six foliated triangles topped by pairs of plumes and flanked on both sides with bellflowers. This pattern is separated by a double circle pattern filled with scrolls and decorated at the bottom with a small winged form. The bottoms of the rim designs are contained by a wreath of scrolls.

In the central river scene a large chalet is at left. Behind it are poplars and large bushy trees. The outline of another chalet can be seen in the background. At right tall elms rise from the rocky river bank. In the foreground there are pieces of a fence and some shrubs. The scenes probably differ on the various items of this pattern, so it is important to discern the border triangle and double circle design.

Marked R.H. and Co., GMK. 1890, 1841-9.

MULETEER
Made by William Davenport

The rim of this scalloped plate is stippled and the outer edge is decorated with a band of beaded ovals. Six oval reserves framed by ruffled C scrolls are set around the rim. Three contain very dark leaves that descend into the well, and three contain small dark leaves, stems and leaves from roses. Flowerlets enter the well beneath the reserves. A pair of large fullblown roses alternate between the ovals with a pair of birds perched on thin branches. A small clump of berries is between the birds and there are other berries and sprays and small flowers near them. A pair of scrolls fringed with beaded lines meet at a four-petaled flower beneath the bird patterns.

In the central scene a man and two women walk with a mule on a road near a cascading stream at left. There is a curving wall beside them and a towered residence behind them. In the distance at right there is a church tower. At left there are a tall tree, some rocks, and flowers. In the foreground there are bushes and flowers. In the middle distance there is a boat on the stream. Tall mountains in the distance complete the scene. The birds and ruffled ovals on the rim are the distinguishing features of this pattern.

Marked (imp.) anchor and Davenport, GMK. 1181a, dated 1836.

NAVARINE

Made by William Adams

The rim of the saucer photographed is paneled and is covered with a printed net. Scrolls run around the edge of the dish and descend over the rim to form a triangular design at four points. Between these triangles are small vignettes of a towered building flanked by trees. The rim design is contained at the base by a pair of narrow white lines. Inside this there is a thick row of short conical designs and finally a wreath of beads and triangles.

The river in the center scene divides a landscape dominated by a castle with tall vertical walls at left. This building is set against Alpine peaks. At right a pair of tall elms rise from the bank and at extreme right there are shorter trees and some castle towers in the distance. An arched bridge can be glimpsed in the center background and there are other buildings and mountains in the distance. A small boat with three people is in the middle of the river, and in the foreground there are a stone wall post and part of a wall at right. Pieces of broken pillars and some reeds are placed in the center foreground.

Marked W. Adams and "Tunstall", GMK. 26, c. 1850.

NEVA

Made by William Ridgway

The rim of the saucer shown is covered with narrow concentric scalloped lines that form a net effect. A wreath of scrolls connects four groups of a trio of dogwood blossoms and long speckled leaves. The well is surrounded by short spearpoint.

The central scene is divided by the river, the Neva of the title. Most of Leningrad in Russia lies on the left bank of the Neva. At left in the foreground there is a large two-handled urn on a pedestal. Another smaller urn is behind it also on a pedestal. A curved railing is at extreme left with some trees behind it. At right there are tall elms. In the background there are castle-like buildings with pointed Gothic rooves, towers, and tall mountains.

Marked W.R., GMK. 3301, 1830-4.

NON PAREIL

Made by Thomas, John, and Joseph Mayer

The rim of this plate is covered with a design of chickweed and small flowers. A band of tiny beads outlines the outer edge. There is no band at the bottom of the rim or around the well. Six pairs of stylized leaves with small dotted circles set in the petals are linked around the rim by a narrow dark vine that bears leaves near the floral pairs.

A small boat with a net hanging from the stern is in the foreground of the central scene. A man with a wide hat stands in the craft and points to shore. Another is seated astern. At right across the water there are Gothic buildings, one has a very high square tower. In the distance there are mountain peaks. At left a pair of tall elms stand on the river bank.

In the foreground of the central scene on the second plate three persons are on the flower covered bank of the river, a man is seated on a log, a woman stands next to him and another woman is seated on the grass. There are tall trees at left. On the right shore there are towers and multi-storied buildings. Some small boats are afloat near the structure. In the center background a bridge crosses the stream. There are other buildings and tall mountains in the distance. Note the difference in the design used on the background of the rims. The second plate is marked T. Mayer, Longport, and dates 1836-38.

Marked T.J. and J. Mayer, GMK. 2570, 1843-55.

350

OBERWESSEL ON RHINE

Made by Enoch Wood and Sons

This plate is deeply scalloped and the outer edge is detailed with a band of dark beads. The rim is decorated with pairs of white flowers that alternate with sprays of bellflowers and bouquets of roses and sprigs. The bottom of the rim is encircled by a twisted rope design interspersed with fleurons.

The central picture depicts the old Rhine River town of the title. In the center is a large round tower. At left in the distance a castle sits on a hill. There are other buildings placed on both sides of the tower. High hills are shown in the background. In the foreground there is a large boat at left on the river and two people stand on the bank at right.

Marked E. Wood and Sons, GMK. 4261, 1818-46.

OLYMPIAN

Made by John Ridgway

The sugar bowl shown carries the rim design around the top part of the body. The pattern shows clearly on the cup plate which is scalloped and its white outer edge is enhanced by a row of small dark beads. The stippled rim is divided by vertical bars that contain narrow oblong cartouches filled with treillage. Pairs of large white roses with dark leaves are placed in the reserves between the vertical patterns. The well is encircled by a wreath of laurel leaves interspersed with pairs of roses placed under the vertical bars. The wreath is the distinguishing feature of this pattern. It can be seen at the bottom of the sugar bowl, around its pedestal and around the stippled band at top.

The cup plate bears a central picture of a small sailboat which approached a domed temple. There are high hills and other buildings in the background. A flight of steps is at left in the middle ground, and there are flowers and sprigs in the foreground. On the sugar bowl the same boat scene appears at left. In the foreground two women in Middle Eastern dress stand on a platform. A man holding a pole sits at left. There is an urn to the right of the women. Flowers are placed in the foreground. There are tall trees at right. In the distance there is a long low bridge or dam and beyond that there are a temple, trees, and mountains.

Marked J.R., and a printed royal coat of arms, GMK. 3258, 1841-55.

ONTARIO LAKE SCENERY

Made by Joseph Heath

The larger plate photographed is twelve-sided and so is the cup plate and the patterns on both plates are identical. A trailing vine interspersed with small flowers encircles the outer edge. A pattern of sprays of flowers separated by a vertical double bar centered with a row of beads. The vine design of forget-me-nots crosses the bars at right. The entire rim design is finished at the well by tiny scallops.

The central scene is European and is dominated by a castle with tall towers at left center. In the background there are tall mountains. A cascade starts in the center rear and becomes a waterfall which spreads into a wide triangular lake area. At extreme right on the river bank there are tentlike structures held up by forked tree limbs. There are tall elms and bushy trees in the background. In the center four people stand on a steep bank and another is seated on the edge of the bank. Shrubs in the foreground and clouds in the upper background complete the circular picture.

Marked J. Heath, GMK. 1993, 1845-53.

ORIENTAL

Made by Samuel Moore and Co.

The edge of this scalloped platter is detailed by a narrow band of printed hearts and beads. Four cartouches framed by foliated scrolls and filled with a large bouquet alternate with four baroque reserves that contain a formal arrangement of fruits, leaves, and sprigs set in a vase that surmounts an oval made from a pair of C scrolls. The baroque designs are placed against a stippled background. The rest of the rim is filled with a diamond diaper pattern. A double row of fleurons and pendant hearts encircles the well.

In the center a building, almost Gothic in character, is at left. It is situated on a river bank. A tall elm rises at center. At far right across the water there are other exotic buildings. A boat with two sails is being poled by two men in the right foreground. At left two small antlered deer, one reclining and one frisking are placed on a grassy bank amidst flowers, bushes, and stones. Behind them, a piece of carved stone has fallen into the water.

Marked S.M. and Co., GMK. 2746, 1803-74.

PALERMO

Made by Joseph Clementson

This plate is twelve-sided and the rim is paneled. A design of stylized lilies and tendrils is printed in a light color over a very dark background. The rim design is contained by a row of small foliated scrolls which is placed on the cavetto.

The central scene is Swiss. There is an elaborate chalet at right which is situated on a lake. At left there are very tall trees and part of a fence. In the distance there are other buildings and towers.

Marked as above, GMK. 910a, 1839-64.

PALESTINE

Made by John Ridgway

The edge of this twelve-sided bowl is detailed with a band of running scallops. The rim is covered with a fine basketweave design. Four scenic vignettes framed with foliated scrolls are placed around the rim. Each has the same scene of a palm tree in the foreground, in the center there is a lake and in the background there are large rectangular buildings and one tall tower. A white band framed in dark lines confines the rim pattern at the well, and a band of arches is placed under the lines.

In the main pattern at extreme left there is a dominant and forbidding two-story building. At extreme left there is a tall arched gateway in a wall and a man and woman walk together on a road through the arch. There are many other formal buildings along the left bank of the river that divides the scene. There are other buildings in the distance and a large one crowns the highest of the distant hills. There are tall trees and a balustrade at left and in the foreground there is a stepped platform and a low domed-top pedestal alongside the platform. At right there are yucca growing from the sandy bank.

Marked J. Ridgway, "Registered 18", GMK. 3256, 1830-55.

PALMYRA

Maker unknown

The rim of this twelve-sided soup dish is covered with a strong diaper pattern of diamonds placed over narrow concentric lines. A wreath of oak leaves and acorns is placed midway on the rim, and the pattern is contained at the bottom by a row of scallops. Beneath this a band of oblong darts and printed scallops forms a dentil design around the cavetto. This pattern differs from the Palmyra and Ionic well wreaths that are ruffled with a diamond and half-square design. Also the diaper design on the rim is much more strongly defined.

The design in the center scene contains the same elements as the other two patterns; tall trees at right, a balustrade, three people on a terrace, a wide river and towered buildings at left in the background. But the transfer is more crisp and the details differ from the other two patterns. (See Palmyra and Ionic, this category).

PALMYRA

Made by Wood and Brownfield

This identical pattern was issued under the name "Ionic" by Clementson and Young who worked from 1845-47. Wood and Brownfield registered it as "Palmyra" in 1845 (See Ionic, this category).

Marked W. and B., GMK. 4243, 1838-50.

PANAMA

Made by Edward Challinor and Co.

This pattern is readily distinguished by its central circular design which is framed by trees and branches and appears on plates of all sizes in the pattern. The scene on the large plate and cup plate are almost the same. Both show a large castle in the left background and an arched bridge crossing a river in the middle. The water is white behind the bridge and dark in the foreground and there are tall mountains in the distance. On the large plate a man and woman stand in the foreground near a woman seated on a tree trunk. The cup plate design omits the standing couple.

The rims of both dishes are paneled. Oval scenic medallions flanked by white foliated scrolls and containing a scene of a wide flight of steps leading to a pair of towers, alternate with a Gothic shield pattern that contains geometric diamonds. These are separated by a field of perpendicular narrow lines. A pattern of shadowy dark foliated scrolls is placed over the linear background. The outer edges of both plates are decorated with a dark band containing a wreath of slanting leaves. The well of each is encircled with running scrolls.

Marked E. Challinor and Co., GMK. 836, 1853-62.

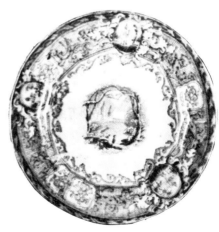

PANDORA

Mark not located

This type of border was very popular around 1845. The back-stamp mark on the platter shown is like that of a pottery that produced dishes in the late '90's, so this is probably a reissue of an old pattern. This is a herringbone border edged with small leaves and small fans around the edge. The border ends in triangles at the well and forms a heavy spearpoint.

At left in the central scene there are several small sailboats with dragonlike prows anchored against a stone landing. There are trees at extreme left. A river divides the scene and on the right bank there are fallen stones from a ruin. Three people stand nearby. Across the water there are large colonnades, temple buildings and towers.

Marked Soho Pottery, Cobridge.

PANTHEON

Made by Ridgway and Morley

The rim of this six-sided vegetable bowl is covered with a wormtrack design filled with tiny sprigs. The well is encircled by a band of spearpoint. The central scene is filled with the ruins of many Greek temples. Tall mountain peaks are in the background. There is a man on horseback at right and a small figure stands nearby. In the foreground there are fallen architectural stones and some bushes.

Marked R. and M. and "Opaque China", 1841-44.

PARISIAN

Made by George Phillips

The rim design for this pattern can be seen on the teapot but is not visible on the gravy boat shown as it is placed inside the top of the gravy boat. It consists of mossy sprigs that are inset with small six-petaled plump stylized flowers. The sprigs are placed in a narrow band around the pedestal base of the gravy boat and around the collar of the teapot. The rim pattern is contained at the edge by a row of small beads and diamonds.

The scene on the gravy boat shows two women in the foreground. One is seated on a rock and points to the water of a lake behind her. The other stands nearby. There are tall lacy trees at right, some bushes, and some flowers. Across the water one sees church-like buildings with fancy windows, tall towers, and an arched bridge at left. In the distance there are other buildings on an island.

The central scene on the teapot also shows two women in the center foreground. One stands at left holding a dog on a leash. The woman at right is in a short skirt and kneels over a basket. Both are wearing hats. There is a lake behind them. At the right there are churchlike buildings in the distance, towers and trees and the arched bridge at far right. At left in the foreground there are over-scaled stylized flowers and two coconut trees.

Marked G. Phillips, see Godden, pg. 492, 1838-48.

PARISIAN CHATEAU
Made by Ralph Hall

Both this plate and the cup plate are scalloped and the edge of each is outlined with pointed beads. The rim design consists of large lilies and small flowers which alternate with a pair of full-blown roses and small leaves. The floral groups are set against a background of narrow vertical lines. Six butterfly-shape dark triangles inset with half a flower and supported by white scrolls are set against the upper rim between the floral designs. Beneath the scrolls and filling the spaces between the flowers, there is a diaper pattern which is contained at the bottom by a pendant scroll design.

The central scene on the large plate is framed by a circle of tiny hearts and trefoils. On the cup plate a simple band of U shape scallops was used. The pictures in the well differ. The large plate shows a man talking to a woman who is seated on a platform in the foreground. A large flower-filled urn on a large square pedestal is at right at the top of a slanting balustrade. At left there are tall trees and bushes. In the background there is a chateau.

The cup plate shows a different chateau at right. It is flanked by bushes and trees. There are tall trees at left, flowers in the foreground, and part of a semi-circular drive which goes around the mansion. There are two tiny dark figures near the drive in front of the chateau. The vegetable dish shows the rim pattern elongated and a different scene from the two plates. The distinguishing feature of this pattern consists of the vertical lines between the flowers and the strong diaper pattern with pendants underneath.

Marked R. Hall (the cup plate is marked (imp.) with a propeller surrounded by beads), GMK. 1888, 1822-41.

PARISIAN CHATEAU (cont.)

PARK SCENERY

Made by George Phillips

Both the dinner plate and the cup plate photographed are unevenly scalloped and the outer edges are detailed by a row of white narrow arches and beads set over a dark background contained by a narrow dark band. Large mossy rosebuds and leaves are placed around the rim on a background of ovals, wreaths of wavy vines, and beads set in a field of narrow vertical lines. The effect is that of moiré. A wreath of sprigs and stylized flowers is set under a band of flattened scallops around the well.

The larger plate bears a center scene containing two cows and two sheep in the center of the scene. In the foreground one of the cows, large and white, is standing in a pool of water. At far right there is a triangular fountain structure placed in front of tall arching elm trees. At left a road leads to a closed gate set between two pillars. Tall trees rise at extreme left. In the distance there is a manor house or abbey with a tall tower. Some deer are on the lawn behind the cattle. The cup plate shows the white cow and two sheep in the foreground, a domed building in the right distance, and part of a paling enclosure at left.

Marked G. Phillips and "Longport" like GMK. 3012, 1834-48.

365

PARMA

Maker unknown

This plate is gently scalloped. The outer edge is decorated with a band of printed narrow scallops and four scenic vignettes are set around the rim. Each reserve is framed with foliated scrolls and each contains a farm scene with different animals in the foreground: deer in one, horses in another, a cow in the third, and goats in the fourth. Pairs of white flowers with dark leaves separate the reserves and small strands of buds are placed on either side of the flowers. The rim pattern enters the well in the form of oval panels which are joined by arches and forms a thick wreath around the well.

In the center scene a cow and a goat are in the foreground near some shrubs, rocks, and flowers. At right there is a building with three tall arches. A tall elm tree rises at right center. At left in the background there is a large mansion with a tower and ornate gatepost that overlooks a river or lake. In the distance there are Alpine peaks.

PEARL

Probably made by Samuel Alcock

The cup plate and 7 inch plate shown are scalloped, and the edges are outlined by a row of ovoid beads. The stippled rim is covered with a design of forget-me-nots. Large oval scenic cartouches alternate with narrow oval reserves containing a double-handled urn with pendant bottom. The scenic vignettes show an entrance gate flanked by tall domed posts, trees, and bushes at left, and at right in the distance across a river there is a single tower. The well is surrounded by a wreath of spearpoint which appears to be scalloped on the cup plate.

The central scenes differ. The cup plate shows only houses and a large dark pine tree at left, and a tower across a river in the right background. The larger scene presents the pine tree at extreme left, and the tower at right. In the center there is a villa, two very large beehives are set in front of it. Two women stand at right near the river which flows across the background. In the distance there are mountains. In the foreground there are some flowers.

Marked with a beehive and "Florentine China", 1830-59. (See Godden, page 28.)

PENNSYLVANIA

Made by Knight, Elkin, and Co.

The vegetable dish and the dinner plate photographed are scalloped and the outer edges are white and are detailed by a narrow band of spearpoint. Four foliated oval cartouches filled with a diamond trellis pattern are placed around the rim. Each cartouche is crowned by a half flower set in a dark background contained by scrolls under which there are horizontal sprays of flowers. At the bottom of the cartouches there are shield designs ˉ flanked by sprays of forget-me-nots. The area between the reserves is stippled, and a very large flower with dark leaves is placed at the bottom of the stippling. This is surmounted by a small foliated heart-shaped design. Garlands of flowers placed beneath the cartouches form an irregular wreath around the wells of the dishes.

The central scene on the platter is dominated by a tall domed tower at right. It is encrusted with scroll work. This is part of a complex of buildings and towers and arches. At left there are tall elms. A river divides the scene, and in the center the stream is crossed by an arched bridge. In the foreground there is a small boat with pointed prow which contains two women and a man. Another man stands on the shore in the foreground. He holds a rope and pulls on the boat. Next to him at right there is an urn. The scene on the dinner plate is slightly different. The towered buildings are at right. The river divides the scene. The tall elm rises at left. The boat is placed in a different position and the man on shore is at left.

Marked K.E. & Co., GMK. 2301, 1826-46.

PENNSYLVANIA (cont.)

PERA

Maker unknown

This soup plate is very gently scalloped and a row of small dark arches is set around its edge. On the rim three tall Greco-Roman incense braziers alternate with three sprays of morning-glories, dahlias and poppies, which are set upon a base of scrolls flanked by long large foliated scrolls whose tips touch the mask handles of the braziers.

The central scene covers the entire well and contains a temple at left with an arched closed paneled wooden door. Its conical roof is crowned with a tall spire. Poplars are placed behind the roof. A large tall tree grows in the center of the scene next to the temple. A man is coming through a gate at the extreme left next to the building and two others are near a niche set in the temple's right wall. A robed man in square hat approaches the building on horseback. Three others wearing turbans are conversing on a castellated rooftop at front left. Part of the castellated wall crosses the foreground and is surrounded by bushes. There are little sprays of flowers in the foreground. In the distance on a hilltop there is a large long building, a pair of tents, other trees, and bushes.

Pera is part of the same series as Tchiurluk and Cialka Kavak (this category.) Laidecker says this pattern was produced about 1815.

PERSIA

Made by William Adams and Sons

Eleven dark fan-shaped designs furled at the bottom and containing a white shell shape over the double furl are placed around the rim of this plate. Each fan shape is flanked by feathery sprigs and these meet and form the mossy background of the design. The edge of the plate is decorated with a double band of dark and light beads topped with triangles.

The central scene presents four persons in the foreground. Two men and a woman are seated on the ground. One of the men smokes a long pipe. The woman leans her arm on a large jug. The standing man holds a pole which he has stuck into the ground. There is a lake behind the figures. At right there are exotic tropical trees: banana, palm, and locust. At left there are parts of buildings with tiled rooves and tall poplar trees. In the distance across the water there are towers and buildings including a round tower and tall mountain peaks. Dark clouds complete the circular scene.

Marked W.A. and S., GMK. 23, 1819-64.

PERU

Made by Peter Holdcroft and Co.

This plate is twelve-sided and the paneled rim is covered with a diaper pattern separated by vertical leafy bars. Three divisions are in a row and each contains a single flower. The trios are separated by larger dark areas that are centered with a stylized white bellflower flanked by white scrolls. At the bottom of each division there is a fleur-de-lis with a bead pendant. Scrolls connect these and result in an arched design around the well.

The central scene is divided vertically by a river that starts at a waterfall in the central background. At left behind some wide leaved plants there is a castle with many domes and minarets. At right there are the same wide-leaved plants and a tall elm. In the distance there are very high mountain peaks. There is a terrace in the foreground flanked by a balustrade, a covered urn on a pedestal at left, and part of a balustrade and an urn on a vertical post and wide steps at right. There are four figures in the foreground, and three others can be seen behind them at the water's edge.

Marked Holdcroft and Co., and "Pearl" (imp.) See Godden, page 328. 1846-52.

PERUVIAN
Made by John Wedge Wood

This rim design is almost a copy of that of Peru. The rim design has been divided into panels by vertical lines. However the dark panels do not contain the bellflower design found on Peru but instead have a diamond containing a rosette in the center. Scrolls are used to contain the bottom of the patterns, and small crosses are placed under the scrolls and around the upper well.

The scene, like Peru, shows a river which originates in a waterfall in the center. There are a castle and minarets at left set against very tall mountains. The elm trees rise at right on the cup plate behind the same covered urn near a pool that can be seen on Peru, but a fountain has been added at left and is distinctive on all pieces of this pattern. The vegetable dish has a different architectural design at right. Neither piece shows the wide flat-leaved plants found on Peru.

Marked J. Wedgwood, GMK. 4276a, 1845-60.

PICTURESQUE

Maker unknown

The paneled rim of this fourteen-sided plate is covered with concentric lines that scallop upward and then dip. A wreath composed of swags of seven fleurons that hang between bonelike branches encircles the rim. A small stylized rose is placed over each swag, and a band of fleurons over fleur-de-lis forms spearpoint on the cavetto.

The central scene is divided by a river that runs between very steep banks. At right columned ruins and arches are placed on top of the bank. There are flowering vines and bushes, trees, and tree roots at extreme right. At left two figures stand on a projection high over the water. A tall ailanthus tree arches over them. There are three figures in the foreground: two adults, one of whom points towards the left, and a child. They stand on a flowering bank supported by roots. In the distance there are a sailboat on the river and some other buildings and mountains.

PICTURESQUE VIEWS

Made by James and Ralph Clews

The border of this large platter and those of the three little plates carries the famous parrot and apple blossom border design by Clews. The birds resemble the Asiatic pheasant designs and are perched on straight bars between scallops and flowers. They can be plainly seen at upper left on the platter rim.

The scenic picture fills the entire well of the platter. There are trees on either side of the river that flows in the center of the scene. A large sailboat can be seen in the middle ground. Across the river lay the buildings of London and Windsor Castle is at left center. There are five people on the flower strewn bank in the foreground.

Note that the smaller plate, (5") "Fort Edward, Hudson River" and the two cup plates "Near Sandy Hill, Hudson River" and the "Hudson River Views — Fairmont" bear wreaths of scalloped beads and dots around the well scene. The pictures used on the cup plates were made from sketches by W.G. Wall of Dublin who came to America in 1818. He furnished them to Andrew Stevenson, a potter in Staffordshire, who sold out in early 1819 to the Clews brothers. Clews used this border for both English and American views. The birds in the rim are the distinguishing feature in the pattern.

Marked (imp.) Clews, GMK. 919, 1813-34.

PICTURESQUE VIEWS (cont.)

POLISH VIEWS

Made by Edward and George Phillips

The subtitle on this plate is "A Tear for Poland". The edge of the unevenly scalloped dish is decorated with a narrow beaded band. Three quarters of the rim is stippled, and a row of white scallops edged with lace separates this from the bottom part which contains a light tracery of diamond trellis. Six large white flowers with dark leaves are placed around the rim against the above background, and sprigs and buds join the flowers on the upper part of the rim. A row of oval beads and dotted lines surrounds the well, and dark leaves and buds from the floral groups cross the beading and enter the well.

A man and woman sit on the grass in the foreground of the center scene. He holds his hand to his face and is weeping. At right there is a church which is topped with an onion-shaped dome and spire. A willow tree is behind the structure. The building sits in an enclosure and a horseman with spear or club can be seen below the wall in the center of the scene. At left there is a pair of tall elms. In the distance there are other buildings and mountain peaks. To the right of the church and in the foreground there are sprigs and bushes.

Marked E. and G. Phillips, GMK. 3009, 1822-34.

POMERANIA

Made by John Ridgway

Both these plates are unevenly scalloped and the white outer edges are set off by rows of beading. The upper rim is covered with a wormtrack design that gives a lacy effect. Four scallop-shell designs set over a pair of foliated scrolls alternate with four bouquets of full-blown flowers, dark leaves and buds, which are placed upon a baroque scroll. In the arches formed under the shell designs, there is a small flower and a swag of flowers, sprigs, and leaves is placed beneath the arches.

The central scenes differ as expected in patterns like this. The larger plate shows several buildings and towers on either side of a river. There is an arched bridge in the center. In the foreground there are two women, one is seated on a flower-strewn bank, the other stands facing the bridge. The cup plate shows a river in the foreground and on the grassy bank across the water in the background there are some houses and a fence.

Marked J.R., GMK. 3253, 1830-55.

POMONA

Mark not located

The rim of the saucer shown is covered with narrow concentric lines. Three oval reserves alternate with three smaller vertical marine scenes. The larger ones show a many-masted large boat that has a paddlewheel. The small reserves show several small sailboats grouped in the center. A spray of small flowers with pairs of forget-me-nots pendant separates the water scenes. A band of scallops and spearpoint contain the rim design at the well.

The central scene is dominated by a very large fountain at right. Three small figures, two standing and one seated, are in the foreground at left. A river divides the scene and at left there is part of a square terrace complete with balustrades and urns. Another fountain can be seen on the terrace. In the distance at left there are trees and buildings with many tall towers, a lake and mountains. At right there is part of a balustrade, plants, and trees.

Marked B.J. and Co.

PRIORY

Made by John Alcock

The plate shown is twelve-sided and the platter is octagonal. A wreath of grapes, leaves, tendrils and vines encircles the upper part of the rims which are covered with a concentric design of wavy lines that give a basket weave effect. In five places leaves from the vines descend across the rim towards the well. A white band contains the rim design at the bottom, and a row of stylized square bells encircles the cavetto.

In the central scene on the plate a stone arched bridge crosses a river. A road passes over the bridge and leads to a large towered building at left which is overrun with weeds. There are tall trees on either side of the bridge. At right in the background there is an arch in a towered entrance set in a high wall. In the foreground there are some rocks and some plants on the bank of the stream. The platter scene is different and shows an abbey in the center background. It overlooks a river or a pond. Three cows stand in the water in the foreground. Tall elm trees rise from both the right and left bank.

Marked as above, with "Cobridge", GMK. 67, 1853-61.

PRIORY by Alcock (cont.)

PRIORY

Made by Edward Challinor and Co.

There are three scenic reserves on the rim of the soup plate photographed. Each contains the same scene of a towered building in the center distance flanked by dark trees. There are some smaller buildings at right. The ovoid reserves are framed with scalloped lines and are flanked by foliated scrolls that terminate in leaf forms. The spaces between the cartouches are covered with a diamond diaper pattern contained at the top edge by a pair of white scrolls and a band of beads framed with white lines. The well is encircled by fleur-de-lis.

In the central scene the priory of the title looms in the left background. A stream divides the scene and there are trees on both sides of the picture. A bridge or a dam crosses the water near the priory. In the foreground a man wearing a top hat is seated on a large rock and a woman and child stand near him. The woman carries a small white parasol over her shoulder.

Marked E. Challinor and Co., GMK. 836, 1853-62.

PRIORY

Made by James and George Meakin

This plate may be later than most shown in this book. It is fourteen-sided and the paneled rim is covered with narrow concentric lines. Four swags of white roses separate four scenic oblong reserves that show a white castle-like building with tall square towers and a dark tree at left. A pattern of thin foliated scrolls links the two designs and forms a continuous line around the outer edge. The rim design is contained at the well by a wreath of pairs of scrolls surmounted with trefoils.

A river divides the central scene. There are tall elms rising from a dark rocky bank at right. At left in the foreground three shallow curved steps lead to a Gothic pointed niche that resembles a shrine. A cross tops the newel post of the stone banister. In the background there is a very large building on the left bank. It has a high tower at each end of its long tall facade. In the distance there is a small dark building with two arches and a tower, a river guardhouse perhaps. Mountains and clouds complete the circular picture.

Marked J. and G. Meakin, GMK. 2598, c. 1851.

PRIORY

Made by Reed, Clementson, and Anderson

This cup and saucer carry a rim design composed of arches centered with three fans on sticks which are joined by a double row of feathers. At the upper part of the rim arched scallops centered with flowers connect the beaded pointed arches below with small quatrefoils. A row of beading encircles the outer edge and a circle of scallops and fleur-de-lis contains the rim design at the well.

In the center picture a large church with spires and a tall tower is set in the background amidst equally tall trees. In the foreground there is part of a ruined capitol of a column and some flowers and leaves. A man and woman stand near a seated woman. The man balances a hoe over his shoulder.

Marked R.C. and A., GMK. 3213, c. 1836.

384

RAVENNA

Maker unknown

A wreath of grapes, grape leaves, vines, and tendrils encircles both the upper and lower border of the rim of this plate. The background is covered with a fine net pattern.

A statue of a woman holding a cup in her upraised arm and a pitcher in the other stands behind a large urn in the foreground of the central scene. The urn is placed on a low pedestal and there are flowers and grass nearby. Tall elms rise behind the statue and urn, and there are trees and part of a low wall at extreme right. A river divides the picture. On the left bank there is a balustrade enclosing trees and plants. In the distance at left there is a large two-storied temple with pediment and columns. Tall mountain peaks and clouds in the sky complete the round scene.

RHINE

Made by Booth and Meigh

The paneled rim of the deep saucer photographed is covered with a net of fine curving diagonal lines. A wreath of small flowers and scrolls is placed over the netting and this extends over the edge and dips in four places towards the well. A band of double arches and small spearpoint encircles the well.

A very large castle situated on a lake is in the right background in the central scene. In the foreground several persons dressed in court costume and a dog are standing on a terrace flanked by stone balustrades. Tall elms rise at either side of the scene and the clouds at the top complete the circular picture.

Marked B. and M. (imp.) 1826-37 (Mark not located).

RHINE

Made by John Meir and Son

The rim of the saucer photographed is covered with concentric narrow lines. A garland of small roses is swagged around the rim over the circular lines, and a wreath of wide white rococo scrolls is placed between the swags. The well is encircled by small thick scrolls that flow to the right and form a double knot that resembles a bone. This is the distinctive feature of this pattern.

The central pictures differ on the various dishes printed with this design. The dinner plates both show castles, a river, small pleasure boats and tall elms. A platter observed at an antique show was distinguished by the row of large scrolls and knots that separates the rim design from the well. The cup plate bears a stylized scene of towers a tall tree and hills at right. It carries only the lower part of the border design. This pattern which may have originated with Meir, is found marked Brough and Blackhurst, Longton. These potters worked from 1872-75. It is also found with the name Moore, made by Cauldon Ltd. who worked from 1905-20.

Marked J.M. and S., GMK. 2633, 1837-97.

RHINE (cont.)

"RHINE RIVER SCENE"

Made by Davenport

The scenic transfer used here covers the entire scalloped cup plate and the outer edge is embossed. The river view shows palisades on the right and a road with a guardrail around their bases. At left there is an island that is covered with bushes. A small, domed watch tower stands on the island next to a very tall tree that rises to the top of the scene. In the distance there are towers and buildings, hills surmounted by white buildings and sloping mountains. Two people are in a boat midstream and there are rocks in the water at foreground. This rocky palisade resembles the Lorelie rocks on the Rhine.

Marked Davenport, GMK. 1181a, c. 1836-60.

RHONE SCENERY

Made by Thomas, John and Joseph Mayer

The rim of this fourteen-sided plate is paneled and is covered with narrow, concentric lines. Five small swags of flowers are placed under branches of foliated scrolls around the rim. The scrolls continue and dip into the spaces between the flowers, terminating in split coils. Small slanted leaves are placed around the bottom rim design which partially enters the well, and their curved, pointed ends form a wreath around the well space.

In the center scene a very large statue of a man with a hat, scepter and shield is placed in a niche in a building at right. The niche is framed by Gothic spires and is located at the top of a double-rounded platform. Side walls descend from the structure on both sides. A river divides the scene. In the foreground on the left bank there are two standing figures and a seated one. In the distance there are other buildings, bushes and trees at right, and clouds above complete the circular pattern.

Marked T.J. & J. Mayer, GMK. 2570, c. 1843-55.

"ROMANTIC"

Probably made by Samuel Alcock & Co.

The soup plate photographed is twelve-sided and the rim is slightly concave. The cup plate mold is completely different and the edge is very deeply cut. The outer edges of both are trimmed with bands of white printed scallops. A circle of scrolls is placed over zigzag concentric lines around the rim and a dark, narrow scalloped line contains the pattern at the well. A wreath of spearpoint is placed under double scalloped lines on the cavetto.

With the exception of a church at extreme right in the distance, the pattern on both dishes is the same. A Gothic building with tall arched windows and large square tower is at center in the middle ground. There are tall trees at right. An arched bridge crosses a river in the center and leads to the left where there is an ornate gate house set above flowering bushes on the rocky bank.

Tall elms rise at left. In the distance there are towered buildings. In the foreground a child with parasol stands next to a man and a seated woman on the river bank. There is a crypt and stone wall near them at right center.

The name on this pattern is illegible only the letters "ma" can be deciphered. This title is used to present the pattern.

Marked with a Beehive device and "Florentine China", c. 1828-59.

ROSE WREATH
Maker unknown

The edge of this plate is very gently scalloped. The rim is covered with a beaded design that gives a marquisette effect. The top of the rim is encircled by foliated scrolls that dip and enclose dark leaves. The "Rose wreath" of the title is placed around the rim and consists not only of roses but daisies and lilies and other small flowers, leaves and buds.

The central scene, framed by scallops and fleur-de-lis, contains a large gate house with open Gothic arch and tower. This building is placed in front of a hill covered with trees and surmounted by a castle. Four cows graze in the foreground. There are tall trees at right and left, and in the left distance there are a river, a square high tower and poplars.

ROSELLE

Made by John Meir & Son

Hanging baskets filled with roses are set in cartouches on the rim of this plate which is covered with narrow concentric lines. The cartouches are framed by vines terminating in clovers which twine and form large trefoil designs between the floral patterns. Beading surrounds the well.

A stream divides the central scene. On the right bank in the middle ground there is an ornate chalet surrounded by trees. In the left foreground there are flowers and shrubs. A pair of tall trees rises on the left bank and in the distance at left there are other buildings and mountains.

The distinctive features of this pattern are the hanging baskets set in cartouche frames.

Marked J. Meir & Son, GMK. 2366, c. 1837-97.

ROUSILLON

Made by James Goodwin

The stippled, paneled rim of this fourteen-sided dish is decorated with a white wreath of scrolls with foliated terminals which is placed over a pattern of vertical, double bars. A circle of small scrolls is placed around the upper well and a second circle of loops over a line is placed beneath this.

A Gothic shrine-like building, complete with statue in an arched miche, is placed at the left in the central scene. Towered buildings appear behind it. The usual body of water divides the picture. At right tall elms grow in a grassy bank that bears flowering bushes, and at far right, there is a covered urn on a pedestal. Four figures are on the riverbank in the center of the scene, one holds a pole. There are rocks in the foreground. Rousillon, in southern most France, became part of France by the Treaty of Utrecht, in 1713. It had formerly belonged to the Hapsburgs.

Marked J. Goodwin, Longton. Registered December 16, 1846. Mark not located.

ROYAL SKETCHES

Maker unknown

The outer edges of both these dishes are detailed with a narrow beading of small hearts. Below this there are triangular groups of flowers alternating with single stylized three-petaled blossoms flanked by scrolls. These are separated by vertical fencing. Five large, identical horizontal sprays of roses and thistles covers the rim, and four larger ones surround the well. The well is encircled by a belt, inscribed "Honi Soit qui mal y Pense", the French motto adopted by King Edward III of England who formed the Order of the Garter in 1839. (Shame to him who evil thinks). The roses and thistle represent England and Scotland.

The center medallion on the vegetable bowl shows Windsor Castle on a tree covered bank in the background beyond the Thames River. In the center of the scene a pleasure boat is rowed on the river, it is covered with a canopy and contains seven figures. Behind it at left there is a sailboat. At left in the foreground there are tall trees. In the center foreground the grassy bank is covered with rocks, bushes and over-scaled flowers. On the outside of the bowl there are scenes of the Crystal Palace.

The pattern on the cup plate is compressed and fills a small area. Note that the cup plate is scalloped and the outer embossed edge is white. The design in the center shows only part of the castle across the river and the boat is omitted.

"RUINED CASTLE"

Made by Robert Hamilton

Coyshe shows this exact pattern on a large plate in Volume I, p. 40. He titled as above and his example is marked Hamilton.

The cup plate is gently scalloped and the rim is covered with a border of wild roses and smaller flowers. A band of dotted beads contains the stippled rim at the well.

In the foreground of the central scene three cows are in a stream. Behind them a dark, triple-arched bridge crosses the water and leads to the ruins of an old castle that appears circular. There are mountains in the distance, tall trees at right, two figures stand on the opposite bank, and there are shrubs and flowers in the foreground.

GMK. 1901, c. 1811-26.

"RUINS"

Made by Benjamin Adams

The rim of this oval sauce stand is covered with alternating vertical scenes. Four show a long, low classic temple set on a plateau at left; the other four vignettes contain a bucolic scene of a seated herdsman with three cows. The rim pattern is separated from the well picture by a band of beaded triangles.

In the center scene a man stands in the foreground with the same three cows as pictured above. He holds a long pole. At right there is a stream crossed by a stone arched bridge at right. The columns, arches and steps of a large ruin are at left.

Marked (imp.) B. Adams, GMK. 10, 1800-20.

RUINS

Made by William Adams & Co.

There are three, scenic cartouches on the rim of this scalloped saucer. Each contains a picture of a man who holds a stick or shovel. He stands in the foreground on a hillside. At right there are tall Gothic ruins; at left there is a tree. The scenic reserves alternate with a trio of large flowers in a stippled field. Six Gothic shield-shaped designs, that are centered with a quatrefoil, separate the two above patterns. A band of small diamonds is placed around the edge of the rim.

In the central scene a man holding a pole over his shoulder walks with a cow and a dog past ruins of tall arch forms and feathery trees. At right there is a pair of columns. In the distance there are a stream, towered buildings and mountain peaks. The foreground is crossed by part of a fence and a dark bank at left.

Marked Adams (imp.), GMK. 18, c. 1800-1864.

RUINS

Mark not located

The white gadrooned edges of these plates are enhanced by bands of very dark arches filled with tiny sprigs. Three sprays of roses, and other large flowers, alternate with pairs of blossoms around the upper rim. Eight, small shadowy sprays surround the central medallion which is framed with beaded white, scallops placed against a dark circular line.

In the central scene of the first plate a horseman with a feather in his hat rides across the foreground accompanied by two small white dogs. Behind him there are large Gothic arches that form part of a church ruin. A man and woman are seated in the right background. A tall tree rises at left and at extreme left there are buildings across a river. Rocks and flowers in the foreground complete the scene.

The second plate shows men fishing in a stream and tall Gothic buildings in the background.

Marked H. & V., and (imp.) Hopkin and Vernon.

"RURAL SCENE"

Made by Andrew Stevenson

The entire surface of this cup plate is covered with the transfer which features tall pine trees in the center. They rise from a bush-covered bank of a river and the bushes resemble pine branches. In the background there are fields and a body of water like a lake. In the distance there are mountains. At right in the center ground there is a cluster of three farm buildings. In the right foreground there is part of a fence. A striped band is placed across the foreground and there is a group of over-scaled flowers at lower right.

Marked (imp.) Stevenson, GMK. 3699, c. 1816-30.

RURAL SCENERY

Made by Joseph Heath & Co.

Both the large plate and the cup plate photographed are scalloped and their white edges are enhanced with small, printed partitions containing tiny leaf forms. The upper rim is covered with a dark diagonal plaid. Four scenic cartouches are placed around the rim and contain a tall urn at left, a sailboat containing three figures in the center and a temple with domed roof and tall trees and mountains in the right background. There are flowers and part of a lawn in the foreground. The reserves are separated by frames of white C scrolls over a band of four diamonds and rosettes. The C scrolls are also placed under the scenic reserves and form a continuous chain around the rim. A lighter plaid pattern is placed behind the diamonds. Triangular pennants attached to a wreath of oval beads encircle the well.

In the foreground of the central scene on the larger plate, a dark and a light cow stand in a stream. There are rocks and trees at right. A church ruin is at left. There are tall trees, a river and mountains in the background.

On the cup plate a single animal is at center. There are a small ruin at left, tall trees at right and flowers in the foreground.

Marked J.H. & Co., an (imp.) propeller mark with beads, GMK. 1994a, c. 1828-41.

PLATE IV

Staffordshire earthernware transfer ware, cup plates and other dishes.

Collection Fountain House East, Jeffersontown, Kentucky.

RURAL SCENERY

Made by Thomas, John and Joseph Mayer

Both the plate and cup plate photographed have the same border of wide, scenic cartouches separated by baroque triangular, foliated scroll designs. A band of zigzag edged with diamonds appears around the upper edge of the cartouches and another band of diamonds on a plain ribbon contains the bottom part. A wreath of small flowers is placed beneath this. Each cartouche contains the same scene of a large mansion at left, three men with fish poles and nets and a dog at center on the banks of a harbor. In the bankground there are house and trees in the distance on either side of the harbor. There are many tall trees in the foreground at right.

The large plate shows a man and woman and boy standing on a road near a small, rustic bridge over a brook. There are boulders and smaller rocks in the foreground. In the center a farmer holds a pole and another one leads three horses which pull a tedder over the fields. In the distance there is a towered building. At left there are tall trees and other trees rise at right center. At right there is a white house behind a fence and a wooden-barred gate. Three cows are faintly visible in front of the gate.

The cup plate shows a man and dog near the bridge; it also shows the man with a pole and the horses pulling the tedder on the field. The trees, towers, and house at right are the same as on the larger plate.

Marked T.J. & J. Mayer and "Prize Medal", c. 1851, GMK. 2570, c. 1843-55.

RUSTIC

Mark not located

The saucer shown is not scalloped. The edge is detailed by a band of printed ovals and swags and the rim is covered with moss over which a grapevine with grapes and leaves are printed in a wreath. In the center a large farm house, with a lean-to shed on the side, is in the left background. A road divides the scene at left. In the foreground there is a grassy terrace and some bushes. Three steps lead up to the right behind a picket fence. Tall elm trees rise at right center.

The second plate may be a reissue of the original pattern. The rim of the dish is scalloped and is covered with the grapes and grape leaves in a thicker wreath than that which is seen on the saucer. The moss has been omitted.

Marked W. & G. Harding. Harding and Cockson potted from 1834-1860, and W. & J. Harding potted in 1862-72.

SALEM

Made by James Edwards

The rims of these twelve-sided plates are paneled and are covered with a dark repetitive design of a ruffled flower set in a baroque frame of foliated scrolls. A half-flower is set between each scroll pattern at the upper rim and is printed against a very dark background. The scrolls at the bottom of the cartouche form a wreath around the well of the larger plate. This was omitted on the cup plate.

A Gothic ruin is at left in the center of the larger plate and there are trees and bushes next to it. At right there are two standing women and a seated man on a riverbank. Tall elms rise from the bank. In the background a bridge crosses a river and there are towers and other buildings and mountains in the distance. In the foreground there are some rocks and bushes.

The design in the center of the cup plate shows a man with his dog at left. There is a lake behind him and mountains rise in the distance. In the middle there is a small temple with a domed roof. It sits on a hill and a tall elm rises above it. At extreme right there are other trees.

Marked J.E., GMK. 1449, c. 1843-73.

SARDINIA
Made by Ralph Hall

This unevenly scalloped plate bears on edging of tiny dark and white quatrefoils. The concave rim is covered with a zigzag, vertical pattern of double lines and beads. Three large oval reserves, framed with ruffles and enclosing a picture of fruits, alternate with three smaller ruffled reserves that show a pair of birds sitting on the edge of a tazza which is flanked by forget-me-nots. A wreath of rosettes, diamonds and tassels encircles the bottom of the rim.

In the center scene a man sits astride a prancing horse. A woman and child stand at right facing him. At left in the distance there is a large building with a domed tower, two steeples rise behind it. A river divides the scene and in the background there are an arched bridge, some buildings and the outline of a mountain. At right there is a large, flower-filled urn on a pedestal with over-scaled flowers at its base and one other in the foreground.

Marked R. Hall & Co., GMK. 1889, c. 1841-9.

SCOTTISH MINSTREL

Possibly made by John Ridgway & Co.

The saucer shown is gently and unevenly scalloped and the white edge is enhanced by a dark line trimmed with small arches containing beads. The upper part of the rim is covered with a diamond diaper pattern. There are five lobed oval reserves, containing oblong fleurettes on the rim. They are separated by long C curves, crested with dark crosses which form the top arches for areas containing a spray of roses and dark leaves. There are small shadowy sprigs set under both rim design elements.

In the central scene there is a large stone mansion in the left background, it is multi-storied, has a rounded low tower section and arched openings. There are tall feathery trees behind it and a lawn at right. Pine trees are at the end of the lawn and in the distance one sees a lake.

In the foreground there are two persons. A lady in white dress stands next to the Minstrel of the title. He wears a kilt, diced socks and is blowing on the mouth piece of a bagpipe.

This dish is part of a set used with "Villa" by Ridgway (this category). It contains exactly the same diamond diaper design on the upper rim and is printed in exactly the same colors (olive green and dark gold) as the set of Villa which is marked J.R. & Co.

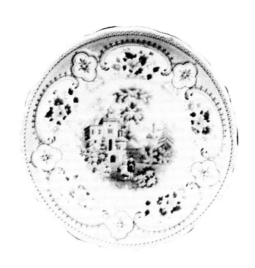

SCROLL

Mark not located

The edges of these scalloped plates are white and a small band of white crosses on a dark background enhances the white area. The rims are covered with a worm-track design on a stippled field which invades the well and ends in a circle of scallops alternating with rounded fleur-de-lis. Tiny lines form a shadow repeat of the edging around the well.

The scene in the center of the dinner plate shows a harbor at right. A sailboat with tall dark masts and nets draped over the prow is placed behind a smaller boat with a white sail. In the distance there are other boats and on shore in the background there are city buildings, a tall tower and a craggy mountain peak. At left on a hill there is a windmill and behind it there are a hill and trees. A man seated on a white horse talks to a standing man on the path that leads to the windmill. In the foreground there are rocks, bushes and over-scaled flowers. A tall tree rises in the center of the scene.

The first cup plate bears a pastoral scene of cows grazing in the foreground. A stream flows through the background and beyond the water there are thatched-roofed farm buildings and tall trees. Mountains rise in the distance and complete the picture. The second cup plate presents a large three-storied mansion in back of a long stone wall with a gate opening in the middle. There are feathery trees at left, a sweep of lawn across the scene, and over-scaled flowers in the foreground.

Marked B.

SCROLL (cont.)

SEINE

Made by John Wedgwood

This soup plate and the cup plate are twelve-sided and the edges are outlined by a row of printed scallops and beads. The rims are covered with a chain design centered with a single flower and leaves placed over a random worm-track background. The oval angular links of the chain are composed of branches. The rim design is contained at the well by a row of scallops hung with small bead pendants.

The central scene is dominated on the dishes by an angled bridge on the right. On the larger plate it has four large openings and the cup plate, two. Both dishes show tall elms in the center of the scene. A stream is in the foreground. There are buildings on top of a tall mountain bluff at right. There is a meadow at left and buildings and trees in the left background. There appears to be a lake behind the central scene.

Marked J. Wedgwood, like GMK. 4276a, c. 1841-60.

SELECT VIEWS

Made by William Smith & Co.

The plate shown is unevenly scalloped and the white edge is outlined by a row of tiny printed beads. Four scenic cartouches, framed with flowers at the top and foliated scrolls below, are placed around the rim. Each contains a different classical scene of towers, temples, domed buildings, trees and water. Two also contain a small dark boat. The spaces between the reserves are filled with a pattern of blossoms and a diamond diaper design, which is framed at the top by a large rose flanked with baroque scrolled ovals. At the bottom of each diaper area there are wild roses and a passion flower, which is a distinctive element of this pattern.

In the central scene a man and woman sit on the ground at right. He leans against a short pedestal that holds an urn. A very tall tree rises at extreme right and arches across the central scene of a river with small buildings and towers on either bank. At left there is a large castle, or columned temple, with a very tall arched entrance and a stone stairway that descends to the water. In the left foreground there are large, over-scaled leaves and dark shrubs.

Marked (imp.) W.S. & Co., and "Queen's Ware" and "Stockton", GMK. 3599, c. 1825-55.

SENATE HOUSE, CAMBRIDGE

Made by John and William Ridgway

The outer edge of this dish is detailed by a row of dentil lines topped with scallops. Four oval cartouches are placed on the rim and contain alternating scenes of two children in classic robes feeding a goat and two scenes showing the children milking her. The cartouches are separated by pairs of very large morning-glories, leaves and forget-me-nots.

The center picture is contained by an octagonal frame and shows two pairs of English scholars in robes. They are on the lawn in front of a large, many windowed building.

Marked J. and W. Ridgway, and "Opaque China", GMK. 3262, c. 1814-30.

SEVILLA

Maker unknown

The rim of the charger photographed bears alternating patterns of three scenic reserves and three stylized bouquets that terminate in five vertical, thick rays. The designs are separated by diamond basket weave which is placed under shell-like scrolls. The scenes are all the same and show a large castle beyond a lake, two small sailboats on the water, and a stone stairway with two rounded urns at right. A wreath of small sprigs is placed around the upper rim. Floral sprays frame the vignettes around the bottom of the rim.

The picture in the center of the well is dominated by a large tiered fountain with cherubs holding up the uppermost basin, and by two swans in the water in the foreground. At left there is part of a balustrade capped with a statue. In the background there are temples and domed church-like towers. At right there are a walled garden and tall trees.

The central pattern is a duplicate in many details of Athens by Adams (this category).

Marked PICKMANY and also (imp.) a large anchor.

SHANNON

Maker unknown

The rim of this twelve-sided plate bears a design of four scenic cartouches which contain a picture of a castle at left, a river in the center, balustrade, bushes and trees in the right foreground, and mountains in the rear. Two small, window-like reserves flank the main cartouches and each continues the picture of mountains, river, and foreground bushes. Between the vignettes a bouquet is set in a frame against a background of concentric, narrow lines that form the background for all the design elements. Scrolls and double spearpoint encircle the outer edge. The bottom of the rim design contains scallops and scrolls under the window reserves. These are joined by beads and spearpoints.

An urn is in the center foreground of the picture in the well. Several small bushes separate it from steps with a stone balustrade at right. Tall trees and bushes are behind the stairs. In the center a river divides the scene and at left behind a tree-lined sloping bank there is a castle set against very high mountains. A low bridge crosses the river in the background and a boat with a man poling two passengers is in the water near the right shore.

SICILIAN

Maker unknown

Both the salad plate and the two cup plates shown in this pattern are gently scalloped and each has an outer edge design of tiny triangles. The rim of the larger plate is decorated with four oval cartouches with foliated scrolls at the top. Two contain a dark ewer at left, some flowers and a scene of Mount Etna and trees at the right. The other two are filled with flowers and an arched scroll with large flat leaves at left. The spaces between the cartouches are filled with garlands of flowers and sprigs at bottom, and a wing-like pair of scrolls at top.

One cup plate shows only the top of the three cartouches, but the wing-like scrolls are present and are distinguishing, as is the scene in the rim that contains the ewer and Mount Etna.

The scenes on each contain fanciful gazebos. The largest plate shows a boat with a high prow in the foreground and both the large plate and one cup plate show mountain peaks in the background.

SICILIAN BEAUTIES

Made by Ralph and James Clews

The white edge and handles of this vegetable bowl are embossed with heavy scrolls. A band of crowned beads surmounts the outer edge. This in turn is enhanced by a narrow string of white beading. The upper part of the rim is stippled and is contained by scrolls. The four oval cartouches on the rim are framed by small fan-shaped scrolls, and are topped with a rosette and three feathers against a very dark background. They are filled with small flowers and leaves. The reserves are flanked by scrolls, and short garlands of flowers are suspended from this outer scroll design. The cartouches are separated by bouquets of large flowers, buds, sprigs and leaves. A band of doubled beaded swags connects these alternating patterns and forms a lacy necklace around the well.

A very large baroque urn, topped with an eagle with wings outstretched, dominates the foreground of the central scene. It is set on a low square base and there are over-scaled flowers at the left on the base. A scroll is placed at the right of the base. In the right foreground there is a part of a fence or wall and a small covered jar is placed on a pedestal at its end. Bushes and flowers are at right.

In the background, across a lake there is a church and tall trees. A sailboat is on the water at center. At left, behind the urn, there is a very large bushy tree and in the left distance there is another religious structure. Beyond the lake, in the distance one sees city buildings and tall mountains.

Marked R. & J. Clews, see Godden, pg. 151, 1818-34.

"SICILY"

Made by Copeland and Garrett

The cup plate photographed shows a castle in the background. A river flows through the center of the scene and there are sailboats afloat on it. A man fishes from a rocky bank in the middle of the picture. The border is distinctive. Large foliated scrolls are placed around the upper part of the rim which is covered with a dark background filled with small trefoils. On the larger plates scrolls encircle the well and frame the central scene. A dinner plate is shown in this pattern, marked "Mount Etna" (Coyshe, Volume II, page 22).

Marked Copeland and Garrett, and "Late Spode", GMK. 1092, c. 1833-47.

SOLAR RAY

Made by James and Ralph Clews

The white scalloped edge of this plate is embossed with beading. A black, dotted line is below this and small beaded scallops form a third edge decoration. The rim design contains three floral swags surmounted with a scroll design that alternate with three sprays of large flowers with very dark leaves. Smaller flowers and leaves from both designs enter the upper well.

A ring of small triangles, trimmed at the bottom with tiny beads, encircles the central-scene which shows the sun rising, or setting, behind hills. At right front there is a castle-like building with rounded towers. A stream divides the scene and it is crossed by an arched bridge at mid center. Behind the bridge there are sailboats and some small buildings. Tall trees rise at either side. The usual over-scaled flowers are placed in the foreground.

Marked (imp.) Clews Warranted Staffordshire, GMK. 919, c. 1818-34.

SPANISH COVENT

Made by William Adams

The white edge of the plate photographed is scalloped and is decorated with a row of beads. Four scenic cartouches are placed around the rim. Two present a river scene in a city and the other pair contain many towered buildings. A shield design is placed between the cartouches. It is framed by foliated scrolls, a trio of roses at top and a large passion flower and a rose at the bottom. The center of the shield is filled with a cellular diaper design. The bottom of both rim designs enter the well.

The central picture is framed by a wreath of sprigs. A man and woman in Elizabethan costume stand in the foreground, in front of them there are over-scaled flowers and leaves. At the right there is an arched, narrow entry through which steps ascend to another closed arch at the right rear. In the background stands the Convent of the title. At left there is a statue in a niche. Behind this there are a pine tree and a tall elm. These are balanced by tall trees and flowers at right.

Marked (imp.) Adams, GMK. 18, c. 1800-64.

SPANISH VILLA
Maker unknown

This platter is scalloped and the outer edge is detailed with a band of large, dark leaves under a row of connecting triangles. A narrow white line is placed between the beads and the rim design, which consists of alternating scenic reserves and an urn with flowers which are separated by large, curving crosses of rosette trimmed ribbon. At the top of each cross there is a dark triangle filled with three white leaves and at the bottom of each triangle there are large, dark fleurettes framed with small dark leaves. Foliated scrolls flank the crosses.

The scenic reserves show a round columned temple with adjacent buildings at left which is set at the top of a flight of stairs which lead down to a river. A small dark sailboat is in the foreground. Behind it an arched bridge crosses to a stony island covered with trees. In the distance there are towers and hills. The floral reserves show a covered urn on a pedestal at the left center. Over-scaled flowers are placed around it. Both vignettes are contained at the bottom by a row of white beads. A ribbon band of geometric design is placed under the beads and this connects the cross designs. A wide design of scrolls and sprigs encircles the upper well.

In the middle of the central scene there are four people on a stone terrace, one of whom points across a river to a statue placed on a pedestal. The statue is surrounded by lacy trees and bushes. There are over-scaled flowers at its base. At left there is a large covered urn on a pedestal and there are over-scaled flowers at its base also. Steps lead down to the water from the terrace and a pair of swans swim nearby at right. In the distance there is a small island and behind that one sees the towers and colonnade of the large villa of the title.

SPARTAN

Made by Podmore Walker & Co.

The rim of this fourteen-sided plate is covered with a design of rounded, oblong cartouches with vine borders; each contains a sprig of bellflowers that are separated by a banister design and set upon a field of narrow, concentric lines. A row of small spearpoint contains the rim pattern in the well.

The central scene shows four adults and a child dressed in Empire fashion. They stand in the foreground on a terrace. A basin supported by a pair of cherubs standing on a pedestal is at right. Beyond that there are tall trees and a vista leading to a pillar. In the center there is a lake and at left there are tall castles and mountains. A fountain throws water high into the air from a large round basin at left. Steps lead to the fountain from the terrace occupied by the group of people.

Marked P.W. & Co., and (imp.) "Stoneware", exact GMK. 3076, c. 1834-59.

STATUE

Made by Samuel Alcock & Co.

The edge of this fourteen-sided plate is outlined by a band of white fleur-de-lis. The paneled rim is covered with narrow, concentric lines that dip at a point between bars made of little sprigs. Garlands of small, white rosettes are placed between the bars. The well is encircled by a double fleur-de-lis pattern.

The statue of the title stands at left upon a square pedestal placed on a stone wall. Trees and hills are to the left of the statue. A large elm rises at center. Some flowers are placed at the tree base and sprawl over the wall. A man in a top hat and cutaway, a lady with parasol, and a child stand in the center of the scene. The man points to a small urn, or statue, at the end of a balustrade at left. In the distance across a lake there are a castle, trees and tall mountains. Part of a wall and pedestal and some small flowers and leaves are in the foreground.

Marked S.A. & Co., GMK. 75, c. 1830-59.

SUSPENSION BRIDGE

Made by Enoch Wood & Son

The rim of this irregularly scalloped plate is covered with five rows of small, pale five-petaled fleurons placed on a dark stippled background. The well is encircled by a deep row of spearpoint. The bridge of the title crosses a river in the center of the scene. At right there is a large tall gate with double towers. At left there are houses and a square tower. In the distance there are other buildings, towers and mountain peaks. Two small sailboats can be seen on the other side of the bridge. A tall elm rises at left. In the foreground two men and a woman stand on the grassy bank of the river. There are bushes at right and over-scaled flowers at left.

Marked E.W. & S., GMK. 4260, c. 1818-46.

"SWISS"

Made by William Davenport & Co.

The edge of this little saucer (3 inches) is slightly scalloped and there is a very narrow band of triangles and pendants around it. The rim design may be abbreviated, but sections of diamond trellis contained by scrolls and a large orchid-type flower alternate with plain stippled reserves contained at the well by large ruffled poppies with dark leaves, small flowers and sprigs.

In the middle of the dish the scene is dominated by a very large chalet at left in the middle ground. It has a big overhanging roof, and what appear to be snow patches are on the steep slopes of the roof. A balcony is placed at left and there is an arched entry in the foundation. A tall dark pine tree is next to the structure at center and there are other trees behind the roof. At right a woman in a long white gown and a man with hat and dark suit stand next to a bushy tree. There are bushes and over-scaled flowers in the foreground.

Marked Davenport, dated with an Imp. Anchor, GMK. 1181a, c. 1836.

SWISS

Made by Ralph Stevenson

The white edge of the unevenly scalloped plate shown is decorated with a band of small scallops and beads. The upper part of the rim is dark and stippled. A wreath of foliated scrolls inset with small white flowers is placed against the dark background. Three designs of hanging baskets filled with large flowers and sprigs are placed around the rim. The oval bottoms of the baskets enter the upper well and are a distinctive feature of the rim pattern. Between the baskets there are sprays of three large flowers flanked by smaller posies and sprigs.

In the center scene a large chalet-type building is in the left background. There are tall trees behind it and its base is set on an arched opening over a stream. Two small boats, one with a sail, are in the foreground in the water. A floating barrel buoy is near the sailboat. At right in the background on a hillside there is a multi-storied house with peaked roofs and many towers. There are other buildings and mountains in the center distance.

Marked R. Stevenson, also an (imp.) Anchor in a circle, GMK. 3704, c. 1810-32.

"SWISS"

Made by Enoch Wood & Sons

The back-stamp is blurred on this unevenly scalloped plate but looks as though it may read "Swiss". The stippled rim is covered with small flowers and root-like lines or sprigs. The outer edge is decorated with a band of sprigs twined over a beaded band. Three pairs of flowers that resemble wild roses and dahlias, flanked by a spray of bellflowers at right and a poppy at left, alternate with a pattern of intertwined ostrich feathers. The feathers are a distinctive design feature. Little forget-me-nots encircle the well in a loose arrangement.

In the central scene a sailboat is at right. It contains five men; four are seated and one stands in the square prow. All wear dark hats and vests. The boat approaches a grassy bank with trees rising from it at left. In the background there is a large edifice under construction and a large chalet is behind the open structure. A tall tree arches above the chalet roof. In the distance there are poplars and Alpine peaks.

Marked E. Wood & Sons, GMK. 4261, c. 1818-46.

SWISS SCENERY

Possibly made by John Swift

These plates are unevenly scalloped and the beaded edges were left white. A band of dark stippling accents the edge. A wreath of foliated scrolls with small flowers encircles the top of the rim, which is covered with baroque scrolls, small flowers and sprigs which alternate with very large cabbage roses, dark leaves and wild roses and ferns. Small bars of trellis are placed under white daisies at three points on the upper and middle rim.

A very ornate chalet is at left in the central scene on the larger plate. There are tall flowering trees behind it and to the left. At right there is a smaller building with a tower. Two small figures stand between the two buildings in the center of the picture. In the distance there are other buildings and tall mountains. The foreground on both plates is covered with over-scaled flowers and baroque scrolls.

On the cup plate the structure and tall tree are also at left. A dark fence leads from the building to the right. A river divides the scene and there are mountains in the distance.

Marked J.S. and "Opaque China", see GMK. 3773, c. 1843.

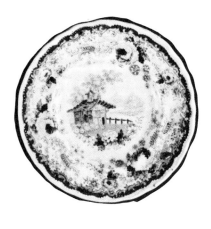

SYRIA

Made by Robert Cochran & Co.

This soup plate is gently scalloped and its edge is detailed by a band of dark scallops. A row of white beading contains the rim design of reserves filled with treillage which are framed by white scalloped bands and separated by vertical posts topped with scrolls and a flower. Three of the reserves present a small scene of a house with a fancy roof and flanked by slanted side buildings. Sprays of flowers are in the foreground and there are trees on either side of the structure. Three floral designs fill the alternatives reserves. A white band trimmed with fringe contains the rim design and forms a hexagonal opening around the upper part of the well.

A river divides the central scene. There are costumed figures on the right bank in the foreground. Tall church-like buildings are on the left bank. At extreme right there are tall trees. Towers and mountains in the distance complete the picture.

Marked R.C. & Co., GMK. 965, c. 1846.

TCHIURLUK

Maker unknown

This plate is from the same series as "Pera" as seen in this category. It is gently scalloped and has an edging of printed scallops at the outer rim and around the well. It bears the same rim pattern as "Pera".

In the central scene a man holding a spear leads a camel who is ladened with bundles. There are barrack-like buildings in the middle ground, and a domed temple and minarets behind them. The houses of a village can be seen at right in the distance. A pair of tall trees rises from a steep grassy bank at right and there are trees and shrubs at left. In the foreground there is a hillock covered with spiky bushes and wide spade-shaped leaves. Laidecker states c. 1815.

TERNI

Made by Cheatham and Robinson

The rim of the soup dish shown is scalloped and the white edge and a beaded line enhance the scalloped design. A floral pattern consisting of pairs of daffodils and poppies, alternating with pairs of peonies, is placed on a stippled ground around the rim. The large flowers are joined by sprays and leaves and buds. A garland of lacy panels is placed around the well and small swags of pendant beads descend from this into the well. Note that the pointed leaves and buds from the six large floral pairs extend over the lacy drapery.

The central picture depicts a mountain village in the background. In the foreground a man dressed in cavalier clothes and astride a horse is at right and listens to a seated peasant girl wearing a large brimmed hat who plays a mandolin. Another girl leans on a wall beside the musician, her plummed hat is on the ground near the horse's front hoofs. There are flowers in the foreground and at left. The subtitle on the back-stamp reads "a romantic District of Italy".

Marked C. & R., GMK. 879, c. 1822-37.

TERNI

Maker unknown

The border pattern on this cream pitcher consists of a wreath of feather-like leaves and forget-me-nots set on a vine placed over a background of vertical lines. The upper edge is decorated with deep pointed scallops interspersed with a pair of small circles. The bottom of the border design is contained by a band of lacy heart-shaped scrolls.

The scene on the body differs on each side but each shows a scene divided by a river, a castle in the right background, and a tall tree at left in the foreground. On one side of the pitcher there are three people standing, on the bank in the foreground; a man, woman and child. On the reverse side of the pitcher, the river is at left. There is a large building at right and there are three adult figures at right in the foreground. There are trees and rocks at extreme left and a brook, a branch of the main stream, which flows across the left foreground.

The back-stamp is indistinct, and may read D. & C. which could be the Swansea Pottery Co., GMK. 3766, c. 1811-17, or it may be R. & C. which would be Reed and Clementson, GMK. 3212, c. 1833-5.

TESSINO

Made by Joseph Clementson

The plate photographed is twelve-sided and a band of leaves twining over narrow rods encircles the outer edge. The paneled rim is covered with a design that resembles bricks. Five stylized perforated baskets with wide rims hang from the rod at the upper edge. There are three flowers in each basket and small sprigs are placed on either side of them. A wreath of foliated scrolls twining over a white band encircles the well.

In the central scene a peddler wearing a wide brimmed hat and carrying a basket on his back is seated on the stones at left. Two women in peasant costume stand talking to him. A road divides the scene; it is bordered with a stone wall in the center of the foreground. Tall elms rise from behind the wall and at right in the background there are many arches that are part of a ruin. A river divides the scene in the distance. A high tree-covered bank is at left behind the peddler. Castle-like buildings and mountains in the distance complete the picture.

Marked J. Clementson, GMK. 910a, c. 1839-64.

TIVOLI

Made by Charles Meigh

The paneled, concave rims of these twelve-sided plates and of the vegetable bowl are covered with concentric lines. A wreath of grape leaves and trios of small cosmos is placed over the concentric lines. A band of leaves, vines and tendrils is set under a white line at the bottom of the rim pattern. The cup plate shows only the lower half of the rim pattern.

The usual romantic scene appears in the center of all three dishes. A river divides the picture and there are tall trees at left with vine-covered roots. At extreme left in the background there is a temple on a hill. At right there are some bushy trees and a castle with many towers is on a hill in the background. In the foreground there are three people, two men, one of whom points to the castle, and a seated woman.

The scene inside the octagonal vegetable dish is the same as that on the plates and is reproduced on both sides of the lid. The temples on the hill at left can be seen most clearly on the vegetable dish.

Marked C. Meigh, and "Improved Stone China", GMK. 2618, c. 1835-49.

434

TIVOLI (cont.)

TYROL

Made by John and George Alcock

This pattern was printed on a twelve-sided plate. The sprigged lattice design on the rim is outlined with a circle of beads which does not follow the molded angles. In each diamond of the sprigged lattice there is a quatrefoil. Three oval reserves are set in the lattice and show an end view of a house with a thatched roof and chimney. There are trees behind the house. In the foreground a man stands holding a cow and his dog is at left. There reserves alternate with three others that contain a pair of flowers, sprigs and leaves.

The central scene shows a large lake or river. In the foreground there are three men with nets. A willow tree rises at right. Across the water there is a fanciful multi-storied edifice with arched windows, thatched peaked roofs and chimneys. In the background there are other buildings and Alpine peaks.

Marked J. & G. Alcock, GMK. 68, c. 1839-46.

TYROLEAN

Made by William Ridgway & Co.

A distinctive fence design encircles the upper part of the rims of these unevenly scalloped plates. Three pairs of large flowers alternate with three triangular scroll and floral designs around the rest of the rim. The spaces between the large designs are filled with sprigs and small flowers. A row of arrow points and short straight lines encircles the outer white edge.

On the dinner plate a man and woman, both wearing wide brimmed hats, are seated on a grassy bank in the foreground. He holds a stick and is probably a herdsman, as there are three white goats at left. There are pine trees on both sides of the scene. At left there is a castle with many towers on top of a mountain. Below it there is an arched bridge with a water tower which crosses a stream, or a lake, which is at center. The road to the castle passes over the bridge around the lake and under a high, arched tower attached to it. In the distance there are other buildings and Alpine peaks.

The cup plate shows two shepherds and sheep in the foreground. A silo tower and barn buildings are at right in the background, and the distinctive pine trees are placed on either side of the scene.

Marked W.R. & Co., GMK. 3303a, c. 1834-54.

TYROL HUNTERS

Made by William Davenport & Co.

The white outer edge of the oval vegetable dish photographed is scalloped and the handles at either side are molded. The upper part of the rim is covered with a diaper design of narrow vertical cells. A band of white scrolls and pairs of flowers encircles the center of the rim and dips to form oval cartouches that contain rosettes. Behind the pairs of flowers there are reserves filled with treillage contained by three beaded ribboned swags caught by rosettes. Behind the cartouches there are garlands of small flowers centered with a keyhole-shaped rectangle.

In the central picture two figures holding guns are in the foreground, one stands and one is seated. Both wear belted jerkins and big brimmed hats. Another hunter can be seen in the middle distance; he is kneeling and aiming his gun. There are tall trees on either side and Alpine peaks in the distance. A lake and some buildings in the background, and rocks and flowers in the foreground, complete the picture.

Marked Davenport, GMK. 1179a, c. 1820-60.

UNION

Made by Edward Challinor

The paneled, stippled rim of this plate is covered with a design of scenic oval reserves framed by intertwining branches. Each scene is the same and shows a man on horseback near two cows who stand in a stream at left. At right there are a barn, a fence and some trees. The reserves are separated by a vertical leaf design, perhaps a sheath of wheat. A narrow band of wheat ears is placed around the bottom of the rim design in the cavetto.

In the central picture a man in farmer's smock, wide brimmed hat and holding a long pole is pointing to the right. A pair of horses, one dark and one white, stand behind him harnessed to a plow. A woman with a pail on her head and two boys stand near the plow. In the distance at right there is a large manor house. A winding road leads to it past a fence and poplar trees. There is a lake in the center of the scene; it is crossed by a flat bridge in the background. Three storage silos stand behind the manor house. In the distance there are a church with a steeple and tall mountain peaks. At left tall elms rise above the group of farm folk. A fence leads off to the left. In the foreground there are bushes, and the soil is striated with furrows made by the plow.

Marked E.C.; the pattern was registered in January of 1852, GMK. 1825, c. 1842-67.

UNITED STATES VIEWS

Made by William Adams

The edges of these unevenly scalloped plates were left white, and the edges are separated from the stippled upper rim by a row of dentils. The distinctive pattern of fans, set on the lower rim in three different spots, alternate with a pattern in three sections consisting of large roses with dark leaves, which are set in small baskets. These designs are separated by white reserves that contain sprigs and which are framed with swags at the bottom.

The central picture on the first plate, framed by a circle of lacy spearpoint is subtitled "Shannondale Springs, Virginia, U.S." It shows two men seated on the grass in the foreground; they are under a very tall tree at right. One is dressed in white and is fishing in a stream that crosses the picture diagonally; the other man is dressed in black clothes and hat. A third seated figure can be glimpsed behind the fishing pole. At left in the rear the building of a resort hotel can be seen on a hill surrounded by trees. The scene on the cup plate in this series is the same as this pattern.

The second plate is subtitled "View Near Conway, N.H., U.S." It shows a man and woman on a curving road that leads past a large log structure at left. There are tall trees behind the building. At right there is a river and in the background there are many tall mountains.

The third plate was titled "Catskill Mtn. House, U.S." It shows two women in a grove of small trees at the foot of a hill which is surmounted by the famous old hotel, the Catskill Mtn. House of the title.

Marked Imp. Adams, GMK. 18, (c. 1800-64) but these Views date from 1830-45. The design of Shannondale Springs was taken from a drawing by Charles Burton which was published in London in 1831. That of the Catskill Mtn. House and the View of Conway were taken from paintings by Thomas Cole which were published in 1830 and 1831 respectively.

UNITED STATES VIEWS (cont.)

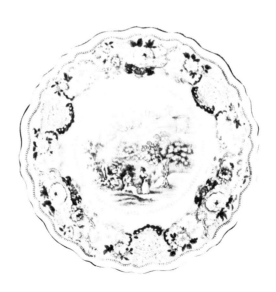

UNIVERSITY

Made by John Ridgway & Co.

The rim of this deep saucer is paneled. Four oval cartouches containing identical scenes of university buildings, flanked by trees, are framed by foliated scrolls and set into an egg-crate diaper pattern around the rim. Small scrolls encircle the outer edge under a narrow plain band. A five-petal stylized flower is placed between the scrolls at the top of the diaper design sections. The well is encircled by a plain band of short fringe.

In the center scene a man dressed in a scholar's gown and hat talks with two others at the gate to the university. At right in the center there are tall pine trees. A large formal building, with a long facade, is surmounted by a tall domed tower in the background. Pairs of students walk on the lawn in front of the building.

The cup plate is identical to the larger dish with the exception that there are no students in the main yard, and the large eagles with outstretched wings that surmount the curved gateposts on the larger plate are omitted on the little one.

Marked J.R. & Co., GMK. 3259, c. 1841-55.

VENETIAN

Mark not located

The oval platter photographed is slightly scalloped and the outer edge is detailed with a band of dark diamonds and light rosettes placed over two small scrolls. A very narrow scalloped line runs along the outside edge. Four identical bouquets are placed around the rim which is covered in its upper half by a design of fans and fleurons and on its lower half, by a mosiac pattern which contains tiny buds. A band of rosettes, set between scalloped lines, encircles the bottom of the rim, and delicate, short strings of beads enter the well from the rim design.

In the central picture a four-tiered fountain rises from its circular base at right. A man and woman stand nearby on a terrace. A dark covered urn is placed on a square dark pedestal and oblong box in the center. Over-scaled flowers are in the foreground. A woman stands with a jug on her head at the top of a flight of stairs in the center. Over-scaled flowers are also placed at the left of the stairs. A domed temple and other buildings, tall trees and a river are in the background.

Marked G.H.

VENETIAN SCENERY

Made by Enoch Wood & Sons

The rims of these scalloped dishes are covered with a design of rectangular forms, topped by a pair of scrolls that meet under half a daisy design. Narrower oblongs alternate with the daisy-topped form and the narrower ones are topped by scrolls that meet at a bellflower. The upper part of the rim above the arches is very dark and small white flowers are printed between the top of the arches.

The cup plate bears an embossed gadroon edge and the oblong patterns are not completed at the base as they are on the platters with small sprigs and a shield or pendant.

Tall trees are placed at left on the dishes and a river separates the scene. All have church-like buildings at right. Those on the platters show many tall towers; on the cup plate the church has a single tower. All have buildings, water and mountains in the background. There are several figures in a large sailboat with covered shelter at the stern and a fancy canopy in the prow on the platters. The boat is omitted on the cup plate.

Marked E.W. & S. and "Celtic China". GMK. 4260, c. 1818-46.

VENETIAN SCENERY (cont.)

VENETIAN TEMPLE

Made by William Adams & Sons

The saucer pictured is scalloped and the outer edge is detailed with tiny triangles and beads. The rim contains semi-circular reserves with beaded edges which contain a large stylized flower surrounded by dark leaves and smaller flowers. These reserves are placed against a stippled field containing a pair of flowers and scrolls placed above a design of a cross composed of oval beads, and a small semi-circular bouquet of buds over a stylized, beaded flower. The well is marked by a wreath of tiny flowers and pendants which gives a spearpoint effect.

The center scene shows an open round temple with twisted columns at right. There are two statues or persons near the structure and one is in the center on a raised platform. A canal divides the scene. A gondola topped with a covered shelter is at left; pennants fly from its top mast and a flag is draped from the bow. There are people in the craft and in the stern a man points to the water. In the foreground there are flowers and ferns. In the background across the water there are towers and buildings. A tall elm rises from behind the temple and arches over the center of the scene.

The cup plate can be identified by the gondola and its super structure. The border has no relation to the rim pattern on the plates. Elements of the fern design from the forepart of the central scene are combined with part of the angles of the stone platform of the temple and placed straight across the design. One of the distinguishing features seems to be the gondola with its draped flag.

The small dish shown does not contain the gondola but does have the distinctive border pattern with the three inserts of flowers.

Marked Imp. Adams, GMK. 18, c. 1800-64.

VENETIAN TEMPLE (cont.)

VENICE

Made by James and Robert Godwin

The saucer shown has both the rim and upper well paneled in sixteen shallow sections. The rim pattern consists of three oval medallions containing a vase of flowers and framed with scrolls like a shield which alternate with three large pairs of scrolled reserves centered with a dark triangle and fleur-de-lis. A narrow band of beaded diamond netting encircles the bottom of the rim. The distinguishing feature is the oval floral medallion.

The scenes probably differ on the various items made in this pattern. On the saucer the picture is dominated by a tower in the left foreground and a large mansion with covered balcony in the center of the middle ground. Tall trees rise at either side of the scene. In the foreground a man and woman stand on a bank of a small pond.

Marked J. & R.G. and No. 125, GMK. 1726, c. 1834-66.

VENTURE

Made by Ralph Hall

Six oval cartouches filled with narrow lines, except for the scenic reserves, appear around the rims of the plate and platter shown. A white Gothic scroll design is placed around the middle of the space in which the scene is centered. Each scene shows a castle with pennants flying from a round tower in the background. In the foreground at right there is a dark urn filled with flowers. Dark bushes are placed on either side. The top spaces between the cartouches are filled with stylized white flowers. There are small scrolls in the triangular spaces at the bottom of the rim design. A white line contains the design at the well and a wreath of small scallops from which small slanted stems and ferns extend, encircles the well.

In the central scene there is a large white Gothic edifice in the background at right. It is set against tall mountains. A path leads from the foreground up a hill to a wooded area at right. There are four persons in the central foreground, a woman and child who carries a parasol and a man and boy. They are on a bank which overlooks a large lake. There is a dark, two-handled urn on a pedestal near them. At left there are tall trees and vine-covered roots that cascade to the water. A small peninsula is seen behind the trees. In the background there is a sailboat on the lake and there are some towered buildings on the left shore. In the distance there are mountain peaks. A white moon peaking through dark clouds completes the scene.

Marked R.H., GMK. 1912, c. 1822-49.

VENTURE (cont.)

VENUS

Made by Podmore Walker & Co.

The rim of this slightly scalloped plate is covered with narrow concentric lines. A very dark line surrounds the white outer edge and this in turn is set off by a white line that is beaded. A row of white scrolls encircles the upper rim and a wreath of dark foliated scrolls is at the bottom of the rim. These rows meet at eight intertwining circles.

This pattern is always distinguished by the pair of white swans floating in the foreground of the central scene. Behind the birds there is a lake, a domed Greek temple-like castle at left and mountains and other buildings in the background. A large urn is placed on a pedestal at the end of a balustrade at right. A man converses with a woman holding a parasol at left. They stand on the steep bank of the lake. Tall elms rise on both sides of the scene.

Marked P.W. & Co., and "Pearl Stoneware", GMK. 3080, c. 1834-59.

VERANDA

Made by Ralph Hall & Co.

The plate pictured is fourteen-sided and the paneled rim is covered with a diamond trellis pattern linked with tiny beads. Six small ovoid cartouches are set around the rim. Each contains the same scene as the others, a picture of a gazebo, trees and bushes at right, two people nearby at left, an urn on a flat pedestal at left, and twin towers in the distance. A roll of spearpoint encircles the well on the convetto.

In the central scene the Veranda (porch) of the title is at right. An oriental archway leads to a grape arbor at right and the trellised railings of the veranda enclose the arch and arbor. There is a column at far right and poplar and tall elms behind the porch. Three people stand on the lawn at the approach to the porch, two ladies, one with a parasol, and a man in a cutaway and a high hat. A river divides the scene and there are towers and other buildings at left across the water. In the distance at left there is part of a wall and there are flowers in the foreground. foreground.

Marked R.H. & Co., GMK. 1890a, c. 1841-9.

VERONA

Made by Edge Malkin & Co.

This plate is a reissue of the pattern first made by George Phillips. For description of the border see Verona by Phillips. Note that this mold is different than that used by Phillips and is not scalloped.

Marked as above, GMK. 1445, c. 1873-1903.

VERONA

Made by George Phillips

The scalloped edge of this plate is outlined by a band of stylized small flowers alternating with small triangles. Four scenic cartouches, framed with scrolls and flanked by pairs of flowers, are placed around the rim. Each contains the same picture, a domed building at right placed against Alpine peaks and flanked by tall trees. An arched bridge across a river is in the center and tall trees, one very dark, are at left. There are three dark clumps of bushes in the foreground. The spaces between the reserves are decorated with realistic flowers, ferns and leaves set upon a base of scrolls and placed over a fine net background. The rim design is contained by shallow scallops set upon a band of squares containing fleur-de-lis. Tiny stylized sprigs descend from this into the well and obtain a spearpoint effect.

In the center picture there are two women in the foreground, one stands and holds an urn placed upon a pedestal, the other is seated on a stone slab and her arms rest upon the pedestal. At left there are other flat slabs, a balustrade, tall elms and a tower in the distance. At right there is a river and across the water one sees classic buildings with domes and towers. A bridge crosses the stream in the center of the scene. A tall hill is in the background and there are buildings at its foot and up its slope to the summit.

Marked G. Phillips, like GMK. 3010, c. 1834-48.

VILLA

Made by John Ridgway

The plate photographed is unevenly scalloped and the white edge is enhanced by a row of dark beads. In four sections of the rim there is a pale diamond diaper pattern which surrounds an oval cartouche containing a small bird perched on sprigs. In the arches formed between the diaper designs there are scrolled reserves which contain bouquets. The top of each of these arched openings is framed by small squares which are centered with beads.

The picture in the well is framed by a wreath of dark scallops and rosettes. In the center scene on the plate there is a Tuscan mansion at right in the background. In the right foreground a small dark figure stands on a bank of a stream which is crossed by a bridge in the middle ground. In the distance one sees village buildings. Tall elms rise from the left bank of the stream and there are tall lacy trees behind the mansion. There are large over-scaled flowers in the foreground.

The tureen contains a picture very much like that on the plate except that the Tuscan mansion is at left in the picture, the bridge is in the right foreground.

Marked J.R. and "Stoneware", GMK. 3253, c. 1840-55.

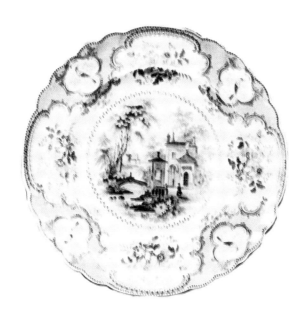

VILLA By J. Ridgway (cont.)

VILLA

Maker unknown

The white outer edge of this unevenly scalloped plate is gadrooned and decorated with molded shells and scallops. A dark band contained by scrolls enchances the white edge. Three different patterns of flowers and scrolls alternate around the rim and sprigs from these enter the well. The most dominant flower group is set upon a dark baroque scroll and terminates in a pair of dark roses and leaves in the well.

In the center the villa of the title is at right. It is of Victorian Gothic architecture. It is situated in back of a large grassy lawn. In the distance at left there are barns and silo towers; tall lacy trees are in the background. In the foreground there are many over-scaled flowers, including a passion flower at center.

VILLAGE OF LITTLE FALLS

Made by Charles Meigh

The rim of this twelve-sided plate is paneled and is covered with a wreath of curved arches composed of forget-me-nots. Ferns fill the spaces created by the arches. The outer edge is defined by a row of oval beads and the outer edge by a geometric pattern that gives a spearpoint effect. The bottom of the rim design is contained by a plain line interspersed with flowers from which small swags form a wreath around the well.

The picture in the center shows tall arching trees at left. A seated person is next to a woman with a parasol and a dog and they are placed on a grassy bank in the foreground. There are small flowers and bushes on the bank. Across the river on the right bank, which is rocky, there are bushes and at top right there are pine trees. In the background there is a group of village buildings dominated by a domed edifice with towers that is situated on a hill above the town. The pattern is one in a series marked "American Cities and Scenery".

Marked C.M. and "Improved Stone China", GMK. 26148, c. 1835-49.

VINTAGE

Made by John and George Alcock

This deep dish is twelve-sided and the rim is paneled. The rim is covered with rows of narrow concentric lines. A wreath of grapes vines, leaves, tendrils and grapes is placed over the striated ground. A row of dentil design descends toward the well from a band of oval beads and rosettes.

The central scene shows four fishermen in the foreground. Two stand holding their pointed nets and one kneels to fold a net; the fourth is sitting under the branches of a tree which is at right. Across the river one sees an old house, a grape arbor covered with heavy vines, a grassy bank, and large stones at the water's edge. In the background there is an island in the middle of the stream. In the distance there are Alpine peaks.

Marked *J. & G. Alcock* and *"Cobridge"*, also *(imp.) "Oriental Stone"*, GMK. 69, c. 1839-46.

VIRGINIA

Made by James and Ralph Clews

The scalloped edges of these dishes are enhanced by a row of dark beading and a narrow printed chain. The rim design is distinguished by the pairs of foliated furled scrolls that resemble goat horns centered with a vertical band of five oval beads. They are joined by swags of large realistic flowers, and garlands of forget-me-nots are placed under them. The area below the little blossoms is stippled. The large swags invade the cavetto.

A band of fine, lacy spearpoint encircles the central scenes. On the platter a man stands with two ladies, one of whom carries a parasol. They are placed in the middle on a grassy bank by a large lake or stream. At right there is a temple with a rounded dome. A sailboat carrying three persons is at left center. Behind it there are trees and a very tall column surmounted with a statue. In the distance one sees a bridge, a lake and some mountains.

The plate bears a different scene. A man and woman stand near a tall tree at right. The lake is behind them and there are temples on the opposite shore. Both dishes contain over-scaled flowers placed across the foreground against a fancy iron fence. A trellis rises at left and it is covered with blossoms. A large willow branch arches from behind the trellis.

This is not usually marked. It dates 1818-34.

461

VIRGINIA (cont.)

VISTA

Made by Frances Morley

This eight-sided plate bears a distinctive rim design of large, veined leaves and tendrils contained at the outer edge by a wreath of small lilies and curving vines.

The central scene shows arching elms on either side. These meet and frame a picture of a large castle in the background, and a lake in the foreground. There are stone steps, balustrades, and a pedestal topped by an urn at right. Three persons, a man and two ladies, in Victorian dress, stand with a little dog on the lawn above the steps.

Marked F.M. & Co., GMK. 2760, c. 1845-58.

WILD ROSE

Possibly made by J. Meir & Son

The edge of this cup plate is detailed with a white, rounded zigzag line. Only half of the famous "Wild Rose" border was used and the central scene of thatched cottage, river and bridge covers the entire well and part of the rim. Most of the left portions of the scene has been eliminated on the cup plate. Coyshe states that the first examples were probably made by Bourne, Baker & Bourne in 1830. (See Little, Plate 12.) Many potters made this pattern. Also shown is a large example of the plate in which the entire rim design can be seen and the complete foreground of fishermen with skiffs is shown.

WINDSOR

Maker unknown

The edge of this cup plate is covered with a wreath of ivy against a dark field. The center scene resembles a decal and shows a girl and boy in Victorian dress seated in a small open carriage pulled by a donkey. A man stands nearby with a pole and a small dog accompanies the donkey. The large round tower of Windsor Castle is in the center background. There are tall trees on either side of the scene. Clouds above the castle and flowers in the foreground complete the circular picture.

WOODLAND

Made by Thomas Fell & Co.

A twisted rope design encircles the outer edge of this plate. The rim bears a design of grapes, grape leaves and tendrils suspended from a vine.

The central bucolic scene shows three cows standing in a brook. There are flowers and reeds in the foreground and forest trees and bushes in the background.

Marked F. & Co., GMK. 1533, c. 1830.

Genre Category

Genre Category

These patterns are dominated by the people pictured in the foreground. The designs contain many scenic elements but the scenes are merely backdrops for the actors. Human activities are pictured against pictures of castles and mountains, rivers and farms, gardens and villas, tropical pampas and the fields of war. The important stars are the farmers, warriors, fishermen, dancers and the others portrayed in their various milieus.

The French word "genre" is used in Fine Arts, particularly painting, to describe pictures of everyday life. This is usually associated with the labors and pleasures of country folk or working people. There seems to be no comparable word to describe the activities of the upper classes, those "to the Manor born". They rode and hunted with falcons, coursed with greyhounds, went on picnics and took along fishing gear, shot arrows at targets and deer. The word "sporting" is used to describe the games of the aristocracy, the word "playing" describes the use of time off from labor by the lower classes. The upper classes disported, the lower classes frolicked. The difference was, of course, determined by the amount of wealth or power the one class possessed and the lack of it by their inferiors.

None the less, all were humankind, all living in the best way they could. All have long ago passed into history, but here in our Genre section that shows human beings in the patterns, the "good life" of long ago still is pictured.

AGRICULTURE

Made by Davenport

The concave rim of this very slightly scalloped plate is covered with a vine pattern of leaf forms, stems, and little berries placed over a design of narrow concentric lines. The outer edge is detailed with a row of beading, and a wreath composed of triangles, beads, and diamonds with bead pendants encircles the well. In the central picture the farmer tills the soil. His plow is pulled by two horses. Another farmer, holding a pole, stands behind the plow. Both wear smocks and brimmed hats. At left there are a rustic, Gothic, two-storied cottage, part of a fence, a wall, and tall trees. At right there is fencing, and in the background some sheep stand under a tall tree. In the distance there are a road and houses. Large flowers and ferns are placed across the foreground.

Marked Davenport and an impressed anchor. GMK. 1181a, c. 1839.

ANGLING

Maker unknown

The rim of this unevenly scalloped plate is trimmed with three lustre bands. In the center a mother stands holding a baby and its feeding dish. Her son sits on the bank of a brook. He holds a fishing rod and clutches at her apron with one hand. Two other small children are beside her. A small cottage is at right and there are trees and bushes in the background. The stream moves from the left past the foreground, and the title "Angling" in quotes appears in the water at lower right.

ARCHERY

Made by the Herculaneum Pottery Company

Both the large plate and the cup plate shown are irregularly scalloped, and the edges are decorated with a row of beads and short palings with interspersions of small flowers. Their rims are printed with four large roses, chrysanthemums, buds, leaves, and forget-me-nots, which alternate with four large lilies with leaves and buds. These are set against a background of tiny arrowheads that form a lace effect on the upper rim. The picture of the cup plate shows the lace pattern clearly. The well is encircled on the large plate by a beaded belt that is divided by two quivers, a target, and a lady's plumed hat. This band is eliminated on the cup plate.

The scenes differ on various size plates. The dinner plate shows a pair of fleeing deer in the foreground. One, the male, with antlers, has been hit by an arrow in his flank. In the background at left there is a tent, and two women with bows stand before it. There is a mansion in the right background, and a tall tree rises from a round platform at right. The scene on the cup plate shows the two women at left. One holds a bow and arrow. Behind them at right is a manor house with a domed center part. Tall curving bushes and flowers are at the extreme right and there are a pair of lacy trees behind the archers at left.

Marked with an impressed Liverbird. GMK. 2012, c. 1833-36.

BEAUTIES I

Made by John Ridgway

The rims of these scalloped plates are covered with three concentric rows of quatrefoils which are graduated from large to small towards the well. They are confined by a band of dark ovals at the outer edge, and a lacy, geometric, pointed design which gives a spearpoint effect at the bottom around the well. A woman in flowing gown and Empire hairstyle is seated on a paved platform in the foreground. A man in court costume leans over her chair. Two greyhounds are at left. In the background a tall pedestal supports a large vase. This is the same vase as shown in "Webster Vase" in this book.

BEAUTIES II
(FALCONRY)

The center picture on this plate shows a woman holding a falcon. Her page and a greyhound are at left. In the distance there are low mountains. Some small flowers are strewn across the foreground. At right the same "Webster Vase" appears. This time it is placed on a low square base.

Marked J.R., GMK. 3253, c. 1830-1841.

473

BEE MASTER (THE)

Maker unknown

The rim design on this platter is distinguished by the oval reserves that contain scenes of pairs of animals: deer, horses, sheep and cows. They are separated by large white garden flowers with dark leaves set in a stippled background. The edge of the dish is decorated with a band of printed deep white scallops, and a row of large white beads separates the rim design from the central picture.

In the scene the Bee Master of the title is at left and is carrying a large skep, (a beehive woven from straw). Two men and a small boy, followed by two dogs, stand near the Master. At right a young man and girl are talking together. In the middleground at right there are three skeps on a shelf in front of a board fence. Behind that there is a large farm cottage. In the background there are trees, a river, hills and houses.

Coysh states that this is possibly an Adams pattern.

BOSTON MAILS

Made by James and Thomas Edwards

The small round plate shown contains a picture of the "Gentlemen's Cabin" aboard the ship "Boston Mails". The square cake plate shows the Ladies' Cabin. Both scenes are framed with scrolls and are identified with labels at the bottom of the frame. The platter in this series shows the 'Saloon' on board this ship, that is, the main salon. The cup plate shown is identical in pattern to the Gentlemen's Cabin scene on the plate. The reserves on the rim contain pictures of sailing ships, each different from the other. The reserves are separated by a square design containing a dark star centered with a white circle. The squares are surrounded by a Gothic geometric frame set against a stippled ground. The outer edges of the dishes are decorated with rows of small triangular dots.

Marked *J.&T. Edwards* and *"Porcelain Opaque"*, GMK. 1455, 1839-41.

Boston Mails (cont.)

CATTLE GROUPS

Maker unknown

The Gadroon edge of this gently scalloped plate is embossed with six interspersals of a fan and flower design. The rim pattern consists of baroque oval cartouches filled with diamond floral diapering over which there are swags of small roses. Garlands of realistic flowers join the cartouches. The central picture is framed with a band of tiny flowers and oval vertical loops. In the foreground scene there are three cows. A man leans on the back of one in the center. He wears a farmer's broadbrimmed hat. There are trees in the left background. A small dog stands near the cows at right. At right in the middleground there is a woman standing who carries a bundle of twigs. There are flowers in the foreground.

Marked "New Stone China".

CHASE

Made by Henry Alcock

The edge of this plate is decorated with a row of dotted squares. The rim bears a design of four elongated scenic cartouches that depict a man on horseback at left and fleeing bulls in the center. The cartouches are separated by oval designs framed with a double, dotted band flanked by fleur-de-lis and containing flowers against a dark background. The well is encircled by a fringe pattern. In the center there are two riders. Their horses are clashing against each other as they race. Both men wear peaked caps. At left in the background there is an Arabic castle. At right there are a tall palm tree and some banana fronds.

Marked as above with "Cobridge", like GMK. 67, c. 1861.

CHESS PLAYERS

Made by William Adams & Sons

The white edge of this bowl is deeply and unevenly scalloped, and a band of small shields, white beads at top and trefoils at bottom set over a white line, defines the upper edge. A very wide band of slanted curving ribbons, placed over a stippled field sprinkled with white sprigs forms the background for a wreath of nasturtiums, leaves and vine. This band covers the outside of the bowl (illus.) and covers one third of the well. In the center scene two ladies, dressed in Elizabethan court costumes are playing chess. A gentleman leans over the shoulder of the player at right. The group is in a grape arbor. In the background there is a lake and across the water there is a Tuscan mansion set against a background of tall mountains.

Marked Adams (imp.) GMK. 18. c. 1830-64

COLUMBUS

Made by William Adams and Sons

The scalloped dinner plate and the smaller plate (5 inches) photographed have different scenes in the center but each show the border design: cartouches containing pairs of animals in tropical settings. One pair resembles buffalos, the other elands or antelopes. Swags of roses are placed between the scenic reserves. A ribbon-type band containing rosettes is placed beneath the swags and sweeps upwards to frame the reserves. A pointed section of the ribbon, flanked by large lilies, is under the reserves. The white outer edges are detailed by a narrow band that has small leaf forms twisted over it.

The larger plate shows Columbus and two of his men as they walk on shore. Indians hide in the bushes and behind coconut palm trees at left. At right there are boats, and in the distance across the water, there are very tall mountain peaks. The small plate shows four men in a row boat. One stands and points to the right. In the foreground there are flowers and grass. In the background there are two small boats, and in the distance across the water, there are palm trees and pines and the very tall mountains that are shown on the large plate. These same mountains are used in the background on the scenic cartouches on the rim.

Marked W.A.&S., GMK. 23, 1819-64.

COMMERCE

Made by Samuel Alcock

The plates shown are irregularly scalloped and the upper part of the rims are stippled. The outer edges are detailed by a band of double arch-like scallops from which very narrow lines alternate with tube forms and descend toward the well until contained by a wreath of small flowers.

Six identical bouquets composed of three exotic stylized flowers with very dark leaves are placed around the rims. The spaces between the floral groups are divided by a ribbon of flowers which are flanked by zigzag lines and spiky stylized branches. These lines and branches are peculiar to this pattern and must be considered the distinguishing feature. A wreath of small flowers, different than the ones above enwreath the well and join the bottoms of the large flower patterns.

Pictured on one plate is an oriental port. At rest in the harbor are a European schooner which is next to a large Chinese junk. In the distance there are tall mountain peaks. At left in the background there are pagodas and other buildings. In the foreground, at center a seated Chinese official reads a list. Another Chinese man stands before him talking to a European in tall hat and Western clothes. Behind the group at left and right there are other figures some working on skiffs at the edge of the pier, others are talking to a street vendor. In the foreground there are some jars, vases and a box.

Commerce (cont.)

The second plate shows a seated Westerner dressed in top hat and holding a cane. He is sitting on a packing crate. Three Chinese men stand near him. There are baskets, boxes and round covered jar. In the background there are towered buildings with upturned rooves, other smaller structures that front on the harbor seen at left. Tall masted ships are in the port, a small rowboat is in the harbor in the middle distance.

The cup plate shows a Chinese merchant who is seated in the foreground. A man stands beside him and reads a list. In the background at left there are tall city buildings, and in the harbor at right there is a sampan. Tall ships can be seen in the background and in the distance there are peaked mountains.

Marked (imp.) Alcock and also a printed beehive. GMK. pg. 28, 1828-59.

COTTAGE GIRL (THE)

Maker unknown

The unevenly scalloped edge of this saucer is detailed with an outer band of scallops and an inner row of beads placed over a white line. Six palette shaped reserves, framed with foliated scrolls and containing white flowers on a very dark ground, are placed around the stippled rim. Small flowers are to the left of the reserves around the upper part of the rim. A band of C scrolls contains the border pattern at the upper well. The central scene is framed with a circle of dotted beads. It pictures a girl at left who holds a hoop around her upper body. At her feet there is a small dog in playful pose and a two-handled wooden pail. At right in the distance there are a cottage and tall trees. Some other trees and bushes are behind the girl at extreme left.

CRUSADERS

Maker unknown

The rim design of this pattern appears inside the bowl and consists of stippled lambrequins that are edged with teardrop designs. Flowers are set in the center of each lambrequin. The upper edge is encircled by a dark row of small scallops topped by rosettes. In the arches formed by the lambrequins there are large flowers, a pair of roses which alternate with a trio of blossoms which includes a passion flower. The floral design is connected around the bottom with a ribbon of sprigs. In the center of the bowl there is a picture of a Gothic castle with many towers, flying buttresses, and portcullis. A road winds to the entrance, and near the building there are two horsemen. Over-scaled flowers are placed across the bottom of the picture. On the outside of the bowl the above castle scene is at right. There is another castle at left, and there are tall trees on both sides. In the center of the picture a man and woman ride on high-stepping horses. He wears a doublet and a hat with many plumes. She rides sidesaddle and wears a long flowing gown and a wide plumed hat, tipped sideways over her hair.

Little attributes a pattern of this name to Deakin and Bailey which would date c. 1828-30.

DANCERS

Made by Ralph Malkin

This plate is gently scalloped, and black and white lines delineate the edge. The stippled rim is covered with four scenes of girls dancing to the music of a seated guitarist and four alternating oval designs bordered by a geometric pattern and centered with foliated scrolls. A band of small diamond pillow shapes and teardrops form a ring around the bottom of the rim.

The central scene on this example of the pattern depicts a Spanish couple dancing to the music of a guitar player who sits at left. Another couple can be glimpsed behind the girl. The dance takes place in a gardenhouse festooned with grapevines. Wine jugs are seen near the musicians in the foreground. In the background at right there are Alpine peaks.

Marked R.M., GMK. 2494, c. 1863-81. (Made later by Ralph Malkin and Sons, GMK. 2494.)

DANCING
Made by Petrus Regout

A ring of double roses with dark leaves alternating with triple interlocking circles containing a pair of large foliated scrolls covers the rim of this plate. The outer edge was left white, and a dark band enhances this. The band dips into the rim design in the center of the triple circles and forms a dark triangle, which contains a white ring-like center. The bottom of the rim is decorated with shallow triangles alternating with small rose festoons. These elements enter the well.

In the center scene, a man and woman dance to the music of a guitar player who is seated at right. Another couple are seated at left on a platform. There is an urn on a high pedestal behind the seated couple. Tall trees rise in the background. There are two little dogs playing in the foreground.

This was made in Holland but is sometimes found unmarked, and like much of Regout's designs, is mistaken for Staffordshire.

Marked P.R. and "Prizemedal". Impressed Maastricht, c. 1850.

DOMESTIC CATTLE
Maker unknown

The outer edge of this deep dish is outlined with dark triangles contained by small white scallops and beads. The stippled rim is covered with three long sprays of wild roses, dark and light leaves and buds, and Sweet William. These sprays are centered with a round basket, tilted open to show some light cherries.

A narrow white band separates the rim design and the central scene which is dominated by two standing mules, one dark and one light, and a reclining goat in the foreground. At right a man crouches near a campfire over which there are a tripod and hanging iron pot. A woman and child sit behind him at the entrance to a rough tent. A tall tree rises from behind the shelter, and its limbs spread across the top of the scene. In the background at left there are tall buildings and trees.

ETON COLLEGE

Made by Edward and George Phillips

The dish shown is gently scalloped, and there is a wreath of entwined rope around the edge. The upper rim is stippled and the lower rim is covered with flowers and sprays that enter the well. Large flowers are placed midway over the stippling, and these are divided in three places by heavy shell-like scalloped lines that form three shallow arches. The alternate dividing pattern consists of three plume-like white scrolls placed over sprigs.

The central scene is the same as is shown in most items of this pattern and is dominated by a trio of persons: a man, woman, and child who stand facing the foreground. The man carries a cane and wears a big hat. Both the woman and child wear long gowns and large hats. Behind them there is a river complete with sailboats, a building under the top of a hill at right and a tall elm at left. The college of the title is in the distance on the left bank of the stream but center in the picture. There are mountains in the distance. The usual over-scaled flowers and bushes are placed at right and left in the foreground.

Marked (imp.) Phillips, GMK. 3008, c. 1822-34.

FISHERMAN
Made by Enoch Wood and Sons

These plates are scalloped and there are wreaths of small scrolled scallop shells around the edges. The stippled borders are covered with alternating designs of shells and goldfish bowls, each surrounded by seaweed which enter the wells. The first plate shows a lone fisherman complete with creel slung over his shoulder, and his net lies in the foreground. He is casting into the stream as he stands on a bank covered with cat-o-nine-tails, bushes, ferns and a small tree. Across the stream there are castle-like buildings and a hill topped by similar structures.

The second plate presents two fishermen. One is seated with a pole lowered into the stream; the other stands and casts his line. A basket with handles is on the ground between the men and a tall tree. At left one sees the riverbank, but in the distance and across the background there are city buildings and towers. The cup plate shows the fisherman in his sailboat. He is hauling in his nets. Behind him at left there is a breakwater, which terminates in a tower topped by a flag. At right there are tall trees, one of which is a pine. Mountains in the distance complete the scene.

Marked E.W. & So., GMK. 4260, c. 1818-46.

Fisherman (cont.)

FORGET-ME-NOT

Made by Livesley Powell and Company

The scalloped white edge of this saucer is decorated with a band of printed beads. A diaper pattern of white circles centered with a dark dot covers the rim. Three sprays of realistic flowers and dark leaves alternate with large groups of forget-me-nots around the rim. A ring of diamonds and tiny double pendent beads encircles the well. A man and woman are seated on rocks in the foreground in the central picture. She is embracing him and looking up into his face as he points to the sea behind them. In the distance at right there are sailing ships. At left in the background there are windswept pine trees.

Marked L.P. & Co., GMK. 2386, c. 1851-66.

GARDEN SPORTS

Made by William Adams and Sons

The edge of the saucer photographed is enhanced with a band of dotted diamonds. The rim pattern consists of three geometric motifs topped with large rosettes set against a diaper field contained by scrolls. These alternate with three sprays of ·stylized flowers and very dark leaves containing large white veins, sprigs and forget-me-nots all set on a stippled ground.

The central scene on this item of the pattern shows a boy and girl playing with a wheelbarrow in a garden. She sits in the back of the wheelbarrow, wearing a hat with ribbons down her back and holds a bouquet as he pushes her along. Two small dogs play at right. There is a scalloped box of flowers in the foreground and a large garden arch at the end of the fence at left. Part of a fence and some bushes can be seen behind the dogs. The scenes may differ on various items of this pattern. The wheelbarrow scene is shown on the sugar bowl. To see other possible scenes, refer to "Garden Sports" by Adams in the juvenile section of this book.

Marked (imp.) Adams, GMK. 18, c. 1800-64.

"GARDENING"

Made by Francis Dillon

This rim pattern is distinguished by the triple ovals of beads that resemble a necklace. These appear in three equidistant places on the rim. A large stylized bird facing right, and perched on flower laden branches, is grouped with scrolls and a pair of flowers with dark leaves, to form the design between the bead patterns. A wreath of white beads runs around the upper edge and a row of dark triangles and dots is placed next to it.

In the center picture a girl, dressed in a jumper, pantaloons and a wide-brimmed hat, stands at the right holding a rake. There are a potted plant and two over-scaled flowers behind her at right. At left a boy in Eton jacket with ruffled collar, and long white trousers stands facing a tall hollyhock. Sprigs and flowers arch across the scene.

Marked (imp.) Dillon, GMK. 1288, 1834-43.

GAZELLE

Made by William Adams and Son

The white edge of this saucer is scalloped and is decorated with a dark zigzag line. The stippled rim is patterned with round white lace-bordered reserves containing spotted lilies. The stems from the lilies all trail to the left, entering the space between the reserves then branching into vertical sprig designs. The same small lacy border scrolls seen above form a wreath around the well. The rim pattern is itself scalloped and forms an arched circle around the central scene.

In the center a lady stands and holds a long pole. In front of her, a little girl approaches the gazelle of the title. She is offering flowers or food to the animal. Behind the group there is a large ornate urn set on a balustrade. There is a pine tree behind them and its boughs can be seen on either side of the urn. At left there is a lake and in the distance there are town buildings and Alpine peaks. In the foreground there are flowers.

Marked (imp.) Adams, GMK. 18, c. 1800-64.

GIPSY

Maker unknown

The rim of this plate is gently indented at four places and its outer edge is dark. The rest of the rim is covered with interlacing scrolls which form ovals which are filled with a small mosaic pattern. Scallop shells are placed at the top rim between the ovals. The bottom of the scrolls enter the well.

The central scene is framed with a filigree of fine scrolls placed within a wide rectangle frame filled with buds on a vine and rosettes on each corner. Note the fan-shaped rosette patterns set in each inside corner of the frame. The picture differs on the various items of this pattern. This one shows a Gipsy pair near their campfire, which is complete with tripod and pot. Their striped wagon is near them at right. The shafts are on the ground. At left there is a tree, and in the background there are city buildings.

GOAT

Made by John and Robert Godwin

This cup has a waistline one-third from the bottom and is decorated with a transfer that shows a scene of a girl kneeling by a goat. Her wooden bucket is on the ground in front of her. Behind them there are a cottage with fenced yard, some trees, and mountains in the distance. A dark band contained by white scrolls encircles the upper edge of the vessel. The rim design is placed inside the cup and consists of three scenic reserves; one contains a horse and colt, the second a cow and calf, the third five sheep. They are divided by a stylized design that resembles a butterfly. This is composed of two scimitar designed scrolls filled with small scrolls which flank a central shield filled with diamond diaper and set over a heart design from which a pair of sprigs are pendent. Two darker leaf shapes are attached to the outer sides of the scimitar curves.

Marked J.&R.G., GMK. 1726, c. 1844-66.

HARVEST HOME (THE)

Maker unknown

The outer edge of the platter photographed is detailed with a running band of heavy white deep scallops. The rim bears a wreath of wild roses, large dark leaves that resemble oak leaves, small dark clematis blossoms and gooseberries. These elements are placed over long baroque scrolls that encircle the lower part of the rim. A band of white beads separates the rim design from the central picture.

A procession passes across the entire well of the platter. It is led by a squire on a horse. He waves his hat in the air as he approaches the entrance to a barn. He is followed by a man in dark suit and tricorn, who is playing a fiddle, a woman in long white gown who plays a type of guitar and a child who beats a tambourine. Men and women with pitchforks, rakes and hoes, others carrying small children, some holding sheaves of wheat lead the ox-drawn hay wagons on the way into the barn. The celebratory procession winds to the back of the scene over hills on curving roads.

HARVEST SCENERY

Made by Job and John Jackson

 The collar of this pitcher is decorated with a large spray of roses, sheafs of wheat, and small garden flowers. Projecting from the spray are farm tools used in the early 19th century at harvest time: wooden rake, flail, sickle, hoe, scoop-shovel, and two-prong pitchfork. Between the sprays there are groups of pond lilies and large lily pads. The mold used was ornate, and the collar is decorated with large embossed fruits, the handle with embossed flowers and scrolls. There is a band of large molded scallops placed around the body of the vessel directly above the scene.

 The farmers' harvest task of bringing in the hay is portrayed in this scene. At far left, girls are raking, and in the center foreground, another girl, holding a water pitcher, stands next to a hay mound as she talks to a man who holds a pitchfork. A small dog is at his feet. Behind him another man with a pitchfork sits in a horse-drawn cart. Another horse is at far right. In the distance, there are hills, farm buildings, and trees. The foreground is strewn with flowers.

 Marked Jackson's Warranted, GMK. 2156, c. 1831-35.

HAWKING

Maker unknown

The collar of this pitcher is decorated with oval scenic cartouches alternating with circular floral reserves. The two designs are set into a stippled background and are joined by swags of drapery at the top. The scenic cartouches contain a picture of a standing man holding a rifle. He is at center and is flanked by a light dog at right and a black one at left. The floral reserves contain lilies. A band of triangles outline the upper edge of the border, and a row of white fleur-de-lis and fringe contains the design at the bottom of the collar.

In the central scene, a man dressed in Elizabethan costume and seated on a white horse, holds out his arm toward a page who is handing him a hawk. Behind them a lady on a black horse holds her arm up while she releases her hawk. There are trees at left, bushes in the foreground, and a castle in the background at right.

HORSE GUARDS

Made by Middlesbrough Pottery Co.

The small deep dish photographed is printed in black. The rim is decorated with four scenic cartouches which contain castles and trees. These alternate with a scrolled circular design in which there are garlands of roses. Both designs are placed over a stippled background and are connected by scrolled buckles. The well is encircled by a jointed scallop design. The central picture shows a large palatial building and pairs of sentry houses which are occupied by guards on horseback. There are two carriages in front of the courtyard.

Marked London, GMK. 2658, 1834-44.

HUMPHREY'S CLOCK
Made by William Ridgway, Son and Co.

The rim of the serving bowl shown is covered with a diaper design of small diamonds centered with crosses. Scrolls contain the design at the outer edges and at the bottom. Vertical baroque scrolls divide the rim area, and these are joined at the well by garlands of small flowers and leaves. Charles Dickens wrote a story entitled "Humphrey's Clock" in 1838. The scenic Ridgway dishes were inspired by the story. This dish shows a canal. A man seated on a mule on the towpath is pulling a flatboat in the canal. A party on board are drinking from mugs. The picture on the lid shows a man and woman standing on a path near a fence. Behind them a man approaches them in his horse-pulled cart. Note the reverse garland design on the rim of the lid. The garlands and scrolls are distinguishing marks in this pattern.

The toy plate (3-7/8" diameter) has no rim pattern, but the edge has a bit of sponging. A boy stands in the foreground at left, his foot on a log. He has food and a bridle in his hand and is trying to catch a pony who is leaping over a fence under a tree at right. There is a house in the background at left. At right a woman is coming through a gate in a fence which stretches across the middle of the scene. There are tall poplar trees and other buildings in the distance.

Marked W.R.S. & Co., GMK. 3309, c. 1838-48.

Humphrey's Clock (cont.)

INDIAN CHIEF

Made by Joseph Heath & Co.

The scalloped edge of the saucer shown is trimmed with a narrow printed line of dark and white scallops. The rim design consists of three triangular reserves filled with zigzag vertical lines which are crowned by a wide dark area containing narrow straight vertical lines enclosed by white scrolls. The reserves are separated by elongated curved stippled sections, centered with a shell at top, crowned with the same dark linear design and white scrolls as described above, and also containing a pair of nosegays at each end. Both rim patterns are contained at the bottom by a wreath of brocaded ribbon that forms C scrolls under the zigzag areas. Three sprays of flowers are placed in the arches formed by the ribbons.

The central scene is framed by a circle of sprigs. It contains the image of the Indian Chief of the title; who stands with long bow in hand on the grassy bank above a small waterfall, which descends from a lake or stream in the middle ground. Across the water there are a pair of deer who stand near some rocks and a tall lacy tree at left. There are palm trees at extreme right. In the distance one sees a temple with an onion shaped dome (!) set against a back drop of tall mountains. Clouds above complete the circular picture.

Marked J.H. & Co. and (imp.) a circular and beaded propellor. GMK. 1994A, 1828-41.

INDIAN SPORTING SERIES
Made by Josiah Spode

The indented rim of the plate is covered with a design of wild animals and a large bird. There are lions, a bear and a boar set in tropical foliage. Behind the bird there is a water scene complete with a small boat. The central design covers the well and shows hunters closing in on a wounded bear. He has been shot by other hunters who are seated on top of an elephant at left, and has been hit by a spear cast by horsemen who are at right. Small white hunting dogs are in the foreground. A coconut tree and other exotic foliage are in the background.

Marked (Printed) Spode and (imp.) Spode 27. GMK. 3648, c. 1810.

INDIAN TRAFFIC

Made by Petrus Regout

The paneled rim of this slightly scalloped soup plate is covered with a design consisting of large pairs of roses with dark leaves that alternate with a circular pattern which contain a pair of small buds flanked by buckles and fleur-de-lis. The white edge is enhanced by a dark band that contains pairs of small white beads. The well is encircled by a band of triangles, alternating with festoons of small roses. Regout used this same band on "Dancing". In the central scene, a man on a horse peddles fruits, pottery and wine. A woman with a child clutching at her skirt stands at left. A man in a tunic is seated at right in a wheelbarrow. Behind wheelbarrow a boy stands and holds a cask. Another boy pays court to a girl who is on a caged balcony in the background. A large building is behind the caged girl. There is a wide-brimmed hat lying in the foreground on the street surface.

Marked P.R. & Maastricht. Made in Holland. See the notes on Petrus Regout in "Dancing" (this category).

LADY OF THE LAKE (THE)

Maker unknown

The white edge of this small (4-1/2") plate is embossed with a gadroon border, and a band of small triangles is placed between the gadroon border design and the rim design. The background of the rim is striated and the design consists of two very large pairs of stylized roses flanked by dark leaves that alternate with a trio of small white flowers set over a scrolled line centered with a triangle. Both designs dip at the outer edge and form shallow curved triangles that effect a clover design. A diamond shaped central area is the result of the rim pattern. In the center the "Lady of the Lake" rides her domain in a swan boat. She is set in a medallion framed with scallops, beads and stylized flowers.

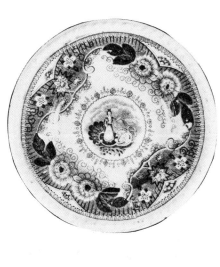

506

LASSO

Made by T. Goodwin

The rim of this unevenly scalloped plate bears four scenic medallions each of which contain the same scene of a white horse who flees to the left and a black one who runs to the right. The upper part of the rim space between the reserves is filled with foliated scroll set against a dark ground, the lower part contains a wreath of flowers and leaves that enters the well. The center scene shows the two horses running to the right and in flight from a pair of cowboys who are in the middleground. Tall pine trees are placed at left. (To see a variation of this design see Lasso in the Juvenile section.)

Marked as above and Seacombe Pottery, Liverpool. See Chaffers, page 764, who states that Goodwin came from Lane End, Staffordshire, in 1852 and established the Seacombe Pottery.

MADDLE JENNY LIND

Made by Edward Challinor

The cake plate photographed is almost square, and the outer edge is scalloped. Scrolls and pairs of small flowers are placed around the rim and there are some small birds set in the rim design. Four larger birds are placed on vines and leafy sprigs in the four corners around the portrait of the great Swedish singer, "The Swedish Nightingale".

Marked E. Challinor, GMK. 835a, c. 1842-67.

508

NAPOLEON

Made by Charles James Mason and Co.

The dishes shown are slightly scalloped, and the white edges are defined by a row of beads and triangles set in a dark scalloped line. Except for the white reserves which are formed by a brocaded ribbon pattern, the rims are stippled. In the areas between the reserves, there is a picture of a statue of a seated woman. She is placed on a circular platform, and there is a horse behind her. She holds a cornucopia on one arm and an apple in her free hand. At her feet there are other symbols: a book, a lyre, a palette, and a Liberty cap on a sticker. These indicate the peace, prosperity, and culture bestowed by Napoleon.

Another female statue alternates with the first. She is standing and holds a bow and quiver under the left arm; in the right hand are the arrows and next to her is a small deer. Presumably she is the goddess Diana. This same figure appears in the Texian Campaign, and because the brocaded ribbon pattern is so similar in design, without close scrutiny, attribution can be difficult.

The white reserves contain identical sprays of large dahlias, dark leaves, small flowers and sprigs. These are surmounted by a crest, consisting of a large baroque ewer, a shield with scalloped edge, and a covered urn set on curved feet. The rim designs are contained at the well by a band of C scrolls ending in leafy sprigs, and small scrolls set with berries that are attached to the bottom of the C scrolls. On the soup plate, Napoleon is seen at center astride his white horse. He is at the head of his troops, his flag bearers are on foot near him. A soldier rides up to him on a dark horse. In the foreground there are large cannon shells and a seated soldier. The platter shows a battle scene. The rims of the cup plates are like those of the large plates. The center of one depicts Napoleon seated backwards on a folding camp chair and holding a telescope. His troops can be seen at right. His white horse is in the left background. The word "Marengo" is printed at his feet. In 1800, Napoleon defeated the Austrians at Marengo in Italy. He defeated them again in 1805 at Osterlitz, which is pictured on the soup dish. The second cup plate shows a desert scene, presumably Egypt, which was invaded by Napoleon in 1798.

Marked C.J.M. & Co., like GMK. 2531, c. 1829-45.

Napoleon (cont.)

OLYMPIC GAMES

Made by Thomas Mayer

The white edges of these unevenly scalloped plates, platter and tureen, are decorated with a dark band of small triangles and a narrow white line. The stippled rims contain four reserves framed in scrolls, two display a bouquet and the other pair a scene of a Greek temple at left which adjoins a tower, an arched bridge in the center and a pair of white over-scaled flowers at right. Between the reserves there is a distinctive design composed of a fan at top set upon a scrolled stem which is flanked by pairs of flowers. The foliated scrolls that make up the lower frame of the reserves invade the well and a row of double spearpoint joins them and forms a wreath.

The scenes differ on the various pieces made in this pattern. The first plate is sub-titled "Spanish Bull Fight". It presents a man in court costume who holds a cape and a sword as he leaps forward on one foot towards a charging white bull. Another man is on horseback behind the matador. A large temple is at right in the background and part of a ring of spectators is shown in front of the building. There are tall trees at left, towers and mountains in the distance, and part of a gate and post flanked with over-scaled flowers are placed across the foreground.

The soup tureen shown has the rim design greatly enlarged on its lid. The sides of the vessel present a scene entitled "Animal Prize

Olympic Games (cont.)

Fight". In the middle of the picture a tiger has downed a gladiator and is lying across his body. Two men with spears and sword are attacking the beast. A columned temple is at extreme left; in the distance there are city buildings and mountains. At right a seated woman, with a child standing near by, watches the fight from a position behind a wrought-iron fence. Larger sections of the ironwork and over-scaled flowers are placed across the foreground.

The stand for the tureen bears a scene which is titled "Victors Crowned". However the picture is dominated by two men in Roman soldiers' dress, (one wears a helmet), who stand in the left foreground. They are slinging large stones at a target which is in the centerground at right. In the background there is a large Victors Arch of Triumph. Beside it at left there are a small temple and tall trees. There are other temples and buildings in the background. Many spectators are seated on the ground in front of the arch and seem to be watching the slingshot contest. Two others are seated in the right foreground next to a curved short wall and domed post.

The cup plate bears the entire rim pattern, and shows a Greek temple in the center distance. There are tall mountain peaks behind the building. A tall tree arches toward the center at left, and there are bushes, an urn and a lacy tree at right. A woman sits on a small tiered platform in the foreground. She is watching a ball game that is taking place on the lawn in front of the temple.

Marked T. Mayer, and "Stoke", GMK. 2569, c. 1826-35.

Olympic Games (cont.)

PASTORAL

Made by Ralph Stevenson

The stippled rim of this gently scalloped plate is covered with a wreath of large single roses and dahlias flanked with dark leaves that are linked by shadowy white veined leaves. The bottom of the floral design enters the well and forms an irregular wreath around the cavetto. The outer edge is detailed with a band of beads on a string which is set against a white line.

In the central scene a woman wearing a hat, veil, long robe and cape, holds a baby against her shoulder and a basket in her hand. Two children kneel on the ground near her. The little girl is clutching her mother's apron. The children are picking flowers or berries. A third child, a boy, stands at her right and points to some bushes. In the background there are a pair of tall trees on a knoll in front of a large white farmhouse. There are cows at left who stand in a pond. A river crosses the scene and in the left background there is a church with tall spire.

Marked R.S. GMK. 3705, 1810-32.

"PASTORAL COURTSHIP"
Made by Andrew Stevenson

A row of oval white beads runs around the outer edge of this platter. The rim is covered with a floral wreath composed of stylized white wild roses, forget-me-nots and a poppy at each corner. The rim design is separated from the central picture by a band of small beads.

In the scene a shepherdress holding a long crook, sits on a grassy knoll in the center of the rural scene. A man, who has a feed basket slung over his shoulder, kneels before the girl. A small dog is near by. A large basket with handles and a broad-brimmed sun hat are on the right upon the knoll. In the background at left there are fat white sheep. A large barn with thatched roof is in the background, and two men and another dog stand in front of the building. At right in the distance there is a windmill upon the top of a hill. Tall dark trees, sloping hills and shrubs complete the scene.

Marked (imp.) Stevenson, GMK. 3700, 1816-30.

PERUVIAN HORSE HUNT

Made by Anthony Shaw

The panelled rim of this dish is covered with four horizontal scenic cartouches each containing the same scene, of a cowboy with lasso who rides a small dark horse. He is at right in the scene and is in hot pursuit of two fleeing wild horses, one white the other black who are at left. The reserves are framed with striated bands that meet at the top center of each cartouche with curved scrolls, and at the botton with a white oval. The forms are linked by scrolls that form circles behind swags of roses. The well is encircled by a plain stippled band, a band interrupted at eight points by scrolls like those at top and a row of fringe.

A cowboy appears at right in the central scene. He is astride a white horse and swings a long lasso towards two fleeing horses in the middle distance. Two other riders are at left watching the chase. There are tall mountain peaks in the distance, and the long sloping hills in the fore-ground are covered with rocks and stones.

Marked Shaws, GMK. 3499, c. 1853.

PET (THE)

Made by William Adams

The edge of the large tea bowl photographed is scalloped, and the rim design which appears on the inside of the cup consists of a wreath of chrysanthemums, dark leaves, and pairs of daisies which are placed in arches filled at the top with scrolls. A stippled band outlines the top of the arches, and is set against a very dark background at the upper edge. The arch forms are closed at the bottom with C scrolls and beading. The rim design is contained at the bottom by a band of scallops linked by diamonds. Tiny dots with two legs depend from the diamond design. The scenes on the outside of the cup and in the center are the same. A woman in a Turkish costume, complete with flowing veil and turban, stands at the right of a fancy domed tent. The tent curtains are open, and a large goat bedecked with floral garlands reclines therein. There are tall trees at right and left and over-scaled flowers in the foreground.

Marked (imp.) Adams, GMK. 18, c. 1845-64.

PICNIC

Mark not located

The plate photographed is unevenly scalloped and the edge is outlined by a row of small dark triangles set in white scallops. The rim is covered with a wreath composed of a band of arches outlined by dark asymmetrical scrolls. Four arches are filled with pairs of large dahlias and prunus, flanked by sprigs, buds, and leaves. These are placed against a stippled background. The spaces between the arches and under four of them are filled with a coarse net design. The well is encircled by a design of double dotted lines which forms an octagonal enclosure. Sprigs are set in the octagonal opening. In the center a girl cuddles a goat. Her ribbon-trimmed leghorn hat is on the grass in the foreground. There is a large tree trunk at left with small branches which arch over the girl.

Marked G.&R.

SCOTT'S ILLUSTRATIONS
Made by Davenport

A row of small printed beads is placed on the unevenly scalloped white edges of these dishes. Next to the row there is a dark band trimmed with white bell forms. The rim design consists of a bouquet of large roses with buds and leaves, a passion flower that dips into the well, and another smaller flower at top. Over the passion flower at the upper rim, there is a scallop shell. Near the rosebuds and at the upper rim, there are three triangular designs containing a rosebud. A Rococo design of foliated scrolls containing diaper cells and flanked by small flowers is placed between the floral groups.

In the center scene on the first plate which is called "The Legend of Montrose", a child in a white gown clutches the leg of a Scottish warrior who holds a shield and long sword as he wards off a larger armed Scotsman who threatens with a dirk. In the background there are towered building, a lake, and mountains. At left there is a tall tree, and in the foreground there are dark thistles and several over-scaled flowers. The platter which is inscribed "Bride of Lamermoor", shows Lucia, the bride of Lamermoor castle, lying unconscious across the lap of her preacher friend. Her brother stands behind them. The castle is at left in the rear. A stream and small waterfall divide the scene. Tall trees are placed in the landscape, and there are over-scaled flowers including thistles in the foreground.

Marked (imp.) Davenport, GMK. 1181a, dated 1846.

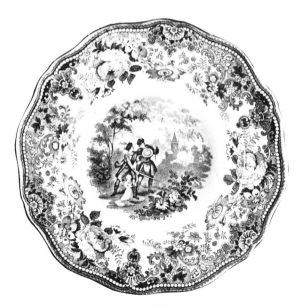

Scott's Illustrations (cont.)

SEA (THE)

Made by William Adam and Sons

Three pictures are shown from this series which includes many different scenes of a shipwreck. One plate shows a man and woman in court dress talking to a seated sailor who has survived a wreck which is shown behind him. In the distance there are a lighthouse and high mountains at left. There is a castellated balustrade on a rocky promontory in the background and a man and woman stand thereon. She is pointing to a large schooner which is at left in the distance. The second plate carries a picture of a man and woman dancing on board the deck of a ship. A seated man plays a guitar, and a standing woman, who is at right, beats a tambourine. In the harbor behind the ships there are other boats, and there is a castle in the distance at left. The third plate depicts the rescue of a man from the sea by three men in a rowboat. In the background a sinking ship is on fire, and flames and smoke rise to the clouds.

The plates are scalloped and their edges are detailed by narrow bands of scallops and spearpoint. The rim design consists of three white reserves containing a large anchor and seashells set against a background of a mountain and a ship at left. The edges of the reserves are scalloped and give a shell effect. Three groups of seaweed on a stippled ground are placed between the anchor motifs. The well is encircled by a wreath of seaweed. The cup plate (not illustrated) displays a picture of a small sailboat sailing toward the castle or fort.

Marked Adams (imp.), GMK. 18, c. 1800-64.

The Sea (cont.)

SEASONS

Made by William Adams

Both the waste bowl and 4 inch cup plate shown depict winter and are so titled on the face. A man sets forth with his dog across the snowy hills. He smokes a pipe and holds an ax. At left there are a cottage and some pine trees. In the right distance there is a castle on a hill. Tall mountains covered with snow are in the background. The complete border is shown inside the waste bowl. Note that the background is stippled, and the four seasons are represented by small classical figures. The white center invades the border at four points and forms a cross design. Bouquets are set in the white areas on the rim.

Marked (imp.) Adams, GMK. 18, c. 1830-40.

Seasons (cont.)

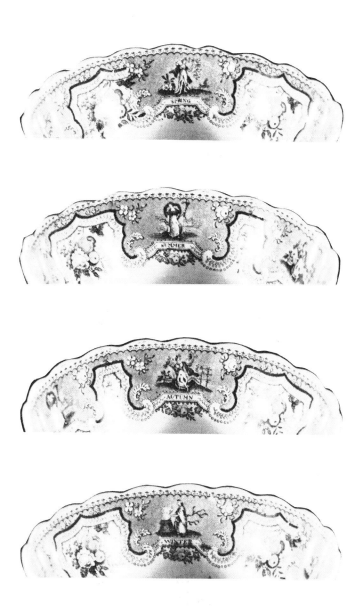

SHELTERED PEASANTS

Made by Hall

The rim of the plate photographed is covered with a wreath of flowers and fruits, interrupted at six points with a design of an oval bell suspended from leaf brackets. The bells are placed over small platforms set upon three round feet. The upper part of the rim is covered with a diamond diapering. The lower rim and outer part of the well are stippled. A band of white oval beads printed with small tridents is placed around the outer edge, and a similar band with larger beads encircles the scene in the well.

The peasants of the title have taken shelter under a large leafy tree. A woman in cloak and bonnet sits at the base of the tree and holds a small child in her lap. A shepherd stands beside them holding his crook. The child cradles a baby lamb and three other lambs lie near the humans. A river flows past the scene at right and in the distance there are some low buildings and a church. Large oak-type leaves are placed in the foreground, and there is a small cask or piggin at left.

Probably made by Ralph Hall (see Laidecker Vol. II pg. 50) c. 1822-49.

SOWER (THE)

Made by William Adams

The edge of the saucer shown is white and is enhanced by a circle of large beads set in scallops. A wreath of flowers and dark leaves separated at three places with a long C scroll capped with a single flower and bud encircles the rim. The picture in the well is framed by a row of scallops and beads, smaller than those placed around the outer edge.

In the center the Sower of the title is at left. He carries a basket and flings seed with his right hand. He is dressed in a farmer's smock and broadbrimmed hat. Behind him there is a tall tree stump topped with bushy branches. At right in the middleground a farmer walks behind two horses. They are pulling a tiller. Behind him there are tall trees and mountains. In the foreground, flowers, reeds, and bushes are strewn across the center. The scene in the bottom of the cup shows no people but has the large tree stump at left and a small barn at right. The cup plates of this pattern (not illustrated) depict the farmer who is working behind the two horses who are pulling a tiller.

Marked (imp.) Adams, GMK. 18, c. 1800-64.

SPORTING SUBJECTS
Made by Thomas Heath

The unevenly scalloped edge of this platter is detailed by a row of light beading followed by a row of small dark dentils. This in turn is next to a narrow stippled ground contained by a wreath of small flowers. The lower rim is covered by sprays of peonies, leaves, and buds that alternate with a smaller spray centered by a striped shaggy flower. The central picture shows a huntsman digging a trap by the light of a lantern hooked on a tree limb above him. His white horse stands at the right and a pair of dogs are at center. A tall tree rises at left and a smaller one is at right behind the steed. The central pictures differ on the various sized plates, but the subject matter shown distinguishes the pattern, plus the described details of the rim.

Marked T. Heath, Burslem, GMK. 1996, c. 1812-35.

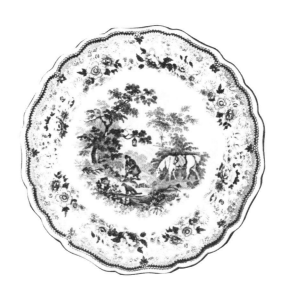

TEXIAN CAMPAIGN

Made by Anthony Shaw

These plates are unevenly scalloped, and the outer edges are detailed by a row of capped beads. The rim pattern on the larger plate is divided by ribbon-like scrolls that arch to form arched reserves against a stippled pale background. Each reserve is topped by a military emblem, guns, flags, drums, and is filled with a spray of flowers. In the panels between, created by the bottom points of the ribbon design, there is a female statue. She holds a bow and quiver under the left arm and arrows in the right hand. A small deer is at right near her. She may depict the goddess Diana. The same figure appears in the rim pattern of Napoleon (this category) and the brocade ribbon designs are very much alike. (See Napoleon). A row of wave-like scrolls filled with ferns closes the rim pattern at the well.

The central scene on the plate shows an officer with tricorn hat seated on a rearing horse. An officer with drawn sword stands beside him. The cup plate does not bear the scroll design and the lower rim or well designs, and most of the ribbon cartouches are absent. However, the military paraphenalia and the statue are clearly identifiable. The scenes differ on the articles of this pattern, and this one depicts an officer in tricorn hat, two officers in shakos, an Indian guide and a guard resting beside a campfire in the forest.

Marked J.B., and mark 3497 has been recorded. c. 1850.

TORO

Made by Charles Allerton and Sons

There are four scenic reserves on the rim of this plate. Each contains the same scene of a South American cowboy astride his white horse, lariat in the air, and in hot pursuit of a pair of fleeing wild horses, one white, the other black. They are placed in a tropical setting with mountains in the distance. Between the cartouches there are four identical Gothic scroll designs set against a very dark background. The rim patterns are framed at the top edge and the bottom of the rim with a beading of white rectangles. There are three other bands on the cavetto, the first plain stippling, the second white arches, the last a lacy dot and dash fringe.

In the center scene, another cowboy has caught a white bull with his lariat. A black bull is fleeing from the scene. In the distance there are wild horses and a small figure of a horseman. Palm trees are at right, oak trees at left and there are mountains in the distance.

Marked C. Allerton & Sons like GMK. 85, c. 1859.

TOURNAMENT

Made by Samuel Moore and Co.

The edge of this gently scalloped plate is outlined by a row of inverted U shaped forms containing beads. The outer edge of the rim is stippled. The rim design consists of three scenic reserves which alternate with floral designs. These are separated by vertical dark rows of foliated scrolls containing a rosette set in a dark diamond. The rows of scrolls are placed on either side of a vertical sprig. The top of the rim design is contained by a band of inverted swags of rosettes and shell shapes. The bottom of the rim design is decorated with a deep geometric fleur-de-lis composed of foliated scrolls and finished at the bottom by spearpoint which enters the well.

The central scene shows a knight with a plumed helmet seated on a rearing horse. A herald blows his trumpet at left. There are other knights and squires standing at left and right. At far left there are standards on poles. In the background at center, there is a canopied spectator box, and at far right in the background there are tents. A few sprigs of underbrush are placed in the foreground.

Marked S.M. & Co., GMK. 2746, c. 1861.

WILLIAM PENN'S TREATY

Made by Thomas Godwin

The edge of this scalloped plate is defined by a row of dark triangles. Two-thirds of the rim is covered with a band of large zigzag white crosses which are placed against a very dark background, some small rosettes are placed at their bases. The lower rim is covered with narrow fringed lines that slant to the right. The upper well carries a band of zigzag lines, and the well is encircled by a wreath of fringe composed of diamond trellis separated by a dark diamond with a bell pendent.

In the center scene, which appears to be set in the tropics because of the trees at right, William Penn, wearing a tricorn hat, stands holding a scroll. He is attended by a hatless young man in a cape who stands at right, and he is addressing a pair of Indians who wear exotic feathered headdresses. One is draped in trailing panels and wears a wide belt, denoting his rank as chief. Behind the chief there is a tent, and several people sit in front of the structure. There are exotic trees and bushes behind the tent and mountains capped with trees in the distance. In the foreground, there is a small spray of flowers with leaves.

Marked T.G., GMK. 1729, c. 1834-54.

ZOOLOGICAL GARDENS

Made by James and Ralph Clews

The white embossed edge of this plate is irregularly scalloped. A dark field around the edge enhances the design. Small white leaf forms are placed around the dark upper rim. These emerge from the top of slanted cartridge forms that encircle the rim. Each cartridge encloses a small dark leaf form set upon a sprig. A wreath of white foliated scrolls contains the rim design at the well. The rim background is stippled. A white lacy wreath enhances a circle of small quatrefoils that frame the central scene. At left in the middle, a man leads a small boy past a circular cage in this scene. The boy points at a small dark animal. At right another boy kneels near the cage, his hand out to the animal. A woman in hat and shawl stands near him. In the background there are buildings and trees, and in the foreground there are over-scaled flowers.

Marked R.&J. Clews. See Godden page 151. c. 1819-35.

Juvenile Category

Juvenile Category

The small plates pictured in this section were produced on the premise that parents will purchase toys that educate and amuse their offspring. A,B,C, plates are in use today. Some of the old alphabet dishes shown herein have the letters printed on the rims, other are embossed.

All the plates carry transfer scenes that are intended to amuse, and instruct at the same time; and some of the instruction was of a moral nature. The plates are of different sizes and are in scale as dishes actually used at meals by children, and as toys to be used with dolls.

For the most part the dishes and mugs are not backstamped. In order to catalogue the patterns they are given working descriptive titles in this book. When they do carry a title and backstamps, these are described, and the dates of manufacture are presented as in the other categories.

ALPHABET CUP

This little cup (2-1/2" diameter by 2" high) shows the first thirteen letters of the alphabet printed on the left side of a scene of children playing on a farm gate made from split rails. The second half of the alphabet appears on the right side of the picture.

ARCHERY
(correct title)

Made by Davenport, GMK. 1179a, c. 1840

The cup shown was made for the use of a child. It is 2-1/2" high. The picture shows a little girl, dressed in long sashed dress, pantaloons and a very large beribboned hat. She is holding a bow and arrow and is taking aim at a target at right. A baby boy dressed in a dark suit with big white collar, and wearing a big round brimmed dark hat is at her right, and at left, an older boy wearing an Eton jacket, long white trousers and dark hat, holds a bow and awaits his turn.

535

BEEHIVES

The edge of the plate shown is outlined with beads and a row of fringe. In the center scene three straw hives (skeps) are set upon a platform at left. In the background at right a woman and child stand on a lawn. The child is pigtailed and the lady wears a bonnet, a long Empire gown and carries a parasol over her head. There is a fence behind the figures and tall trees in the background. A swarm of bees can be seen in the center.

BERLIN
(correct title)

Made by William Alsagar Adderly, marked W.A.A.
GMK. 47 (1876-85)

This is a later pattern than most shown in this book. It is a good example of a child's plate (5-1/4" D.). The rim is decorated with oblong floral reserves separated by a Gothic geometric knot. A dark band encircles the outer edge, and white bands contain the rim pattern at both top and bottom. Small beads and pendants descend from the white line at the bottom into the well.

The central scene shows a mansion at left. It has ornate pointed Gothic roofs that are topped with spires. There are trees next to the house. A river divides the scene and at right there are tall elms with exposed roots spilling over a steep bank. In the background there are other towers and some hills. Clouds above complete the circular picture.

536

BIRD AT FOUNTAIN

The slightly indented rim of this plate is decorated with a scalloped wreath of small pointed-petalled flowers and leaves set on a continuous vine. The upper rim is covered with a diamond diaper pattern contained at the top edge by a row of beads. A scalloped band of rosettes and dots is set under the wreath at the lower rim and there are diamonds and a drapery design under the rosettes and on the slope of the well. A peacock sits on the rim of a fountain basin in the central scene. There are several over-scaled flowers at the right and a spray of leaves and a few blossoms at left.

537

BOY WITH PUNCHINELLO
(correct title)

The dish is covered with the classic drawing of a cherubic boy seated on an oval platform. He is dressed in a draped toga and holds a small clown doll or puppet balanced on his knee. The figure has a stone statue quality in contrast to the realistic bushes in the background.

CHINTZ I

Made by John Ridgway & Co., like GMK. 3259a, 1841-55

This child's plate is covered with a paisley design that includes stylized butterflies.

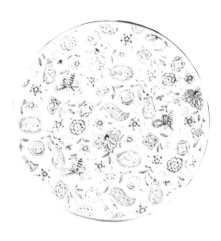

CHINTZ II

Maker unknown

This scalloped plate (4") is covered with a background of small squares. A swirling pattern of feathered, curved scrolls and tiny black star-shaped flowers is placed over the net background. This may be a cup plate.

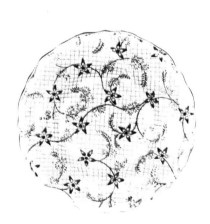

CLOCK

This dish was meant to teach many basic lessons. The clock in the center is surrounded by the names of the months of the year. The alphabet appears printed around the upper part of the rim, and the numbers from 1 to 52, the number of weeks in a year, are printed on the lowest part of the rim pattern which enters the well.

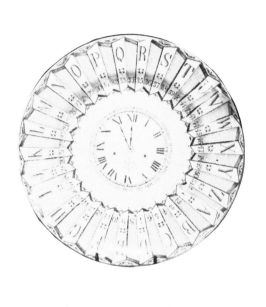

COW AT REST

The rim of the plate shown is covered with embossed figures of animals (monkeys, foxes, a wolf) and two oval designs; all are heavily over-coloured. In the center a reclining cow rests by a little brook.

DEAF AND DUMB BUNNY PLATE

Hand signals for letters are printed in a circle around the center picture of a pair of rabbits walking in their Sunday best. The rim carries an embossed alphabet.

541

FARMER (THE)

Made by J. and G. Meakin
GMK. 2598, c. 1851

The edge of this plate is decorated with a gold band. The rim is wide and is embossed with long sprays of wheat and flowers. In the middle, the transfer shows a farmer standing by a horse-drawn, two-wheeled cart laden with bundles and sticks. In the background there are barns and trees behind a long fence.

FISHERS
(correct title)

Made by Cork, Edge, and Malkin, marked C.E. & M.
GMK. 1101, 1860-71

The outer edge of this dish is decorated with a row of beading. A wreath of linked hearts encircles the rim. In the center, two children are fishing from the bank of a brook. A little girl stands behind a boy who lies on the bank. Behind them there are two cows wading in the water. Tall trees rise on either side of this scene, and there is an arched bridge in the background.

FISHERS (cont.)

FRANKLIN AND THE KITE

The edge of this slightly scalloped toy plate (3-1/16") is detailed with a row of beading, and the narrow rim is covered with a pattern of white darts with dark centers that gives a triangular effect.

The central scene shows a man standing at right center. He is dressed in Colonial clothes; a dark tail coat, knee breeches and a tricorn. At left in the background there are Dutch-type buildings behind a stone wall, and at left in front of a brick wall there is a large church. The man stands, his arms folded, and watches a boy fly a kite. At right a boy is rolling a hoop. A monument is in the center background. There are over-scaled flowers in the foreground.

The little sauce boat is 3-1/4" from edge of handle to end of spout. It is 1-3/4" high. It is possible to see the kite and the buildings but the transfer was cut off in the middle and there are no figures in the scene.

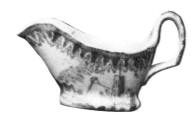

GARDEN SPORTS
(correct title)

This is a variation on the pattern which is described in the Scenic section. The border has been changed and the rim design of little sprigs is more appropriate in scale to these toy dishes. The plate is 3-1/2", the vegetable dish is 4-1/4" by 3-1/4", the platter is 6" long, and is decorated with the wheelbarrow motif used on the large adult set.

GOOD EXERCISE
(correct title)

A seesaw made from a board placed over a tree trunk is used by two little boys in the scene shown on one side of the mug photographed. The other side (not shown) shows two men sawing wood and is titled "The Sawyers".

GREYHOUND

This toy dish is 2-1/2" in diameter. The upper half of the rim is covered with a design of scallops that contain ovals. Little beads are pendent from the arches between the scallops. In the middle of the well there is a transfer picture of a reclining greyhound. He lies in the grass, and there are some bushes and part of a fence behind him.

HARBOR SCENE

The top rim of the child's mug shown is decorated with a narrow double line, then a band of white triangles, white beading and dark scallops. Many ships, with sails down, are anchored in the harbor which can be seen behind the sloping hills and long sheds shown in the foreground. Across the water there are other hills and mountains. The cup is 2-1/4" high and 2-1/4" diameter excluding handle. Coysh shows a cup about this size in his volume II (1800-50) and calls it a coffee cup. (Plate 32, top right.)

HEN AND CHICKS

Made by Enoch Wood & Sons, marked (imp.) as such with "Burslem"
GMK. 4257, 1818-46

This little plate has embossed flowers on its rim. The flowers have been over-coloured and a lustre ring outlines the outer edge and another is placed around the bottom of the rim. The central transfer presents the hen and her chicks, one of whom perches on her back.

JOSEPHINE AND L'AIGLON

The wife of Napoleon is pictured with their son, the "Little Eagle". She is seated on an "Empire" styled couch. Narrow lustre bands encircle the edge of the plate and the well.

JUVENILE
(correct title)

Made by Podmore Walker & Co., marked P.W. & Co. and (imp.)
"Pearl Stone Ware" GMK. 3075, 1834-59

This plate is twelve-sided and the panelled rim is covered with an irregular fish scale pattern formed by small branches. The outer edge is outlined with a row of scallops and beads, the bottom of the rim design is contained by a band of spearpoint.

In the central scene a girl dressed in dark bodice and long white skirt is seated at left on a garden bench. Behind her there is an urn on a tall pedestal. At right a girl wearing the same costume is jumping rope. There is a fence behind her at right in the middle ground. In the distance there are a mansion and tall trees.

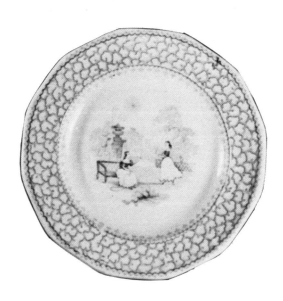

LASSO
(correct title)

Made by John Thomas Hudden, marked J.T.H., GMK. 2104, c. 1859-85

The article photographed is a saucer from a child's set of dishes. Three reserves are formed on the rim by a continuous band that encircles the lower rim, and by scrolls that form frames at the top. Each reserve contains the same scene of a white horse towards the left, and a black one who runs to the right. In the space between the scenic reserves are small flowers beneath the band, and foliated scrolls against a dark background above it.

In the center, both a black horse and a white one are running toward the right. There are palm trees and tall white mountain peaks in the background with rocks and tree branches in the foreground. The scenes probably differ on the various items of the set because the title infers the presence of horse hunters who are in pursuit with ropes. (See *Peruvian Horse Hunt* and *Horse Hunters* in the Genre category for comparable patterns.)

Note, the LASSO pattern, made by T. Goodwin and described in the Genre section of this book, is probably the original design and presents the complete rim design.

LITTLE BO PEEP

The rim of this gently scalloped plate is covered with embossed roosters, flowers, and small animals. Blobs of lustre have been scattered over the embossing. The central picture shows a maiden leading a small girl. They stand at left under a willow branch. The older girl points to a flock of sheep who are in the meadow at right.

LONDON DOG SELLER
(Correct Title)

Here is an alphabet plate with the outer edge detailed with a red band and embossed letters. Another red band is placed around the bottom of the rim. The center picture shows a man in tattered tall hat and rumpled suit. He holds two small dogs, has one sticking out of his coat side pocket and another on a leash near his feet. He stands on pavement in front of an arched doorway.

LUSTRE VINE WITH LAMBS

The edge of the scalloped plate shown is outlined with double lines of lustre. Twelve lustre groups of flower petals are placed around the upper rim and are linked by swags. Another band encircles the well. The pale yellow print is hard to distinguish, but it shows a lamb with its mother.

MARY AND HER LAMB

Mary feeds her lamb from a bottle as they stand in the center of the scene on this plate. There are trees in the right background and one in the left distance. The edge of the very gently scalloped plate is decorated with a band of beads and an inner row of small straight lines that give a fringe effect.

MONASTERY HILL

This miniature platter (3-1/2" by 4-1/2") has a border of lilies, leaves, and morning glories. In the center scene, a farmer and his cow walk at the foot of a hill surmounted by a large tall square building that is placed behind a wall. There are a shed or small cottage in the right foreground and a tall bushy tree at left. (W.H. Little states that the pattern, which is shown on a miniature tureen included with a set of Willow pattern dishes, should be attributed to Hackwood of Eastwood, Hanley. Plate 27.) (Laidecker Book II, pg. 71, describes a miniature set that must be very much like this.)

552

PARENTAL CARE
(correct title)

The edge of this child's plate is embossed with little beads and the rim is covered with small embossed flowers. A child says her prayers at her Mother's knees in the center of the scene. A canopied bed is in the background.

PASTORAL

The child's supper plate shown is completely covered with the transfer print of two cows, one standing, the other reclining in the foreground. Behind them there are bushes and white tree trunks. At far right in the distance there is a cottage. Small daisy-type flowers are strewn in the foreground. The edge is decorated with oval beads.

PET GOAT

Made by Edge Malkin & Co.
GMK. 1440, c. 1871

Two items from a child's set of dishes are shown. The plate displays the border of lacy semi-circles and triangular lines. At the outer edge there is a row of straight lines, like paling; at the bottom of the rim there are small rosettes set against a stippled background which is contained by a row of spearpoint design formed by small arches.

The central scene pictures a young girl with long flowing hair, wearing a long dress. She leads a small goat by a tether of twisted rope. In the distance at left there are small classic buildings and tall trees. Flowers and grass in the foreground complete the scene.

The sugar bowl displays the distinguishing rim design on its lid. The scene on the body of the bowl is the same as described above.

PET PAIRS

Made by Thomas Godwin, GMK. 1730, 1834-54.

The top of this mug is detailed with an embossed narrow band of beading. Inside the top rim is decorated with a printed row of triangles over a band of diamonds. One side of the cup shows a pair of small dogs, the other presents two cats, one of whom plays with a ball.

PLAYING MARBLES

Three boys, wearing suits complete with short jackets and long trousers and wearing little caps, are playing with marbles in the scene shown on this cup. The picture is framed with flowering branches and small scrolls.

PLOWING TIME

Here is another alphabet plate with embossed letters on the rim. The edge is outlined by a narrow black line. The well is covered with the transfer showing a farmer guiding his plow in the foreground. In the background behind a fence there are a cottage and some trees.

POOR BOY AND THE LOAF (THE)
(correct title)

This child's plate carries a moral message in words and pictures. The slightly scalloped rim is embossed with a shell-shaped scroll design which alternates with embossed flowers, which are over-coloured. The central scene shows a well-dressed boy and girl and large dog in front of a shop window. The boy is offering bread to a poor lad with no shoes.

POTTERS ART (THE)
(correct title)

This dish is embossed with an alphabet on its rim. The middle picture shows three potters standing at the wooden bench in their workroom. They are making plates, according to the description below the scene.

RAINY DAY

The mug shown is printed with a picture of a lady dressed in a long gown, bonnet, and shawl. She carries an umbrella as she talks to three small children, two girls and a boy, who share an umbrella. Behind them there are a fence and some flowering bushes.

RESURRECTION
Made by J. & G. Meakin
GMK. 2598, c. 1851

The edge of this plate is detailed by a narrow red line and the rim is covered with the raised, embossed letters of the alphabet. In the central scene, the religious transfer shows Jesus calling up the dead.

ROBINSON CRUSOE AND FRIDAY
(correct title)

The indented rim of the plate photographed is printed over with the alphabet. Some flowers are used to fill in the extra space at the bottom of the border, and the edge is outlined with a row of sprigs. The central transfer fills the well and shows Crusoe with Friday. There are palm trees and mountains in the background.

ROSE CHINTZ

Made by Livesly Powell & Co., GMK. 2386, c. 1851-66

This is a small toy plate. The ten-sided dish is covered with small six-petalled very dark flowers and stylized rosettes flanked by three dark leaves. These designs are placed over a background of sprigs. This pattern is very much like "Rose and Bell" made in mulberry by the same potter.

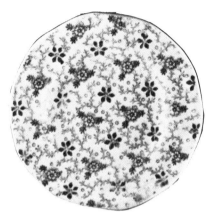

RUSTIC
(correct title)

Made by Whittingham, Ford, and Riley
GMK. 4131, c. 1876

The mug shown is printed with a scenic transfer and colour was added over the print. Two boys are in a wooden cart pulled by a large dog who is in hot pursuit of a fleeing rabbit. In the background there are tall trees and a lake. Across the water are farm buildings. The border pattern of leaves twisted over a vine is placed inside the rim of the mug. Another mug is paired with this, according to some who have seen it, and shows the cart overturned.

561

SEESAW, MARJORIE DAW
(correct title)

This alphabet plate has embossed letters on its rim. The edge is detailed with a band of embossed roping, and there is a narrow embossed band of scallops around the bottom of the rim. The central picture is of a boy and girl on a seesaw, which is made of a long tree limb placed over a log.

SHUTTLECOCK

The small (2") mug shown pictures boys dressed in Eton jackets and long trousers. They are holding small rackets with which they strike two feathered shuttles back and forth. The game of Badminton was evolved from the old game of "Battledore and Shuttlecock".

SOLDIERS ON HORSEBACK

These little dishes (3") show cavalry officers on the battlefield. One is leading a charge, and his title of 'Field Marsin' is at the bottom of the rim. The other shows one of the men ready to draw his sword. It is titled "Battlefield". The men are dressed in the uniforms of Hussars. Two of every three cavalrymen in the British Army of the early 1800's were Hussars.

SPRAY OF FLOWERS

 Two dishes are shown that were part of a child's toy set; the larger is 3-3/4", the smaller 3-1/4". Each has the same border consisting of dark triangles centered with white dots. A narrow shadowy stippled wreath of triangular forms is placed next to the outer hand. The larger plate contains a spray of garden flowers surrounded by sprigs. A butterfly is in the space under the top large flower at right. The smaller dish omits both the top flower and the butterfly.

TAKING A WALK

Made by John Rogers & Son
GMK. 3369, c. 1814-36

The edge of this plate is outlined with a black band, and the rim is embossed with fleur-de-lis joined by swags at the well. The scenic transfer covers the well and shows a woman in a long gown and large hat leading a small boy by the hand. He is dressed in Eton jacket, long trousers and lacy shirt.

TEA TIME

This plate is 4-1/4" diameter and may be a cup plate. The plain edge is outlined by a band of narrow vertical lines. A dark band encircles the upper rim and contains the rim pattern of fleur-de-lis, asterisks, and intertwined arches. A row of beads runs through the bottom of the design.

The well is wreathed with a double line design that curves into a scrolled peak at 10 points. The central scene shows three young ladies *dressed in Regency fashion. They are seated at a round table which bears cups, a teapot, and little plates which resemble cup plates. A band frames the picture and the words on it read: "Ladies all I pray make free, and tell me how you like your tea".*

TIGER HUNT
(correct title)
Made by Cartwright & Edwards
GMK. 796, c. 1857

At right in the foreground of the scene on this mug, a large tiger with a smile on his face hides in spiky bushes. There is a cocoanut tree behind him. In the background there are three mounted men armed with spears. Two hunting dogs are in the middle of the picture. Mountain peaks and clouds complete the scene.

VIRGINIA AND HER GOATS
(correct title)

The name of this design appears on the bottom rim under the fruits and leaves strewn in the foreground. The scene occupies the whole dish and shows a girl in a long white gown who leans her arm against a large boulder. A white goat stands on his hind feet at left, and a small dark goat grazes under some ferns and flowers at right.

WATER HEN
(Correct Title)

The edge of the plate shown is outlined with two narrow lines. The upper part of the rim has a design of zigzag lines with beads placed in each angle formed by the lines. The central picture covers the well. The Water Hen of the title is at right. She seems to be reaching for something in the water which is sprinkled with reeds and lilies. At left and at right there are tall flowers. The sprigs from the floral design at

567

WATER HEN (cont.)

right arch across the top of the scene. Two small birds are at upper left. There is a small oval vignette in the center. It shows a lake, a road and some castle-like square buildings under many banks of clouds. The American coot is a water hen.

WILLOW BUTTERFLY

This toy dish (2-3/4") is printed with part of the stylized butterfly that appears in the rim design of many Willow patterns. The half-flower with double hooks, from the same design, can be seen on the rim under the butterfly.

WILLOW PATTERNS

*The tureen stand shown is part of a child's set of dishes. It is 5-1/4"
long including handles. It is marked Edge Malkin & Co. GMK. 1445 c.
1873. Notice there are two men on the bridge in the left lower
foreground, and the pair of birds overhead are very large. The small
plate (3-7/8") is marked Copeland, GMK. 1072 c. 1850-72. Note the
diamond diaper pattern on the rim and the absence of bridge and men.*

YOUTH
(correct title)
The rim of this scalloped plate is embossed with three rows of rosettes. A narrow lustre band outlines the outer edge. The center transfer shows the faces of two maidens, one dark, the other fair, and that of a young man. They are framed in a circle trimmed with flowers and leaves. A butterfly is at top and a bouquet at the bottom of the frame.

Polychrome
Chinoiserie with Lustre

Polychrome Chinoiserie with Lustre

These patterns are printed in polychrome and the colours are predominately rose, lime green, dark red, buff, salmon, and dark green. The colours are placed over a black transfer outline. All are decorated with gold, tan or bronze lustre which has worn off on some of the dishes. On some the effect is brilliant with vivid colours, others are subdued when pastel shades were used. Most are printed on plain molds without scalloped edges.

The pattern themes are similar and include Chinese figures of nobles and their attendants in garden settings. Dealers refer to the most popular pattern as "The Tea House" pattern or "The Chinese pattern". As a matter of fact one plate shown is entitled "Chinese Pattern" (Ashworth). None is labeled "Tea House". These two designs show two Oriental maidens in a garden; one holds a vase, the other a lute. Both are looking out of the garden to the left. A figure who may represent a chaperone is seated in a garden house at right, she can be seen through the open window. The seated figure is a recurring theme and appears in the famous Timor patterns made in Holland, Germany and France. Timor pictures an Oriental princess standing in a garden. She holds a wand or fan in her upraised right hand. A young man is leaping off a fish trimmed roof at left. He steadies himself by grasping a tree branch. His black boots are on the ground. A pointed pagoda with a pennant flying from its spire is behind a lattice fence in the right background. A constellation of seven linked stars surrounding a new moon is above the tower. On the larger items such as the toddy bowl shown, the chaperone figure sits in a tea house at right. These designs are related to the Willow story derived from Chinese Canton patterns which usually included the figure seated in the tea house.

Some dishes are marked with titles, other bear numbers consisting of four digits painted on the back. These are artists numbers and refer to the location of the design in the pattern books owned by the pottery. The numbers impressed on the back are usually mold numbers except when a year date is impressed such as that used by Copeland.

Most of the patterns shown date from 1870-1880 and are later than the others pictured in this book, but are included to illustrate the continuing fascination with the old Chinese designs and also as an intriguing facet of the artistry of the Victorian pottery artists.

CANTON *(plate) Marked B.F., Could be Boch Freres of Belgium. Tea House pattern with very deep colours.*

CANTON *(bowl) Made by the Societe Ceramique (Holland) Flow Blue quality in background with deep soft pastels in Tea House pattern.*

CHANG *(square plate) Marked E.M. & Co. B. Made by Edge Malkin. Gardener at left putting plants into a jardiniere. Personage with staff, holding a pitcher, stands at right. Rim design of zigzag fretwork over a row of fringe.*

573

CHILI *(pitcher) Marked M.T. & Co. Houses at right, curved bridge, plump bird above. Same pattern as found on Yin by Ashworth.*

CHINESE CHING *(tureen stand) Made by William Adams & Co. Tea House pattern.*

CHINESE PATTERN *(plate)* *Marked H & C, made by Hope and Carter #16210 Tea House pattern. Also found marked L.S. and S. and (imp.) Ashworth #16210. Very pale print.*

HONG *(plate) Landscape made by Petrus Regout.*

575

HONG KONG *(plate) Marked P.B. & S., made by Powell, Bishop and Stonier. Floral design.*

INDIA TREE, THE, *(plate) Tree of Life pattern made by Meakin.*

576

JAPANESE *(sauce stand) Marked with "D", Made by Thomas Dimmock (1828-59).*

KYBER *(pitcher) Made by William Adams & Co. Famous Flow Blue pattern.*

577

"MANDARIN" *(pitcher) Marked #242, quatrefoil border.*

MANILIA *(saucer) Marked R.H., made by Ralph Hammersly.*

MELTON *(plate) Made by Wedgwood & Co. Combines birds with oriental border motifs.*

NANKIN *Marked J.F.W. Made by James Wileman.*

NING PO *(saucer) Marked C.H., made by Charles Hobson.*

"PAGODA" *(plate) Mark illegible, German.*

PA JONG *(rice bowl) Made by Petrus Regout.*

PEKIN *(cake plate) Marked J.B. Made by James Beech.*

PEKIN *(plate) Marked (imp.) Holland & Green.*

PEKIN *(water cress bowl) Marked R.K. & Co.*

PEKOE *(egg cup and plate) Ashworth (imp.).*

POTISCHE *(relish tray) Made by Petrus Regout.*

SANA *(plate) Made by Petrus Regout.*

SANA *(plate) Unmarked, looks like caricature of SANA by Regout.*

SHANGHAI *(plate) Marked T. Till and imp. Till.*

SHANGHAI *(plate) Variation of above.*

SLAMAT *(bowl) Made by Petrus Regout.*

586

"TEA HOUSE" *(sauce tureen stand, lid and ladle) Marked with a Chinese mark and #2232, brilliant colours and lustre.*

"TEA HOUSE" *(sugar bowl) #6372 Unmarked. Bright colours, tan lustre.*

PLATE VI

Tea House, Detail.

"TEA HOUSE" *(cake plate) #6369 and (pitcher) #6369. Marked B.W. & Co. Made by Bates & Walker. Very high quality printing, all molds marked with date of issue. Also found with later mark (imp.) G.W. & Co., Gildea Walker & Co.*

TEA POT *Unmarked. Lustre band over printed fret design on handle.*

TIMOR *(plate and serving bowl) Made by Petrus Regout.*

TIMOR *(coupe plate) Marked K.G., Made by Keller & Guerin, France.*

TIMOR *(tea tile) Made by Villeroy and Boch, Germany. (Also found with Utzschneider*

TODDY BOWL *Marked B. or E.*

TREE OF LIFE *(soup plate) Marked (imp.) R.S.R. Made by Ridgway, Sparks and Ridgway.*

VASE WITH PEONY *(plate) Made by Copeland and Garrett.*

YIN *(small platter) Marked Ashworth, Hanley. (Large platter) Ashworth #9447.*

Miscellaneous Category

Miscellaneous Category

This is the catch-all section of the book. If a separate chapter were to be devoted to each of the several subjects shown here, this book would be a tome. There are only a few patterns in each class, none fit easily into the established categories, so they are listed here in alphabetical order. The topics are Marine, Avian, Zoological, Religious, Moralistic, Gothic Geometric, and Botanical (other than floral). A few other patterns, including "Railway", the "Farmer's Arms", and "Arms of the States" are in a class by themselves and are also presented in this group.

AESOP'S FABLES
Made by Josiah Spode

The plates in this pattern are irregularly scalloped, and the edges are decorated with a band of dotted ovals and arrowheads set in small upright rectangles which are interrupted by large floral trefoils at six points. The upper third of the rims are covered with a stippled field contained by scrolls. Trios of large flowers are placed around the border and are joined to a large hydrangea blossom at the right, and a scroll design containing a large wild rose and terminating in the head of a fox at left. A white daisy is placed on the upper rim near the stylized fox head.

The first plate is subtitled "The Lion in Love". It shows a man kneeling by a large lion. He is removing a thorn from the lion's paw. A man and woman stand nearby. In the background there are trees, a lake, and a large manor house. The second plate is subtitled "The Dog and the Sheep". Here are a dog facing a sheep and a masked animal (the fox) behind them. In the background there are trees and mountains. In the foreground on both pictures there are over-scaled flowers.

The first plate is marked Spode, GMK. 2650, 1805-32. The second is marked Copeland and Garrett and "New Blanche", GMK. 1090, 1833-47.

ALBERT STAR

Made by Ridgway, Morley, Wear and Co.

The edge of this eight sided platter is white and the rim is covered with a dark background. Six large teardrop shaped designs flanked with scrolls are placed on the long sides and on the corners of the rim. Between these there is a smaller design of scrolls topped with a chevron containing diamonds and crowned by a pair of horn-like scrolls. White foliated scrolls are woven through each side of the second design. The well is framed on the cavetto by a geometric pattern interrupted by acanthus leaves and small fleur-de-lis. An oval frame decorated with triangles and scrolls encloses the central medallion which is composed of eight petals surrounding a circular band and a rosette.

Marked R.M.W. and Co., exact GMK. 3275, 1836-42.

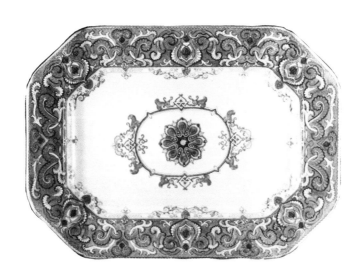

AMERICA

Possibly made by Thomas Furnival

The upper half of the rim of the twelve sided cup plate shown is covered with a gothic geometric pattern of triangular reserves filled with leaves that are separated by a pair of hooked scrolls back to back tipped with fleur-de-lis. The lower part of the rim is covered with small flowers and leaves which as can be seen on the platter, are just a part of the entire rim pattern which consists of hexagonal reserves set over triangular scrolls on the bottom part of the rim. The scrolls from the upper rim are set over the triangles on the lower rim, and vice versa. A band of zigzag beading contains the rim designs just below the cavetto. The central pattern shows an eagle with wings spread. His head is turned to the right, his right talon holds three arrows, the other holds olive leaves. He sits on top of a globe of the world. A dark halo of rays surrounds the bird.

Marked T.F. and Co., and (imp.) 'Real Ironstone', GMK. 1645, 1844-6.

AMERICAN BIRD

Made by James Edwards

The edge of this plate is trimmed with coils of ribbon over a narrow band. On the rim there are three groups of wild roses and three of a form of lily. In the center a mockingbird perches on a flower-laden branch.

Marked (imp.) as above, see Godden, page 230, 1842-51.

AMERICAN MARINE

Made by Francis Morley

The cup plate photographed has a border similar to the larger dish but lacks the reserve that carries a picture of a large steamboat with side paddlewheel, rowboat and trawler. The central scenes differ on these plates as is usual, but each shows sailing vessels in a rough sea. The well is encircled on both by a row of printed scallops. The distinctive feature that is the same on all pieces of this pattern is the rope design that is used for framing the reserves on the rim and which forms a cross between them.

Francis Morley and Co. first produced this design GMK. 2760, 1845-58. G.L. Ashworth joined the Morley company in 1859-62 and then in 1862 Ashworth took over so these plates are found with the marks F.M. and Co. and later Ashworth (imp.) and also G.L.A. & Bros. GMK. 139, 1862-90.

ARMS OF THE STATES

Possibly made by T. Walker or Mellor Venables

These plates are fourteen sided and the rims are paneled. The edges are detailed with a cobalt band that flows into the upper rim. In the center of the first plate, a medallion, created by a flow blue circle, contains the arms of the state of Delaware. This encompasses a shield flanked by a sailor and a hunter. The other plate shows the arms of Virginia. The medallion contains a man who holds a spear and stands upon a group of shells. These designs were also produced with medallions around the rims containing arms of different states and printed in many colors.

Marked "Ironstone" in an impressed curve, 1834-51. See Laidecker, part one, page 24.

"ASIATIC BIRDS"

Probably made by Charles Meigh

The two cup plates photographed illustrate the difference that the flow blue printing and a pastel printing can affect in a pattern. It is possible to see the rim design on the lighter dish. A dark band outlines the outer edge and is succeeded by a row of white beads. The upper rim is stippled and is contained by foliated scrolls, pairs of six petaled flowers, large roses, and five petaled blossoms. However the distinguishing feature is probably the rosette type large flower inset with a dark center that contains a five pointed white star. These are surrounded by very dark leaves and a C scroll at right, and occur equally spaced in three spots on the cup plate rim.

In the center a pair of exotic birds are perched on flowering branches. There are over-scaled flowers at right and in the foreground there is a tazza filled with fruit.

Marked with a Chinese mark, GMK. 2617, 1835-49.

ASIATIC PHEASANTS

Made by Bovey, Tracey Pottery Co.

For a description of this pattern, see "Asiatic Pheasants" by Hall. Note that the central bouquet differs from Hall's and that the bird is not at all the same.

Marked B.T.P. and Co., GMK. 498, 1842-94.

ASIATIC PHEASANTS

Made by Ralph Hall

The outer edge of this unevenly scalloped plate was left white and was enhanced by a row of printed white beads set in a shaded band against a black background. Three passion flowers are placed around the rim and alternate with a pair of large flowers surrounded by buds, sprigs, leaves, and smaller flowers. The floral designs are separated by the distinctive triangular design composed of a beaded band at the top which is a part of the outer edge design. It has scrolled sides and a flower at the apex. The triangle is filled with slanting lines that meet to form a chevron pattern.

In the center of the dish, there is a large bouquet of exotic flowers including passion flowers. The birds of the title are pictured with one flying above the flower arrangement and the other perched on a flower stalk and snatching at a butterfly who hovers at left.

Marked R. Hall, GMK. 1888, 1822-49.

ASIATIC PHEASANTS

Made by John Meir and Son

The dish photographed is scalloped and there is a printed narrow deep scallop band containing beads around the outside edge. Sprays of flowers are placed around the rim and small sprigs are placed above the flowers against a second dotted line. The floral designs are separated by triangular patterns topped by a curved line terminating in scrolls at each end. The triangles are formed by the lines and by scrolls terminating in a flower flanked by leaves at the apex. The triangles are filled with straight lines that form chevrons, and this distinguishes the rim pattern.

In the center the two birds for which the design is named are placed on either side of a large sprawling bouquet of roses, dahlias, and other flowers. Sprays of prunus and forget-me-nots surround the central bouquet. This is very like the Hall version, but the outer rim treatment is different. The flowers on the rim are different, and the central bouquets are not the same nor are the exotic birds.

Marked J.M. and Son, GMK. 2635, 1837-97.

ATHECUS

Made by William Adams

The upper edge of this cup plate is dark and stippled. The lower part of the rim is also stippled in a lighter shade. A band of scrolls, small flowers, and leaves surrounds the middle of the rim.

The central scene is dominated by a large lyre in the center. At left a hanging basket full of flowers slants and touches the harp. At right there is a small quiver full of arrows placed above an over-scaled passion flower. There are sprigs and small flowers in the background.

Marked with an (imp.) eagle, mark not located.

BANDANA

Made by John and William Ridgway

This scalloped plate bears the typical Ridgway gadroon edge. On the rim there are four lambrequin reserves filled with trelliage and containing a rose, forget-me-nots, and leaves. Small bouquets separate the reserves and are linked to them by garlands that dip into the well. In the center scene two exotic birds stand on stone slabs at right. A tall bamboo tree rises behind them. At left there are over-scaled flowers and large leaves. A third bird chases a butterfly at center top.

Marked J.W.R. and "Stone China", GMK. 3260, 1814-30.

BANDANA (con't.)

"BASKET"

Made by Charles James Mason and Co.

The edge of this scalloped plate is fluted and a band of floral spearpoint is placed around the outer rim. A wreath composed of six sprays of small leaves surrounds the basket full of flowers which is placed in the center of the well.

Marked "Mason's Patent Ironstone China", GMK. 2530, c. 1845-8.

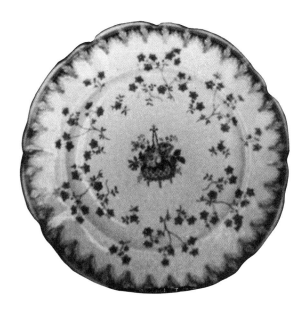

BEEHIVE

Made by William Adams

Six dark baroque triangular designs filled with diamond lattice and small flowers are set against a background of small rosettes on the upper rim of this saucer. A tiny band of sawteeth is placed around the outer edge. A wreath of large flowers encircles the lower rim. This same design appears in the upper inside part of the teabowl. The Beehive of the title can be seen at left in the picture in the well. It is surrounded by flowers and there are flowers in the foreground. There is a tall lacy tree and a second shorter one in the background behind the hive. A brook cuts diagonally across the scene toward the right and an urn filled with flowers sits upon a platform on the opposite bank from the hive. In the distance there are mountain peaks. The same scene is placed around the outside of the teabowl, and the Beehive occurs again in the bottom of the cup.

Marked (imp.) with a crown and "Adams Warranted Staffordshire", GMK. 20, 1810-25.

BERRY

Made by William Ridgway

The edge of this plate is decorated with a chain made of thorny vine stems. The entire plate is covered with a dark print composed of very large leaves and groups of raspberries. A pair of butterflies are opposite each other and perch on sprigs which are placed on the rim.

Marked W.R., GMK. 3301, 1830-34.

BERRY (con't.)

BIRD PATTERN
Made by Job and John Jackson

The scalloped edge of this plate is white and is decorated with beaded molding. A dark scalloped and looped line from which triangles of tiny beads suspend towards the well separates the edge from the rim design. Four different small exotic birds perched on sprigs alternate around the rim with four different large flowers with dark leaves and forget-me-nots.

In the center of the well two birds, one at right with a crown crest and long tail and one at left, plainer but larger, are perched on small branches. Sprigs of flowers are behind them. In the foreground there is a dark basket with a fancy oval edging. Large flowers are placed in front of the basket design and two are placed within it.

Marked Jacksons Warranted, GMK. 2156, 1831-5.

BIRD PATTERN (con't.)

"BUTTERFLY JAPAN"

Made by George Miles and Charles James Mason

The entire surface of the well of this lobed soup dish is covered with a pattern of ovals and stylized flowers. A large dahlia and leaves is at center right and a butterfly is at left. A band of dark beads encircles the top of the cavetto. The lower rim has a pattern of parts of large flowers. The upper rim carries a dark brocade band.

Marked (imp.) "Mason's Patent Ironstone China", GMK. 2539, 1813-29.

CABINET (THE)

Made by Elijah Jones

A row of printed beads is set around the unevenly scalloped edge of this soup plate. Eight divisions are marked on the rim by a coil of ribbon wound over a bar. In the center of each section there is a cane with knob at top and pointed bottom. Large feather-like leaves are wound around the canes and form scrolls on either side of the knobs at the top of the rim. The background of the canes is partially shadowed and a diaper pattern of diamonds and sprigs covers most of this and ends in points toward the ribbon coils. A band of ribbon arches encloses the rim pattern at the bottom and forms an octagonal frame for the central scene.

In the well some precious objects are laid on a table that holds a large vase containing over-scaled flowers. There are coins, beads, rings and a miniature snuff box in the foreground. A teacup with double handle and a saucer are behind the treasures. In the background there are trees, urns, a balustrade, and part of a silhouette of a mansion.

Marked E.J. GMK. 2214, 1831-39.

CALEDONIA

Made by Ridgway, Morley, Wear and Co.

The edge of this scalloped plate is white. The rim is covered with a plaid design that descends into the well and is contained there by a white band filled with zigzags. A wreath of clover and daggerpoints encircles the well on the cavetto. The central medallion contains an escutcheon in a white circle which is surrounded by the eight points of a star design. Small sprigs are placed between the points of the star.

Marked R.M.W. and Co., GMK. 3271, 1836-42.

CEYLONESE

Made by George Phillips

The rims of the two plates shown and the ring around the lower body of the pitcher are decorated with a design of sprigs interspersed with pairs of small flowers and dark leaves. A small semicircular feather is set around the outer edge of the plates underneath a dark band containing oval beads. This design can also be seen inside the upper part of the pitcher. The semicircular feather is a distinguishing element in this design. The patterns on the items shown differ in background detail, but left and center they all contain a peacock. On the cup plate he stands next to an urn at right. On the creamer he is next to a bush at right, and an urn can be seen at extreme right. On the dinner plate the bird is at center and perches on a classic urn and his long train cascades to the pedestal that supports the vase.

Marked G. Phillips, like GMK. 3010, 1834-48.

CHARMONTEL

Made by John Ridgway

The rim pattern on this saucer resembles a wallpaper pattern. Five vertical lines form the background for wide strips of bamboo leaves that alternate with a band of flowers and fruit. The latter terminates in the well with a pendant blossom. Swags of ferns connect the blossoms and form an open star design with the central medallion which is composed of spokes of flowers and shadowy ferns around the dark circle.

Marked J.R. and a ptd. coat of arms, exact GMK. 3258, 1830-55.

CHUSAN

Probably made by John Ridgway

The upper rim of this twelve sided plate is covered with a lacy net composed of diamonds and contained by baroque scrolls. Eight shield-shape reserves filled with the diamond lace and framed by baroque scrolls descend from the border and enter the well. Large dark ruffled flowers are placed on either side of the shields. Smaller flowers and leaves are beneath the shield. In the center a small basket is suspended by its handle from a leafy stalk that terminates in small blossoms. At left there is a peony tree.

Marked with ptd. coat of arms, GMK. 3258, 1830-55.

"CLEWS DOUBLE PRINTS"

Made by James and Ralph Clews

These cup plates are printed with a very dark vivid blue which is typical of the work by the Clews brothers. These are decorated with a double transfer half of which appears upside down. In one, Oriental buildings can be seen at upper left and at top right there are some willow fronds. A different building is at lower left. Some of these are reverse prints and seem to be printed upside down facing each other. In some cases the transfer has been moved so that the full scene does not appear on both halves. This use of reversing bits of transfer seems to be peculiar to Clews.

Marked Clews Warranted Staffordshire, GMK. 919, 1818-34.

CONCHOLOGY

Probably made by Thomas Dimmock

The rim of this gently scalloped plate is covered with a design of small C scrolls against a stippled ground. The white edge is outlined with a narrow dark band and the rim design which invades the well is contained by another narrow dark line. A band of small triangles and quatrefoils is placed inside the line and surrounds the well. A cluster composed of conch shells, seaweed and smaller shells is placed in the center of the dish.

Marked D. and "Stoneware", like GMK. 1299, 1828-59.

CORAL BORDER

Made by Thomas Dimmock

The soup dish is unevenly scalloped. The rim and most of the well are covered with a stylized pattern of coral branches set with small blossoms that form six large reserves which contain big stylized flowers and leaves. The central bouquet of flowers, seed pods, and sprigs, is also stylized.

Marked D. and "Stoneware", GMK. 1297, 1828-59.

CORNICE

Made by William Davenport

The small object photographed is a knife rest, one of a pair made to hold carving knives above the dinner table cloth, in order to prevent soiling the cloth.

Marked Davenport, like GMKS. 1185, 6, & 7, 1820-60.

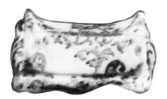 

CORONATION

Made by James and Ralph Clews

The white edge of this octagonal platter is decorated with a twisted band of dark sections. The well is encircled with a white ribbon band filled with small Y or bone shapes. The rim is covered with a wreath of berries and leaves. In the central scene a large vase filled with over-scaled flowers is at left. It sits on a white table top. There are peaches and other fruits, sprigs and leaves in the center of the table and a small bird perches at the right on the surface.

Marked Clews Warranted GMK. 919, 1818-34.

DEAD GAME

Maker unknown

The dish photographed is a tureen stand. It is gently scalloped and the handles are embossed. The outer edge is detailed with a narrow band of moss and the rim is covered with a sprawling wreath of stylized dotted leaves and flowers.

In the center scene three dead game birds lie in a heap on the ground. There are some flowers in the foreground. At left there are an imposing gate and gatepost, a balustrade, and a pair of tall trees that arch over the center of the scene. At extreme right in the background there is a manor house on a hill. Mountains in the distance and clouds above complete the circular picture.

EAGLE

Made by Podmore, Walker, and Co.

The rim of this plate is decorated with a design of gourds with blossoms and leaves set in five scrolled semicircular reserves which are flanked by scrolls and lilies set against the linear background of the upper rim. Stylized bellflowers suspended from double scrolls separate the reserve patterns. In the central scene a pair of eagles perch on some tree limbs which are growing from a rocky cliff high above a lake in the background. At left in the distance there are mountain peaks.

Marked P.W. and Co., GMK. 3075, 1834-59.

FALLOW DEER
Made by John Rogers and Son

The pierced dish photographed has a border pattern of crocus. The cavetto is decorated with a band of large triangles and beads. In the center scene two spotted deer are in the foreground. Behind them there are cottages and farm buildings with rooves covered with snow. A stream of water, which appears to be frozen, is behind the animals. There are stylized large trees in the background. Fallow deer are Eurasian in origin, called "Dama, dama" and have a yellowish coat.

The gravy boat shows four deer in the foreground. A round open temple is on a steep bluff at right. The rim pattern appears inside the vessel.

Marked (imp.) Rogers, GMK. 3369, 1814-36.

FARMERS ARMS (THE)

Made by Burgess and Leigh

This large (4¼ inch high) mug is covered with pictures of farmers' implements; single bottom plow, scythe, rake, pitchfork, churn and spinning wheel. There is a picture of a farmer at right and his wife at extreme left. The banner says "God speed the Plough, Success to the Farmer". The farm scene at the bottom below the motto shows horses behind a rail fence at left and a lane leading to a building in the center and cows at right.

Marked B. and L., GMK. 712, c. 1862.

FEATHER

Made by Wood and Challinor

The feathers of the title are abundant on the rim of the scalloped plate and in the center. Stylized flowers which are overpainted are placed over peacock feathers to form this design.

Marked W. and C., GMK. 4244, 1828-43.

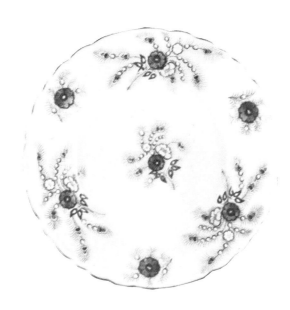

"FERN"

Made by James and George Alcock

The rim of this scalloped cup plate is covered with swags of small dark flowers that alternate with vertical sprays of delicate ferns set with tiny flowers and buds. The latter enter the well.

A pinwheel of the fern sprays is placed around two dark flowers and leaves in the center.

Marked (imp.) J. and G. Alcock and "Cobridge", GMK. 68, 1839-46.

FLENSBURG

Possibly made by James Edwards

The rims of these twelve sided dishes are covered with an outer wreath of very dark foliated scrolls and an inner one of lighter small leaves. The second band is contained by a dark band which is very apparent on the cup plate. The center design consists of a Prussian eagle with wings outspread and head turned to the right. He sits on top of a two handled urn. An over-scaled rose is at the base of the urn and an equally large lily and stem are at right. Delicate willow branches and buds are placed behind the bird. Flensburg is in Germany and is located near the border of Denmark.

Marked (imp.) Warranted, 1842-51. Mark not located.

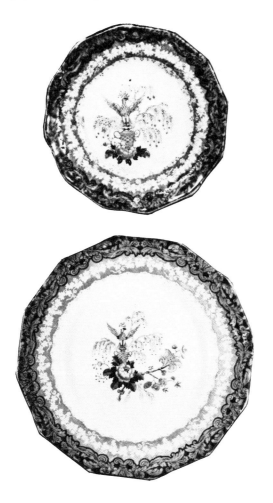

FLORILLA

Made by Edward Challinor

The twelve sided plate shown is decorated on the upper part of the rim with arches composed of scrolls. The outer spaces are filled with concentric lines. A trio of flowers of a peony type is set in each of five spaces under the upper arches, and trailing scrolls on either side and a vine underneath each trio form a framed reserve. The spaces between the floral groups are decorated with a bud and leaves that extend from the vine.

A tiny gardenhouse with Oriental roof is at upper left in the central scene. A willow and a flowering tree are behind it. In the foreground there is a square platform set upon a floral and scroll base. A large scroll extends from the platform to stairs at the left which ascend to the gazebo. A vase is set upon the platform. It is filled with over-scaled flowers that are like those on the rim. A tiny crested pheasant flies above the vase.

Marked E.C., GMK. 835, 1842-67.

FLOSCULOUS

Made by William Ridgway and Co.

The pinwheel pattern on the scalloped plate shown starts at the center of the well. The three scrolled arms rotate to the right and stems composed of bellflowers on each arm split into other stems bearing stylized flowers and dark leaves that curve around the indented rim. Between these dark dominant patterns there are three sprays of stylized carnations, sprigs and leaves that originate at three center curves of the pinwheel.

Marked W.R. and Co., GMK. 3303, 1834-53.

FOREST

Probably made by Samuel Alcock and Co.

The pattern shown on the cup plate is composed of two stylized trees made from a reverse printing of branches and leaves.

Marked with a beehive and "Florentine China". See Godden, page 28, 1830-59.

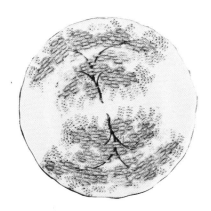

FRANKLIN'S MAXIMS

Maker unknown

This small mug is only two inches high and probably was intended for use as a coffee cup.

FRUIT AND FLOWERS

Maker unknown

The plate shown is unevenly scalloped. Its outer edge was left white and a band with small cherries and leaves linked with stylized flowers enhances the edge. A molded wreath of scrolls is placed around the middle of the rim. Three large differing groups of fruits flanked by leaves and sprigs alternate with three smaller sprays around the middle and lower rim and enter the well.

In the center medallion there are peaches and cherries flanked by dark leaves, and topped with flowers and berries; these are surrounded with a wreath of cherries and dark leaves set over a beaded circle.

FRUIT BASKET

Maker unknown

The edge of this plate is unevenly scalloped and the indented rim is paneled. The upper rim is decorated with six tasseled spearheads filled with a diaper design containing rosettes. A pair of rosettes flanks the triangular designs and small scrolls connect the patterns. Large fruits are pictured around the rim. The well is deeply indented and it is circled by a band of scrolls and rosettes crowned with fleur-de-lis.

In the center a basket with tall handle is filled with fruits, leaves, and sprigs. An insect hovers above the handle. In the foreground there are large fruits and leaves.

This is attributed by Coysh to William Smith and Co. on page 68 Vol. II, GMK. 3598, c. 1845.

GIRAFFE

Made by John Ridgway

The white edge of this plate is indented in eight places. The upper rim is stippled and is covered with a diamond diaper design. Eight scrolled arches alternate around the center of the rim with a large flower that surmounts a pair of smaller blossoms, leaves and scrolls. The arches contain a shadowy pattern of entwined leafy stems.

Three giraffes are placed in the middle of the central scene. One is seated near a bush at center left, one stands nearby and a third who has a chain around its throat, leans its head upon the standing one. Two men in Arabic clothes are at right. One stands, the other is seated facing him. A sword lies on the ground nearby. At left in the background there are tents. There are two other men and tall palm trees near the tents. Behind the men at right there are a circular stone well, bushes, bamboos, a feathery palm, and a large coconut tree. In the foreground there are pineapple plants and some firm fronds.

Marked "Published August 30th, 1836 Agreeably to the Act" also "Stoneware", and "Jn. Ridgway", like GMK. 3255, 1830-55.

GRAPE

Probably made by Joseph Furnival

The edge of this saucer is slightly scalloped and there are oval arched moldings on the rim. A vine runs around the outer edge and three large bunches of grapes alternate with three smaller ones in the molded arches. Single grape leaves are placed between the fruit designs. This plate was printed in dark green and the grapes were colored purple.

Marked J.F., like GMK. 1643, 1845-70.

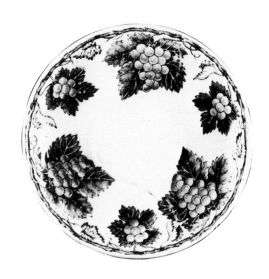

HAMPTON COURT

Made by John Ridgway & Co.

The rim of this unevenly scalloped plate is covered with a design of bold vertical stipes formed of a combination of dark and light bars which are separated by narrow horizontal lines. A wreath of foliated scrolls contains the bar pattern at the bottom of the rim, and small sprays extend from the scrolls into the well.

In the center a leafy branch bearing three plums is flanked by the same small flowers described above.

Marked J. Ridgway & Co., GMK. 3259a, 1841-55.

HOP BORDER

Made by Joseph Clementson

A twisted double vine that forms oval loops is printed around the outer edge of this plate. Six large groups of hops and leaves descend from the outer vine and converge toward the open center.

Marked J. Clementson with a Phoenix bird, GMK. 9108, 1840-64.

"HOT WATER DISH"

Made by William Davenport

This dish is made in two parts which consist of a plate sitting on a shallow basin. It is 10½ inches diameter. Hot water was poured into the spout at right. The Oriental design is overpainted with rust and blue.

Marked (imp.) Davenport, GMK. 1179a, c. 1805.

INDIAN

Made by Livesley Powell and Co.

This twelve sided plate is printed with a design of five panels which are created by white curved lines that interlock with each other and form a vertical oval design that is centered with a quatrefoil at five points. In each of the reserves there is a floral pattern consisting of a pair of flowers with leaves and buds placed against a dark stippled background.

The central design contains a tall double handled urn which is placed on an Oriental table with curved short legs. This is at right. Dark flowers and other small blossoms and daffodils are placed around it. At left there are over-scaled flowers and a small insect hovers over them.

Marked L.P. and Co. and "Ironstone", GMK. 2386, 1851-66.

JAPANESE

Made by Samuel Alcock and Co.

The plate photographed is unevenly scalloped and a band of dark beads is printed around the edge. The stippled rim bears the design of four white foliated scrolls embracing a pair of rosettes. Dark scrolls are placed on the upper rim between the dark designs. The well of the plate and the lower part of the rim are encircled by a wreath of prunus blossoms on thorny branches. At four spots exotic Asiatic pheasants are placed on the branches. Triparted Arabic arches were left white on the rim in order to frame the bird figures. A bouquet of over-scaled flowers set in a flared Japanese flowerpot, complete with scrolled feet and scalloped lip, is seen in the center of the dish.

Marked S.A. and Co., and "Stoneware", GMK. 75, 1830-59.

JESSAMINE

Made by John Wedge Wood

A garland of very small flowers encircles the edge of this saucer. The rim is covered with short straight branches composed of tiny beads and having the same small flowers that are found in the garland. In the center a rosette is set in a frame of beads and petals that form a medallion. This is surrounded by a wreath of the same spiky branches as found on the rim.

Marked J. Wedgwood, like GMK. 4276a, 1841-60.

LEAFACE

Made by John Ridgway, Bates and Co.

The soup dish shown is printed in luster. The outer edge is detailed with a dark band containing light oval beads. A wreath of leaves, running scrolls and tendrils surrounds the rim. A row of beading contains the rim design and this in turn is encircled by a row of tassels connected by a swag on the cavetto. In the center there is a stylized round flower design surrounded by a frame of six pointed arches containing spade shaped dark leaves. Small stylized sprigs are placed between the points of the star design.

Marked J.R.B. and Co., GMK. 3269, 1856-58.

LILY

Made by Wood and Challinor

The major portion of the transfers used on these plates was placed upon the rims of the dishes. The design was printed in mulberry and overcolored with blue, green, and mustard. Spiky forms that resemble coral extend from one end of the floral spray, and sprigs that resemble seaweed are placed around it. The lily of the title appears in the center of the larger plate. It sways on a curved stem and has three stylized leaves. The central flower was omitted on the cup plates.

Marked W. and C. and "Stone China", GMK. 4244, 1828-43.

LONG LIVE THE KING

Made by Joshua Heath

This is a very early example of transfer printing and is pre-Victorian. The dish was made in honor of King George III. It is printed in a soft blue that is not greyish. The border is Oriental and resembles those used on early Willow patterns. Note the butterflies, the cellular reserves and the fret motifs. A wide band of honeycomb oval cells is placed around the cavetto.

In the center a wreath of laurel leaves joined at the top by a bowknot surrounds a circle of bellflowers joined at top and bottom by a circular design containing an asterisk. The wreaths enclose a crown placed over a swag and under that the words of tribute appear.

Marked (imp.) I.H., GMK. 1991, 1770-1800.

MARBLE

Made by John Wedge Wood

The rim of this twelve sided soup plate is paneled. The entire surface of the dish is covered with fine dark transfer that resembles the veining found on marble.

Marked J. Wedgwood, GMK. 4276a, 1845-60.

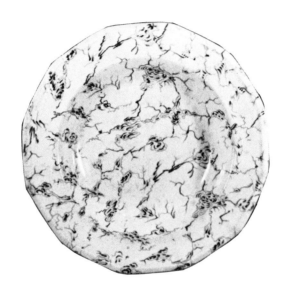

MARIGOLD

Made by Wedgwood

The rim of this plate is covered with framed narrow panels that contain stylized flowers. The well is surrounded by a wide band of linear motifs that resembles primitive letters. The center design consists of five stylized marigolds, four of which are framed by semicircular foliated bands that are joined by a fan design. These surround the fifth central flower.

Marked (imp.) Wedgwood, and dated c. 1876, GMK. 4075.

MILLENIUM

Made by Ralph Stevenson & Son

This pattern was made to illustrate the biblical prophecy believed by the early Christians to predict the second coming of Christ who would rule for a thousand years before the last judgment. The open Bible is shown at top under the large eye of God. The stippled border is covered with flowers and plants that produce grain.

In the center picture a child is seen embracing a lion. Lambs and other domestic animals, as well as a wild beast lie nearby. Above them, in the rays emanating from Heaven a banner proclaims "Peace on Earth" as a dove carrying an olive branch flies on high. In the white area beneath the figural group is printed "Give us this day our daily bread" in a curved line under the body of a praying man.

Marked (acc. to Laidecker Bk. II pg. 80) R.S.&S. GMK. 3706, 1832-35.

MORAL MAXIMS

Made by Ralph and James Clews

The edge of this scalloped plate was left white and is decorated with a band of dark quatrefoils edged in white. These alternate with three ribbons that contain beads and rosettes and which are placed over three scenic reserves and bear labels identifying the reserves. The first says "Industry" and is over a picture of a beehive placed beside a seated woman who is showing the hive to two children. The second reserve is labeled "Knowledge" and below the label is a picture of a woman holding a scroll. She is seated next to a large overflowing cornucopia and is looking at a child who stands behind a globe of the world. The third reserve labeled "Temperance" shows a seated elderly scholar holding a tome. A young man is seated at his feet. Between these scenes there are mottoes on ribbons twisted around flowers and shells that bear an oval rosette. The first ribbon appears next to the industry scene and states "Industry, the Key. Integrity the lock. Wealth and Fame the Treasure"; the second pertains to knowledge and states "Knowledge is not acquired but by attention and application"; the last, which applies to temperance states "Learn Prudence. One vice is more expensive than many Virtues".

The well is outlined on the cavetto by a deep row of lacy spearpoint. The scene in the center presents three women in the middle. Two are seated on the grass under tall trees at the right. The third, holding a basket, stands and faces them. A river divides the scene and on the right bank in the background there is a large churchlike structure with a domed tower. On the left bank there is another building of the same type. A dark tall arched bridge connects the two.

Marked R. and J. Clews. See Godden, p. 151, dated 1818-34.

MOSAIC TRACERY

Made by James and Ralph Clews

The background for this design of scrolls and leaves surrounding a vase form filled with poppies, is a diaper pattern of beaded hexagons filled with quatrefoils. The pattern covers the entire cup plate.

Marked (imp.) Clews Warranted Staffordshire, GMK. 919, 1818-34.

NEPTUNE

Made by John and George Alcock

The edges of these unevenly scalloped plates are decorated with a narrow band of fencelike design composed of uneven palings. The slightly concave rim is covered with a paisley pattern made from curved branches of seaweed. A large three masted sailing ship flying the Union Jack rides the waves in the foreground of the central scene. There are other ships in the background. The cup plate is gently and unevenly scalloped. No pattern was used on the rim but the entire central transfer was placed on the dish and covers the cavetto and part of the rim.

Marked J. and G.A. GMK. 69a, 1839-46.

OAK AND IVY

Made by Joseph Clementson

The rim of the saucer shown is paneled and is covered with a wreath of oak and ivy leaves on a vine with sprays of acorns and smaller oak leaves descending from the vine into the center of the well. The large leaves and the acorns are overcolored.

Marked J. Clementson and "Ironstone", and a Phoenix bird, GMK. 910a, 1839-64.

ORIENTAL BIRDS

Made by John and William Ridgway

The distinctive scalloped mold used on the rim of these plates is embossed with small flowers between each scallop. A tracery of rosettes flanked by ferns is printed on each embossed scallop. The rim is decorated with three large roses and forget-me-nots that alternate with three bouquets of anemones, poppies and leaves.

Crested birds perch on the branches of a prunus tree in the center. At the base of the tree there are flowers, grass, and some small stones. The soup plate shown with two birds in the pattern is multi-colored with painting placed over the blue transfer printing.

Marked J.W.R. and "Granite China", GMK. 3260, 1814-30.

ORNITHOLOGY

Made by William Adams

This slightly scalloped plate is a reissue of an earlier pattern (see Ornithology by Meir). It is presented in order to show the complete rim detail. This pattern is composed of rows of tassels joined by slanting lines that form diamond designs that terminate at the well with a tassel effect. The outer edge is decorated with a row of tiny scallops containing dots. The six cartouches that are placed around the rim are framed with beaded scrolled curved bands and each contains a picture of a bird in a natural setting.

The central scene shows a mountain lake with rocky formations covered with pine growth on both sides of the water and Alpine peaks in the distance. In the foreground a large bird with swanlike neck is at left standing on a bank. At right a smaller version of the same bird stands on a bit of land on which there are ferns and bushes.

Marked W. Adams, GMK. 26, c. 1891.

ORNITHOLOGY

Made by John Meir and Son

The sides of this sugar bowl are covered with a picture of a large long-billed bird seated in the foreground on a sunken log. Behind him at right another bird roosts in a tree. The scenery includes a large lake, rocky banks, pine trees and mountains in the distance. The collar design is composed of a fine network of tassels in which are set small oval reserves containing pictures of different birds. The design is the same on the lid as on the base but the bird portraits are omitted on the base.

Marked J.M. and S. GMK. 2634, 1837-97.

PARADISE

Made by Livesley Powell and Co.

The rim of the soup plate pictured is ten sided and the edge is decorated with a row of small circles. Three sprays of lotuslike flowers are placed on the rim and are flanked with long large foliated scrolls. Small flowers and leaves are placed among the scrolls at the right of the sprays. In the center a bird of paradise is perched above an arrangement of very large exotic flowers, leaves, buds, bamboo sprigs and whirling foliated scrolls.

Marked L.P. and Co., GMK. 2386, 1851-66.

PEACE

Made by Robinson, Wood and Brownfield

The ring of this scalloped saucer is covered with a repetitive design of concentric dark lines interspersed every half inch with a small rosette. The spaces between the lines are filled with wreaths of square white crosses centered with dark beads. The effect is that of a diamond pattern. The well is encircled by a ring of arches centered with an arrowpoint.

In the center scene a kneeling child embraces a friendly smiling lion. A small lamb lies at left near the child. There are flowers and sprigs behind the figures and other small flowers in the foreground. Two palm trees are placed in the distance at right.

Marked R.W. and B. GMK. 3345, 1838-41.

PEACE AND PLENTY

Maker unknown

The upper rim of this dish is covered with a wreath of swags and pendants. Ears of wheat are placed in the swags and on either side of the pendants. In the central scene, which covers the well, a large seated figure of Ceres, goddess of plenty, sits at right holding a cornucopia which contains fruit. She is sprinkling seeds from her upturned arm. A large bird stands on the ground at left. Two children stand near her with hands lifted to catch the seeds. Another child sits on a railing at right holding a scroll that says "Peace". An angel with trumpet flies above the scene at upper right and holds another peace scroll. There are formal buildings, a chapel, and a dome at right. Budding trees and clouds complete the background.

PHEASANT

Made by Ridgway and Morley

The three plates shown are gently scalloped and thick scrolls encircle their outer edges. Each has three scenic reserves framed with foliated scrolls on the rims. The vignettes on the two larger plates show two birds facing each other, an over-scaled flower in the foreground and mountain peaks in the background. The cup plate reserves contain a single bird each different from the other. The distinctive rim pattern consists of concentric scalloped white lines on a dark field. The white dotted arch forms at the base of the rims are dominant on all three plates. The larger plates have small bars that depend from the arches and these form a design around the well.

The dinner plate bears a central scene showing a garden terrace and balustrade and tall elm at left. Two pheasants are placed at right amid flowers at the foot of a pedestal surmounted by a tall vase filled with flowers. In the distance there are a gazebo on a hill, a river, other buildings, and mountains. The bread and butter plate shows the pedestal with an urn filled with large flowers in the center, a balustrade at left, and two birds in the foreground. The cup plate contains one large pheasant nestled in some flowers. There are bushes and trees in the background.

Marked R. and M., GMK. 3276, 1842-44.

POLISH STAR

Made by Thomas Godwin

The edge of this plate is unevenly scalloped and the rim is covered with vertical bands of alternating patterns of light and dark floral strips that resemble wallpaper. A row of tiny short lines is at the base of the rim and a wreath of fleur-de-lis encircles the well. The central medallion is composed of an eight petaled star set against a background square design of scrolls and having acanthus leaves at the four corners and a crown shape on the other four sides.

Marked T.G., GMK. 1729, 1834-54.

POMPADOUR

Maker unknown

A *stylized pattern of flowers and leaves is placed over the entire surface of this mug and its handle. The design is a combination of line engraving, and stippling. Enameled beading was also applied on some of the flowers. J.B. may stand for James Beech, but this piece looks earlier than Beech's era. (see Texian Campaign which has the same back stamp). Marked J.B.*

PRINCESS FEATHER

Made by Edward Challinor

Four different curved sprays of garden flowers are placed around the rim of the dish photographed. The sprays are composed of sprigs and ferns as well as of flowers and resemble feathers. A butterfly perches on the design at top. The trio of flowers, dominated by a large rose and buds which appears on the bottom of the rim, is repeated in the center of the plate. The very dark leaves at the bottom left on the rim were omitted in the composition of the center bouquet.

Marked E. Challinor, GMK. 835a, 1842-67.

"PRUNUS WREATH"

Made by John Rogers & Son

A row of white beads is set against the dark edge of this cup plate. The entire little dish is covered with a cellular design and a wreath of dark bars, white prunus and large dark leaves surrounds the rim and extends to the center of the well.

Marked imp. Rogers, GMK. 3369, 1814-36.

QUADRUPEDS

Made by John Hall

The cup plate and fruit, or salad, bowl photographed illustrate how the components of a pattern could be arranged on different articles in the set of dishes produced. The bowl is decorated on the inside rim with cartouches. Each contain a picture of an animal set against a mountain scene (a ram, a boar, an hyena, and a caribou). Between the cartouches there are a harlequin diamond field and vertical lacy designs on a pedestal that supports an urn shape. These resemble incense braziers. These vertical designs enter the well and are attached at the four corners of a scrolled frame that surrounds the central scene.

In the central picture a husky dog stands on a rocky seashore. A boat and a dory and mountains are behind him. The outside of the dish is decorated with the same diamond background. A chain of white diamonds confines the design at the top and bottom. Large foliated scrolls flank a trio of large leaves on both the body and pedestal.

The cup plate resembles the large dish only in the background of the diaper pattern on the rim and the chain of diamonds around the outer edge. Three large classical floral basket designs alternate with three inverted shells set upon a base of two vertical scrolls which flank dark leaves. The central medallion contains a hyena and is encircled by small scallops. A lion appears on the ten inch dinner plate, not shown.

Marked I. Hall, GMK. 1885, 1814-32.

QUADRUPEDS (cont.)

RAILWAY

Maker unknown

This transfer is the same as that described on Railway Mug. The mug is 4¼" high. (Marked P.V.)

"RAILWAY MUG"

Maker unknown

Many potters made mugs with pictures of trains on them. George Stevenson had built a steam locomotive in 1814 which was able to draw a train of eight cars. This was a great achievement and was commemorated by the potteries. In this example the engine pulls a coal car, two passenger cars and a flat bed with a landeau upon the platform complete with driver and three passengers. Note name plate "Pilot" on the side of the steam engine. The background and rim linear patterns differ on the mugs but most bear this transfer.

"RAILWAY MUGS"
joined to show entire pattern

663

"ROGERS' ELEPHANT"

Made by John Rogers and Son

This plate is lobed and the outer edge is defined by a row of white pointed arches containing a dark triangle. The stippled rim is decorated with a wreath of large white flowers and dark leaves. The rim pattern descends into the well and is contained by a band of hairpin curved white lines on the cavetto.

In the central picture a small figure wearing dark clothes and holding a pole stands at right next to a white elephant whose ears appear scalloped or decorated. There are a pool of water and flowers and plants in the foreground. At left a dark gazebo stands on top of a small hill. Below it and in the center of the scene there are small latticed buildings and a fence. Some trees rise from behind the compound and gardenhouse. At right there is a very large tree which rises and crosses to the center of the scene. Behind the tree there is a tall mountain peak.

Marked (imp.) Rogers, GMK. 3367, 1814-36.

"ROGERS' ZEBRA"

Made by John Rogers and Son

These plates are slightly indented and the outer edges are detailed by a band of inverted vs and straight lines that terminate with a bead. The rim is printed with a wreath of leaves and large white flowers, morning glories being the most distinctive blossom. The rim pattern on both plates descends into the well and is contained by a narrow band of a Greek key design.

The central scene on the larger plate and the cup plate as well is dominated by a zebra ridden by a man who wears a fancy wide brimmed Oriental hat. Two other figures stand in the center, one in dark robes wears the same headgear and the other is garbed in a long white tunic. There are buildings at left and a pagoda, a tall ornate tree and very dark bushes. There is a large stylized cherry tree at right. There is an open space which perhaps represents a lake behind the figures and one sees a peninsula with three tall trees on it across the water.

Marked (imp.) Rogers, GMK. 3367, 1814-36.

ROYAL STAR

Probably made by Samuel Alcock

This plate is small (5 inches) and may be part of a toy service. It is scalloped and the indented rim is covered with a pattern of zigzag lines which form triangles. The rim pattern invades the well and is confined therein by a band of small sprigs that resemble stylized pine trees set in triangles. The dark six pointed star in the center is filled with a diamond diaper pattern. Six other rays composed of wavy lines are set between the points, so that the entire pattern seems to have twelve rays.

Marked with a beehive device and "Florentine China", 1828-59.

RUSSELL

Made by William Ridgway and Co.

This saucer is printed with a stylized eight petaled rosette in the center which is surrounded by a wide wreath of realistic roses, daisies, poppies, leaves and sprigs. A band of triangles and beads outlines the outer edge of the dish. The upper rim is decorated with a deep scalloped band; small sprigs and dark beads alternate above the band. Small treelike designs are set below the band in the arches formed by the scallops and they terminate in spearpoint towards the center of the well. Mossy sprigs are placed between the points.

Marked W.R. and Co., GMK. 3303a, 1834-54.

SEA LEAF

Maker unknown

The rim of the saucer shown, the outside of the cup, and the upper rim inside of the cup are covered with large clumps of seaweed. A small medallion of the weed is centered in the well of the saucer and in the bottom of the cup.

667

SEAWEED

Made by John Ridgway

The edge of this twelve sided plate is trimmed with a narrow band of Greek key design. The indented rim is covered with a two tone pattern of coral-like branches. In the center of the well there are a large conch shell, three smaller conical shells, large lacy sea leaves, and some coral.

Marked I. Ridgway, GMK. 3256, 1830-55.

668

"SHANNON (H.M.S.)"

Made by John Rogers and Son

Her Majesty's ship, The Shannon, was an English naval sailing ship of the late 18th and early 19th century. She had a tall rigging and was heavily armed. She defeated an American ship named the U.S.S. Chesapeake on June 1, 1813 which had carried 38 guns. Here the frigate is shown under full sail in the center of the scene. A smaller boat is in the foreground in front of the boat. This would seem to be a landing boat. Other sailing ships are seen in the background. The border is composed of branches of seaweed at top and bottom with cowrie shells and coral framing the oblong picture. The Chesapeake was commanded by Captain Lawrence.

After her defeat at pistol range distance by the Shannon, Lawrence, who was dying, said "Don't give up the ship". However, she was completely disabled. The Shannon towed her to Halifax where she was converted into a British ship. A series of paintings by a British artist, J.C. Schetky commemorated this victory.

Not marked. 1814-36.

"SPODE'S ORIENTAL BOUQUET"

Made by Josiah Spode

This soup plate bears a rim pattern composed of a wreath of three identical sprays of stylized flowers and small dark round fruit. In the center there is a bouquet of flowers, buds, and berries, stylized in the Oriental manner.

Marked Spode and "Newstone", GMK. 3652, 1805-20.

670

SUN OF RIGHTEOUSNESS (THE)

Made by Enoch Wood and Sons

The two plates shown are scalloped and the rims are divided into six sections by vertical Gothic designs topped with leaves and scrolls set against a dark ground. These Gothic bars are joined by three scalloped bands, an outer one of spearpoint, a second one of double line scallops, and lastly by large round beads. The spaces between the bars are filled with pattern of wheat or fruits, or flowers. The reserve at the top contains a landscape over which a very large sun is rising. Its rays are divided like a fan. Under this is printed the title "The Sun of Righteousness".

The central medallion scenes are formed by a band of elongated bellflowers and oval seeds. One plate pictures the infant Samuel and his words of prayer "Speak, Lord, for Thy servant heareth", are placed under his image. The other portrait of a young boy is labeled St. John. Ledicker states that these plates were labeled KEB.

The above plates are unmarked. Ann Hudson Moore in the Old China Book, on page 23, attributes the design to Enoch Wood and Sons, 1829-40. Laidecker states some of these plates were marked KEB. KEB was used by Elkin Knight & Bridgwood see Godden pg. 234 re Gm 1464, 1827-40.

SWANS

Made by Podmore, Walker and Co.

There are three reserves on the rim of this dish containing a scene of a fountain basin set amidst over-scaled flowers and flanked by foliated convoluted scrolls. These alternate with three large pairs of flowers, one dark and the larger one white against a stippled background. A band composed of diamonds and beads broken at six points by fan shapes filled with scrolls and a rosette contain the rim design at the bottom. Under the diamond band there are triangles and small vertical scrolls. At the outer edge of the rim there is a narrow row of angular S lines.

The swans of the title are swimming in the foreground. One is black, the other white. A man in a toga and swirling scarf held in his right hand, is pointing towards the swans with his left hand. At right there is a tall tropical plant, and in the background there is a pagoda with double upturned rooves. Tall trees and some bushes complete the picture.

Marked P.W. and Co., GMK. 3075, 1834-59.

TEMPERANCE SOCIETY (SO-CALLED)

Maker unknown

The outer edge of the larger plate photographed is encircled by a band of shallow scallops printed in white against a dark background. The rim is covered with a lacy design and nine small bouquets are placed against the lace at the upper rim. A printed row of small scallops contains the rim design at the well.

A large shield appears in the center of the plate. At top center there is a semicircular banner placed over an oak tree that surmounts the shield. The banner reads "Firm as an Oak". A man and woman stands on either side of the shield. The man holds a flag stating "Sobriety" and she has one stating "Domestic Comfort". A streamer held up by two children is placed at the bottom of the shield and states "Be Thee Faithful unto Death". The cup plate bears the name of a temperance group and states "Peace and Plenty are the Rewards of Temperance". The shield of this order has an angel at left and a woman at right.

TORONTO

Probably made by Samuel Alcock

The rim of this saucer is covered with a design that resembles flag bunting. The outer edge is decorated with a row of short slanting lines, and the upper rim is covered with a wallpaper type design of vertical stripes between vertical sprigs. The design that appears on the outer edge also encircles the well. In the center of the dish there is a six pointed star composed of striped triangles. Striped spikes are placed behind the star.

Marked with a beehive and "Florentine China" 1830-59.

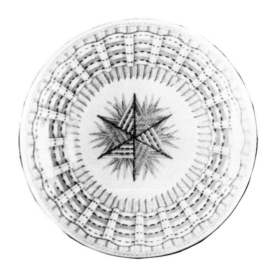

VINE

Made by John Rogers and Son

The embossed white edge of the plate photographed is unevenly scalloped and a row of printed beads accentuates the scalloped line. The uppermost part of the rim is very dark. A wreath of grape leaves and vines encircles the rim. Six triangular vertical sprays of grapes and grape leaves, forget-me-nots and large pointed leaves descend to the well and across it to the central circular frame. Between the vertical patterns there are large white flowers.

The central medallion shows a large tree at right. A man stands in its shade. Another is seated nearby. There are three grazing animals in the foreground. A river divides the scene diagonally, and in the left background there are temples, trees, and mountains.

(Imp.) Rogers, GMK. 3369, 1814-36.

VINTAGE

Made by James Edwards

This pickle dish is molded in the form of a shell and a woman's head framed in a ruff is molded at the handle end. The outer edge is detailed with a printed band of spearpoint. Large sprays of grape tendrils and leaves are placed on the sides and a single bud with leaves is at either end of the dish.

Marked as above with Dale Hall (imp.). See Godden, page 230, 1842-51.

WATER LILLY

Made by John Ridgway

This plate is gently scalloped. Its rim design carries into the well and consists of six panels separated by very dark bands which contain short white scrolls. The dark band is flanked by a lighter one, also bearing the small scrolls. The reserves are filled with flower designs, three of which are stylized small roses and ferns, the other three are stylized angular leaf forms.

The well is encircled by a white band from which small curved panels separated by spearpoint point towards the central motif of ferns and four-petaled flowers which forms a circular design composed of the elements found in the rim panels.

Marked J.R. and "Imperial Stone", GMK. 3253, 1830-55.

WESTERN STAR

Made by William Ridgway

The rim of this unevenly scalloped plate is covered with dark diagonal curving bands that contain lines interspersed with diamonds. A floral and sprig pattern alternates with a rosette and feather pattern against diamond trelliage in the spaces created by the diagonal lines. A wreath of rosettes set upon a band of narrow lines is placed around the well over a band of fringed scallops. In the center the star medallion is encircled by quatrefoils and framed in large baroque elongated violin shapes. Small scrolls flank the points of the star.

Marked W.R., GMK. 3301, 1830-34.

ZAMARA

Made by Francis Morley

The plate shown is twelve sided and the rim is slightly concave. The outer rim is decorated with a band of arches interrupted at twelve points by small fan shapes. Beneath each band, a straight line topped with a fleur-de-lis and interrupted by a large bead divides the rim into twelve sections. On the rim arabesque scrolls against a stippled background alternate with a stylized lotus design which is flanked by a pair of foliated scrolls and crowned with a lily. The color of the rim background becomes lighter towards the well and is contained by a white scalloped line interspersed with fleur-de-lis at twelve points.

A stylized eight point petaled flower is placed in the center medallion in a dark quatrefoil. Four foliated scrolls terminating in large leaves alternate with four sprigs around the central motif.

Marked F. Morley and Co., (imp.). GMK. 2761, 1845-58.

PLATE V

"Delaware", Made by Charles Harvey and Sons. Collection of Debra Pond, Glastonbury, Connecticut.

Unascribed Patterns

Unascribed Patterns

The dishes shown in this section have no backstamps nor any other identification, and therefore cannot be attributed in this book. So that more may be learned about their origins, they are presented here with an abbreviated description of each item. The pattern names and/or makers may be forthcoming from further study and research, and will be published in future editions of this book. The author welcomes assistance by collectors, students and experts.

In order to facilitate correspondence it is necessary to formulate a list and assign a code number and letter to each design. The list follows the format of this book. The letter "U", meaning Unascribed, precedes a letter denoting type, such as "G" for Genre or "S" for Scenic. Each list will be numbered so that if you write and wish to mention that you recognize U.G.4, we will know you are referring to Unknown Genre pattern #4. The word ascribe means to credit in writing or speech, let us hope that the words will be forthcoming so these patterns can be ascribed.

U.F. 1 (cup plate). Fourteen-sided, edge outlined with a black line. Slightly paneled rim covered with a bold design of quatrefoils separated by small scrolls. A large rose, leaves and long stem is placed across the well, a pair of blue bells on curving stems is at right. This example is polychromed.

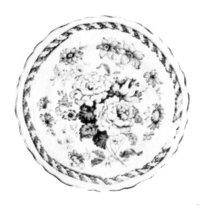

U.F. 2 (cup plate). Scalloped edge embossed with beads. A rope band of leaves entwined over a dark band encircles the upper part of the concave and paneled rim. A bouquet of large roses, dark leaves and several varieties of smaller blossoms covers the well and advances over the lower rim.

683

U.F. 3 (cup plate). Slightly scalloped and edge is embossed with tiny beads. Upper part of concave paneled rim decorated with wreath of linked trefoils interspersed with dark heart shapes containing quatrefoils. A spray of chrysanthemums, dark leaves and forget-me-nots is placed across the well.

U.F. 4 (cup plate). Outer edge decorated with tiny dark triangles and pendant bowknots. A single dahlia-type flower with long stem and three stylized flowers at base crosses the well and part of the rim. Three small butterflies, two on rim, one in well; two leafy sprays on either side of large flower on the rim.

U.F. 5 (cup plate). Large swirled vase filled with bouquet of overscaled flowers. Handle of vase is figure of woman. Border and cavetto covered with two large shaggy flowers and leaves facing across plate, alternating with two large curled fern leaves. Spaces between filled with scrolls and forget-me-nots.

U.F. 6 (cup plate). Deeply scalloped white edge enhanced by dark band of quatrefoils. Stippled rim filled with white fleurons contained by scrolls. Large dark patterned vase at left in well contains some small sprigs. An overscaled cabbage rose in center at foot of vase, and a pair of asters at left.

U.O. 1 (cup plate). Embossed white border with gadrooning. Band of trefoils and triangles surrounds central scene of tall pagoda tower and large house with upturned rooves. Very tall bamboo tree behind house and equally tall pine at extreme left. Arched bridge at right crosses stream that flows across scene. Sailboat at right in front of island containing another pagoda which has four rooves. Water and mountains in distance.

U.O. 2 (cup plate). Edge outlined with tiny beaded scallops. Rim and cavetto covered with wreath of wild roses, leaves and philodendron. Medallion in center framed with white scallops against a narrow stippled band. Round two-storied domed structure with double overhanging rooves in center of scene. Scrubby pine trees on either side. Two small figures on lawn in foreground.

U.O. 3 (plate). Odd figural border shows a dignitary, shaded by parasol held by attendant, who stands in a garden between two pillars. Another personage is seated at right next to a large white jardiniere. Between the figural reserves there are gazebos, trees, a stream and rock forms. Central scene shows Chinese palace garden with terrace overlooking a stream. Man stands on terrace holding the reins of a horse. Palace buildings at right, cliffs and gazebo across river at left and pagoda on mountain in distance. Note statue of seated dog on tall column at right near large tree.

U.O. 4 (plate). Concave rim idented at eight points and covered with a wreath of dahlias, foliated scrolls, poppies, and small fruits like berries and grapes. An area of worm track pattern forms an octagonal frame around the central scene which shows a Greco-Roman Temple set above a landing stage on a river. A rowboat with many figures approaches the landing. A man leads a camel past an arch at left and Byzantine city buildings can be glimpsed through the arch. Tall palm trees appear behind the temple.

PLATE VII

Oriental Birds, Detail

U.O. 5 (plate). Man on raft poles on stream and passes three figures on bank in front of round columned gazebo at right. Across the river there is another round open garden house and two figures stand therein. In distance there are buildings set against conical mountains. Border contains scenic reserves showing second gazebo and man on raft separated by stylized trees and scenes of the distant buildings and conical mountains.

U.O. 6 (platter). Deeply scalloped white edge enhanced by band of small triangles and scrolls. Rim pattern of passion flowers and scenic reserves showing towers in middle flanked by distant tall mountain peaks invades the well. Central scene has Asiatic domed temple in left middle ground, a curved wall and tall dark post at left; two figures, one stands holding a spear and shield, the other seated nearby. Overscaled flowers both right and left foreground, a river and towers and trees in background.

U.O. 7 (cup plate). Willow type with large seven rooved pagoda at left. Arched bridge at right with two men. Odd large trees with white veins in middle and left (looks like Coysh Book I #13 by Spode, dated 1790-1805).

U.O. 8 (plate). Eight oval scenic reserves set in a diamond diaper design show overscaled sunflowers alternating with scene of two women, one of whom is seated in a garden with a dog. They are near a large round table. Quatrefoils around outer indented edge and an octagonal frame of quatrefoils frames central scene which presents the sunflowers in the foreground. A man and child who seem to be preparing something for a figure with crown and scepter seated at left. There is an ewer on the table. They are under the shade of a tall tree on the left bank of a stream that divides the picture. In the background on a hill at right there are large buildings with castellated towers. Two overscaled birds fly over the scene.

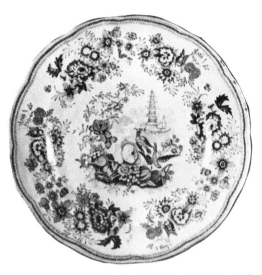

U.O. 9 (plate and cup plate). Both dishes gently scalloped. The white outer edges enhanced by double rows of saw teeth design. Pattern on cup plate rim was cut in half but larger plate shows three long sprays with butterfly perched at right end. In center a large upturned basket of flowers is at left and a tall branch of bamboo and blossoms rises behind the basket to curve into top center. At the right of the basket there are grapes and striped melons, two large Asiatic birds perch on them near an overscaled rose. In the distance there are pagodas, a river and islands. (Pattern Located PAGODA, by Enoch Wood & Sons – See ADDENDA, page 759)

U.O. 10 (cup plate). The design of a winged dragon, spiky branches, stylized flowers and leaves covers the entire scalloped dish (marked with an impressed eight point asterisk).

U.O. 11 (soup plate). Five scrolled shields set around edge of unevenly scalloped dish, and joined by brocade placed over sprays of peonies and leaves. Well medallion, framed with brocade trimmed with wide spearpoint, shows peony tree at left rising from a geometric base of three triangles. Rock forms and flowers placed around base. Stream crosses picture and at right across the water there is a pagoda. Two small figures stand under a bamboo tree near the building. An insect flies at upper right. (Marked L.B.).

U.O. 12 (plate). Two fishermen in dark belted robes and big hats stand in foreground near stream. Across water there is a large horizontal building set upon a base containing oval apertures. A small hexagonal structure is in center background and at upper right is another building with curved roof. Tall exotic trees rise at left. Central scene invades cavetto. Indented rim covered with wreath of loops formed from foliated scrolls, dahlias, dark and light leaves, large leaves shaped like an elephant's ear. (Looks like Roger's work as figures dressed like those in "Zebra", plate mold the same, and colour the same.)

695

U.O. 13 (plate). Garden scene with man reaching with bud in hand towards a large flower filled urn at right foreground. He holds small basket. A child stands near him. House with curved roof in background under the shade of large willow. River in left background with high prowed boat bearing covered section and flying a pennant. Arched bridge in distance leads to hills surmounted with a pagoda. Distinctive border with four areas of bold plaid diaper design alternating with flowers, foliated scrolls and a half dark daisy at rim.

U.O. 14 (change dish, advertising dish). Willow pattern. Three men on bridge, large doves above, angled fence in foreground, cavetto covered with brocade, rim covered with geometric key design, small stylized flowers and advertisement.

U.O. 15 (change dish, advertising dish). Willow type; pair of large birds above scene, three men on three-arch bridge, angled fence. Two sections of honeycomb diaper pattern over key scrolls on either side of advertisment. Note small sprigs on cavetto.

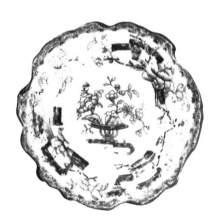

U.O. 16 (cup plate). Edge cut deeply and unevenly. Wreath of peonies set between and over dark geometric bars. Peony tree in center rising from wide brimmed basket composed of curved bars and set upon part of a table-like base.

U.O. 17 (cup plate). *This cup plate is printed in a very light shade of blue. It presents the standard Willow pattern in the well. The rim design incorporates stylized butterflies, and has sections of a half flower with hooked twin stems at the top of the rim. W. Little shows this pattern on plate 48 and presents a saucer and a cup. The fence with the four swastikas is clearly seen and so is the odd flower which appears inside the top rim of the cup shown. Little states the mark is a printed one, attributes it to William Ratcliffe, GMK. 3199, 1813-40.*

U.O. 18 (Child's plate). (4¾") *Has all the elements of the Standard Willow pattern. Pair of doves, three men on three-arched bridge. House, cherry tree, apple tree at right. Willow at center. Angled fence crosses foreground. Only part of rim pattern used. Entire rim pattern shown and band around well shown in Coysh Vol. I, pg. 80, attributes to Josiah Spode 1810-25. (Marked "Stone Ware").*

U.S. 1 (sugar bowl). A bay at right and tall sailing ships at anchor, a steam paddle wheel at extreme right. A man sits on beach in foreground. He wears tall hat and white trousers. Two women stand nearby, one is stooping towards a child. A parasol, hamper and small dog are in foreground. House on hill in background. Water and other ships can be seen behind hill at extreme left. Rim pattern contains stylized passion flowers alternating with a dark fan design, and with arches containing daisies. Row of oval beads at bottom of rim pattern.

U.S. 2 (cup plate). Double print. Half shows two women in long gowns, bonnets and a parasol at left on a lawn near a river. Round small temple on hill at upper right and castle across water in left distance. Other half shows single arched bridge over stream in center. Gothic buildings and towers in right background, tall lacy trees at left.

U.S. 3 (plate). Rim has distinctive design of bent tree branches placed between vignettes of cottage and tower in ruins, an abbey with Gothic entrance and a mansion in ruins. Picture covers well. Tall bridge with four arches crosses large stream bearing a boat with two men, which is in foreground at left. In center and left backgrounds there are a castle and towers. Tall stylized trees are at right and behind them one sees the same cottage and tower that appears on rim. (See Coyshe Vol. I pg. 102, and Little plate 35.)

U.S. 4 (plate). Elaborate border design on unevenly scalloped dish carries scenic cartouches with large urn on tall pedestal at left, overscaled flowers at its base; a river divides scene, and a small dark boat is at right. In background across water there are three towers and mountains. Alternating vertical scrolled bands containing rosettes and quatrefoils divide scenic reserves from floral designs of peonies. Wide lacy band of pennants, sprigs and quatrefoils is placed around upper well. In center garden scene a woman and child stand on a lawn, a servant, wearing a scimitar, bows low before them. In left background wide steps lead to a colonnaded temple. Arches and domes are in the background and a castellated wall and tower is at right. There is water in the distance and a dark boat and mountains. (Marked (imp.) with asterisk.)

701

U.S. 5 (platter). Edge scalloped and detailed with band of stylized bellflowers and beads. Stippled background on rim with wreath of wild roses, both dark and light. Sprigs and leaves below roses enter upper well. Three cows standing in small pond in foreground. At left a shepherd and sheep rest in shade of large trees. In background right there is a large farmhouse with gabled roof. Part of a fence and some shrubs are in foreground.

U.S. 6 (creamer, and saucer). European river scene with large dark round tower dominant. Tall Gothic spire behind saucer contains rim pattern of alternating scenic reserves showing river with small dark boats and buildings across water, separated by pairs of wild and cultivated roses against stippled background. A wreath of sprigs surrounds well and is placed under rim design on creamer.

U.S. 7 (plate). Rim covered with baroque scrolls and pairs of large flowers. Six trios around upper stippled rim, shadowy sprigs around lower rim. A large white house in background of central scene. Tall white trees next to house, tall very dark trees at left. Two men with canes stand with a small dog and a child in center foreground on light road that winds around to front of house. Dark rocks, shrubs and small white flowers are across entire foreground (marked "Semi-China" in a cartouche).

U.S. 8 (cup plate). Scalloped white edge set off by printed white darts against dark band. Classic rim design of scrolls, rosettes and horn shaped pendant double scrolls. Center scene of a major temple surrounded by smaller shrines and out-buildings. Flowers and sprigs placed across foreground.

U.S. 9 (platter and cup plate). Border of lace swags pinned at top with rosettes. Large poppies alternate with smaller blossoms on the swags. Note rosettes and small dogwood type blossom on cup plate rim. Scene on platter shows ruined monastery or church in background, man and woman in foreground near tall tree at left. River in background, sailboat on water, castle in distance. Cup plate has church at left, river with boat at right, towers in distance. (Note similarity to "Monastery" in Scenic category.)

U.S. 10 (cup plate). A little girl stands on steps of terrace in formal garden. Large covered capped stone post at right, lion on tall pedestal at left. Border of coral sprigs. Edge detailed with dark diamonds linked with scallops.

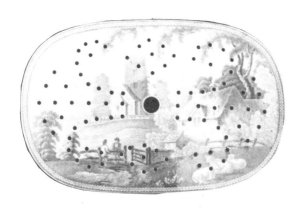

U.S. 11 (drainer and sauce tureen stand). Village church on hill in background. Two men talking across fence in foreground. Thatched roof cottage at right. Pair of sheep in foreground at right. Border of large white roses, dahlias and leaves on very dark ground. Heavy white double scallops around edge. May have been made by Rogers as same embossed rose handles were used by him. Drainer omits border. (Re mold shape, see Coysh Vol. I pg. 62, #83.)

U.S. 12 (bowl). A design of ruined church arch and a picture of woman reading at base of partial column, river in background, towers and arches across river, large bird above. Both scenes set in triple arched openings. Large floral pattern of lilies and ruffled blossoms between scenes. Small stylized blossoms in background of floral pattern.

U.S. 13 (plate). Five distinctive pointed white-veined rose leaves in trios are set around edge. White roses, daffodils and light leaves form wreath with above. Plate edge indented at eight points and decorated with white ovoid beads. Central scene covers well; shows cottages with thatched rooves and chimneys in background, farmer with hoe over shoulder at right, castle on hill in distance, river with sailboat below hill, tall trees at extreme left and pair of cows, one white the other dark in foreground near bushes.

U.S. 14 (cup plate). Resembles plate above (13) Daffodilas and wild roses in border, connected with angled string. Central scene shows thatched cottage left background, tall trees on high bank at right, man in foreground holding pole.

U.S. 15 (plate). A cottage terrace scene in center containing women and children on lawn in foreground and on porch under a grape arbor. Tuscan gate and tower at right in background. Border of unevenly scalloped dish stippled and covered with faint hexagons. Six floral groups around rim separated by curved slanting lines topped with plumes and linked at the bottom with stylized daisies and carnations. A wreath of feathery fans placed around well is crossed by leaves from the large floral designs.

U.S. 16 (plate). Border with distinctive quartets of dark rose leaves, heavily veined. Passion flowers and roses, leaves and buds between large leaf groups. Central scene shows two women in long gowns and bonnets, one holding a parasol, seated on grassy bank. Man with top hat and cane stands nearby. Waterfall in center. Two cows in right foreground. In background, beyond a lake, there are arches and a round tower with conical roof.

U.S. 17 (plate). Edge indented at eight places. Four cartouches on rim, framed with foliated scrolls and containing an eagle, wings outspread head turned to the left. Spaces between filled with cartridges topped with triangles and based with diamonds on a background of narrow concentric lines. River divides scene. At left a round gazebo under tall elms is on high bank. Castle in right distance set on cliff, with tall round tower from which a flag is flying. Two women in long gowns, and seated man are in right foreground on the sloping bank.

710

U.S. 18 (saucer). Distinctive bold rim design of diamonds and rosettes in a chain set against stippled dark upper rim and white lower rim. Scene presents two fishermen in oriental dress on river in high prowed skiff. In background at right there is a colonnaded pavilion on a high bank. Tall lacy trees and pointed mountain peaks are in background and in distance.

U.S. 19 (cup plate). Sixteen-sided dish, paneled rim covered with sprigs and dots. Darker sprigs form uneven chain around rim. Mountain scene in center appears Mediterranean; stone buildings, many towers, houses on hills and century plant in left foreground.

U.S. 20 (cup plate). Rim pattern dominated by three large Asiatic pheasant-type birds, wings outspread, head to right, perched on straight branches of flowering tree. Floral design and scrolls between birds. Small quatrefoil chain around center scene of little dark sailboat in right foreground, which contains three figures and approaches a large stone Gothic rectangular building on left bank. Overscaled flowers across foreground.

U.S. 21 (cup plate). Rim design of double arches composed of feathery fans filled with sprigs under sprays of small dark branches and berries. Rosettes between tops of arches. Picture of Tuscan tower and buildings at right. River, trees and mountain peaks in distance. Very tall stem of lilies at left and other overscaled flowers in foreground.

U.S. 22. Medallion in center shows church graveyard, large white cross on monument at right. Two figures on path at left. Border contains two scenic cartouches showing city scene with round domed tower and two showing four buildings with spires. Reserves separated by scrolls and lattice. Pairs of white rosettes set at top of each cartouche may be distinguishing feature.

U.S. 23 (cup plate). Twelve-sided rim divided into five wide panels by large five-petaled rosettes surmounted with fleur-de-lis against a very dark ground. Scrolls across tops of panels centered with a large fleur-de-lis. Scrolls placed around central scene of twin-towered church set in Alpine scenery.

713

U.S. 24 (cup plate). Dark upper stippled rim circled with rosettes at top of scalloped dish. Lower rim covered with arches which contain ovals, with sides ending in spears at the well. Central picture of white gothic church, perhaps in ruins, at left. Tall dark lacy tree at right.

U.S. 25 (cup plate). Very dark quatrefoils around outer gently scalloped white edge. Wreath of large realistic flowers around rim, notably wild roses and half of sunflowers or large daisies. Also some scrolls between flowers. Central scene of a country church on lawn overlooking a brook. Tall pale lacy trees in the background and at right.

714

U.S. 26 (cup plate). Rim pattern distinguished by large butterflies with wings outspread at each side of design. Wild roses and dark cosmos with leaves between butterflies. Woman stands in middle of center picture. A tall round tower and slanting wall with two arches is at right. Trees and part of a fence on slope at left. White edge enhanced by band of dark beads.

U.S. 27 (cup plate). Upper rim of twelve-sided dish covered with concentric lines that step upwards. A row of fringed white crown shapes placed around lower rim. Center scene divided diagonally by river, large castle with towers at right. A very tall tree in center at left. Other buildings and mountains in distance. A white cow or horse in foreground.

U.S. 28 (cup plate). Picture covers entire plate, large Gothic church in center background. Scene looks French. Large mimosa tree at left, another lacy tree at right, lady with large dark hat and dark Empire gown in foreground. Scalloped edge outlined with small feathers and lace wreath.

U.S. 29 (cup plate). Partial border design shows white scrolls and rosettes against a stippled upper rim. Two sprays of wild roses with dark leaves alternate with the formalized double rosettes. Slanted single-arch bridge in background of scene may be distinguishing feature. Towers in right distance and city buildings at left are placed against soaring Alpine peaks. Woman wearing hat with peaked top is on shore in foreground. A small boat is nearby and contains two small figures wearing hats.

U.S. 30 (tea pot). A river scene is placed on sides of the vessel. There are towered buildings on both sides of the stream and mountains in the distance. The part of border shown contains pairs of roses separated by a triangular pattern of rosettes and scrolls.

717

U.S. 31 (platter). The border is distinctive and contains large sheaves of leaves flanking small scenes of fields, a castle in the distance, a river and mountains. Floral bouquets are place against a stippled ground between the vignettes. Scrolls and sprigs encircle the upper well. In the center a pair, dressed in French court clothes stand on a terrace at right. There is a river in the background and towered buildings across the water. At left there is a triple tiered fountain and in the center there is a very large urn set on a tall sculptered pedestal and filled with overscaled flowers (this may be "Seine").

718

U.G. 1 (bowl). Abraham about to sacrifice Isaac shown in well. Border of scalloped dish appears inside at top and in enlarged version around outside; consists of alternating scrolled dark large spearheads and fleurettes surrounded by sprigs contained at edge with band of running triangles and finished at bottom in a row of triangular beaded pennants. Small scrolls are placed inside pennants and between them.

U.G. 2 (cup plate). Cartouches in border contain peregrine falcons. Gently scalloped edge decorated with row of diamonds and trefoils. Alternating oval reserves contain a fancy flower-filled urn. Small branches placed over stippled rim. Wreath of triangles and vertical sprigs surrounds central scene of a nobleman with plumed hat, on horseback. A yeoman stands nearby and has just released three falcons. Towers and forest in background.

U.G. 3 (plate). South American horse hunters. Cartouches on rim show buck deer fleeing from two small dogs. Triangular shield shapes formed of foliated scrolls, contain a diaper pattern of quatrefoils and are centered with acanthus leaves. Heavy white spearpoint around well. Scene of gaucho on white horse waving a lasso and pursuing a pair of horses, one white the other black. Another rider and horses in background; steep mountains in distance.

U.G. 4 (plate). Horsehunters. Four cartouches on rim contain four different scenes, horse fleeing, cowboys in pursuit, two giraffes fleeing from a cowboy. Separated by Gothic foliated scroll designs over a diamond diaper design. Band of small squares and a deep row of white spearheads around well. Center scene covers well; a gaucho on black horse at full gallop, he has coiled his lasso and is about to capture the white horse in foreground. Herd of black and white wild horses in background, and tropical trees, lake and mountains in distance.

U.G. 5 (cream pitcher). Scattered large flowers at top, band of narrow ovals containing tiny vines at foot. Ovals repeated on handle, which shows part of the bottom of a lacy framed reserve. A bird seller in doublet and feathered cap holds a tray which is suspended from his shoulders and surrounds his body. Small doves perch on edges of tray. Lady in veil and long medieval gown stands on terrace, holds a dove on her hand, there is a greyhound at her feet. River in background and buildings and mountains in distance.

U.G. 6 (cup plate). Unevenly scalloped edge outlined with dark triangles, white band, a row of beads. Stippled rim shows exotic birds with outstretched wings, fruits and flowers. Mourning scene in center, man leans on monument near willow tree. River, arched bridge, towers and round buildings in background. Overscaled flowers in foreground.

U.G. 7 (cup plate). Scalloped edge shows bottom lines of four cartouche frames separated by row of small arches. Rim covered with daisies and sprigs on a stippled ground. Elephant with blanket and rider is escorted by man on foot who carries pole. Towers with onion dome against Alpine peaks in background. Tall lacy trees at left.

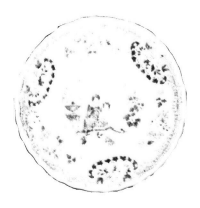

U.G. 8 (cup plate). Two girls resting on ground in garden. Bird cage between them. Covered dark urn on square pedestal and tall lacy trees at left. Castle in right background. Distinctive border pattern of dark beaded semicircles filled with flowers alternate with wide arched openings containing overscaled sprays. Wreath of scallops around well.

U.G. 9 (cup plate). Troubadour and lady. He sits on terrace steps. Large covered urn on square pedestal in left foreground. Tall odd tree behind urn. Looks like trees shown in "Canova". Temples at right across lake. Outer rim beaded and an inner band of embossed gadroon molding.

U.G. 10 (sugar bowl). Rim pattern appears on lid, scenic reserves contain a two-storied house with the upper story overhanging the lower, tiled roof and a small tower, pine trees and part of a fence made of curved branches at right. Four scallop shells, one in each corner of lid, connected with scrolls. Small scrolls and feathery fans around base of pedestal. Milkmaid carrying yoke and two pails, dressed in Tyrolean or Swiss peasant costume in foreground of central scene. Rustic buildings and tower at right and pine trees at left.

U.G. 11 (saucer). Rim cartouches contain alternating scenes of hussar on horseback or elephants bearing howdahs, both set in Alpine surroundings. Lattice fragments around outer edge and between scenic reserves. Bouquets of large flowers also alternate with scenes. Center shows soldier carrying battle standard; he is on horseback, foot soldiers with spears near him. Snowy mountain peaks in background. May be Adams "Hannibal". Marked with an impressed eagle.

U.G. 12 (plates). Edges decorated with a twisted band of beaded ribbon in which large roses are entwined, and small forget-me-nots are placed over the dark portions. One plate shows three hunters riding at the gallop. Pack of hounds at left. Tall trees, a lake and mountains in background. Second plate shows spotted deer leaping a fence, a dog in hot pursuit and the three riders close behind. Lake, trees and mountains in background.

725

U.G. 13 (cup plate). Girl in peasant costume holds bridle of donkey in center scene. Border of mosaic and rosette background has pair of scenic reserves containing a man or boy in middle, a church at right rear. A pair of scalloped wide reserves alternate with scenes and contain half of a large dark sunflower, and sprigs. Well framed by row of unequal length narrow oval cartridge forms.

U.G. 14 (plate). White edge encircled with small dark beads. Wreath of wild roses and Sweet William covers rim. Well scene, framed with white band shows boy sitting on basket at knees of woman who holds his hand. Small dog at right. Jug on bench at right. Trees and hill in background.

U.M. 1 (cup plate). An American eagle perched on the base of a shield containing thirteen stars. Thunderbolt arrows in talons. Dish ten-sided with cobalt edge.

U.M. 2 (cup plate). White outer edge scalloped and embossed. Printed dark wreath of scallops and sprigs surrounds transfer of a pair of exotic birds placed at left on sprigs next to an arrangement of large melon-like fruits at center. Small flowers placed around face of dish.

U.M. 3 (platter). Six oval reserves containing a scene of woman holding basket and a child standing on path in front of stone cottage. Part of fence and tall tree at left. Fans of seaweed between vignettes. Central scene shows three men in skiff in foreground. Boy at tiller wears high hat, others wear tasseled tams. Boat filled with strips resembling cork. Large wooden house and tall trees across water at right. Tall oak on left bank. Towers and other town buildings in distance. Two small sailboats in background (marked with a large impressed crown and curved ribbon; may be Middlesbro Potter).

U.M. 4 (cup). Central medallion shows kneeling cupid holding up tazza to swan which is behind him and curves its neck forward to drink. Border design around outside and upper inside consists of dark scallops at top over a point d'esprit pattern. Lower part of border covered with running circular scrolls embracing a star and emanating from vertical foliated scrolls.

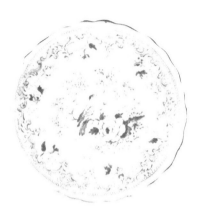

U.M. 5 (cup plate). Scalloped white outer edge decorated with band of beads. Scrolls and floral sprays alternate with pairs of pears on rim. In center a bird perches on leafy tree branches next to an overscaled rose with leaves and sprigs.

U.M. 6 (waste bowl). In center medallion girl with large plumed hat, holding a water pail, stands in garden. Tuscan buildings and towers at left, mountain peaks in distance. Tall trellis and trees at right. Distinctive border consists of point d'esprit over a swag of large flowers alternating with semi-circular pattern of rosettes and dark beads set in swags over a dark ground.

U.M. 7, U.M. 8, U.M. 9 (cup plates). No. 7 has a dark stippled background and picture of single lily at left, a planter box at its base full of cactus type leaves. No. 8 has light stippled ground, double camellia flower with dark leaves in center. No. 9 has light stippled ground, shows triple camellias and buds with very dark sprigs at bas. All are on same mold and all have border design of pairs of speckled lilies, dark leaves and buds. All stippled grounds are composed of coarse dots.

U.M. 10 (platter). Large classic two-handled vase filled with overscaled bouquet sits on a flower-strewn table at left center. Lake in background, buildings and trees across water in distance. Floral border contains white blossoms that resemble those used by Wedgwood. A sprig of lily-of-the-valley is placed in each of the four corners.

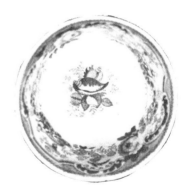

U.M. 11 (tea bowl). A small figure wearing a peaked hat and playing a mandolin is seated on baroque scroll in border design which is seen on the outside of the vessel. An exotic bird is perched near the musician at left. A vase full of flowers is on tiny table between them. Floral panels alternate with the vignettes. Upper rim is stippled and is contained by scrolls. In bottom of bowl there is a group of shells.

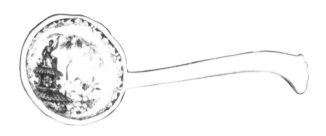

U.M. 12 (sauce ladle). Figure resembling Neptune holding a trident or spear, is set on tall pedestal decorated with a large oval rosette in center. Overscaled flowers at right. Border design of rosettes, and pairs of flowers flanking a triangular design.

U.M. 13 (tooth brush box). Sides covered with a continuous grape vine with leaves, grapes and tendrils. Top decorated with large two-handled jar on pedestal in center flanked by overscaled flowers.

U.M. 14 (sugar bowl). Scenic vignette presents lady in large head-dress, holding a bird on her upright hand and riding a white horse away from the foreground. In the right distance there are oriental-type buildings. Upper part of bowl is stippled and small flowers and scrolls are placed around edge. Wild roses are placed between the scenes.

U.M. 15

U.M. 16

U.M. 17

U.M. 18

U.M. 19   U.M. 20

U.M. 15, 16, 17, 18, 19. 20, (all lustre trimmed cup plates). No. 15, wide outer band, shows a stag in the woods. No. 16, inner circle around scene of very large classic temple set on a hill and surrounded by tall pines. No. 17, embossed white edge, double lustre lines, woman sits and holds basket, a large urn filled with stylized flowers is placed at her feet. No. 18, embossed white edge, double lustre lines, center shows man and woman standing on bank of stream. Double-arched bridge in background, large house behind bridge. Water trees and mountains in distance at left. No. 19, (may be child's plate), white edge, wide lustre band, mourning scene in graveyard. No. 20 famous "house" pattern.

PLATE VIII

Andalusia, Detail

A Selection
of Backstamps

Backstamp Art

No attempt has been made here to match the backstamps or marks shown to the patterns presented in this study, but they were selected from the specimens photographed. They are of interest in themselves and warrant reproducing. There is a difference in meaning between the word "marks" and the word "backstamp". Marks, in the ceramic field mean the letters, scratches, insignias, printed, impressed or otherwise noted on any product produced by a potter. Marks are usually found on the base of a piece because the early European potters copied Chinese potters' imperial era marks. The marks we refer to in this book are the Trademarks of the Staffordshire potters.

Backstamps, on the other hand, relate only to transfer printed china, and were part of the sheet that held the transfer pattern. The stamp was cut away from the margin of the paper and affixed to the bottom of the dish, while the main design was placed on its face. Both marks and backstamps can be aesthetically interesting, but the backstamps are fascinating. They reflect the versatility and imagination of the artists who composed the patterns. Each is a small, charming expression of individual artistry. They are shown here in order to present another facet of the Romantic expression of the Victorian potters.

Columbian Star
Octr. 28th 1840
Jno. Ridgway

THE DOG AND
THE SHEEP
ÆSOPS FABLES

Japan
Flowers
Stone
China
IWR

1240

MILLENIUM

VR
Villd
STONE WARE

BOSPHORUS

CHINESE LANDSCAP

CATSKILL MOSS
MEREDITH
C.C

E.K.B.
Canton Views
OPAQUE
CHINA

EW&S
SUSPENSION
BRIDGES

Senate House
Cambridge
J. & W. RIDGWAY

DOMESTIC
JAs EDWARDS

COPELAND & GARRETT
NEW
BLANCHE
4

CALEDONIAN

Oriental

CALEDONIA

COLUMBIA
ADAMS & SONS

BARONIAL HALLS
T.J. & J. MAYER
PATENT

SPANISH VILLA

MAZARA
IRONSTONE

ARABIAN
F.D.

IMPERIAL STONE
Water Lilly
J.R — C.P.

IRONSTONE CHINA
MARBLE
WEDGWOOD

WESTERN STAR
W.R.

NONPAREIL

MARCELLA

Milanese Pavilions
J.H. & Co.

IRONSTONE
MONTILLA

RUSTIC
W. & G. HARDING

AGRICULTURE
DAVENPORT

India Temple
Stone China
J.W.R.

IRONSTONE

INDIAN

I.P. & Co

MANHATTAN

R. Stevenson

VENUS

P.W. & Co.

BERRY

W.R.

ALBERT
STAR

R.M.W. & Co.

Carstairs
on the Clyde

BELLE VUE

ADELAIDE'S
BOWER

Stone China

HOLYWELL COTTAGE
CAVAN.

WARRANTED

Asiatic Pheasants.

R. Hall.

WEBSTER
VASE

Italian
Villas
J.H. & Co.

Parisian
Chateau.

R. HALL.

TERNI

SINGANESE

R. H. & Co.

VERONA

Patterns Which Could Not Be Located or Photographed

We would be grateful for information about these designs.

ALPINE

ANCIENT ROME

ANCONA *(mul?)*

ARCADIA *(F. & W., Wormtrack border, thatched cottage at left. Village in background, figures in foreground-see GMK. 4435).*

ASIATIC MARINE *(Pratt).*

BOWER

BRITISH BIRDS *(S. Alcock).*

CASTENET DANCE *(Shaw).*

CHINESE JUVENILE AMUSEMENTS

CLARA

COLUMBIAN

EGYPTIAN

FLORENCE

FLORENTINE FOUNTAIN

FRUIT AND FESTOON

GOTHIC BEAUTIES

HABANA *(Adams).*

HIBERNIA

HUNTSMAN, THE

INDIAN SCENERY *(Hall).*

IONA

IRISH SCENERY

LAKE

LAUSANNE

MESSINA

MONTREAL

NILE, (The) *(Shows upper and lower river map on backstamp).*

OLYMPIAN *(R.C. & C. Scottish figures in kilts dancing on terrace. Border large flowers alternating with shield shapes).*

ORIENTAL BEAUTIES

PAVILION

RUSTIC SCENERY *(Clementson).*

SOIRO *(Challinor).*

SWISS *(Clews).*

WINDSOR *(Mellor Venables).* 745

Bibliography

The Dictionary of World Pottery and Porcelain, Bolger. 1971

The Old China Book. N. Hudson Moore. 1903

Encyclopedia of British Pottery and Porcelain Marks. Geoffrey A. Godden. 1964

Staffordshire Pottery. Wedgwood and Ormsbee. 1947

British Pottery and Porcelain. Geoffrey A. Godden. 1963

Marks and Monograms on European and Oriental Pottery and Porcelain. W. Chaffers. 14th Revised Edition.

Staffordshire Pottery and Its History. Josiah Wedgewood. 1912

History of the Staffordshire Potteries. Simeon Shaw. (1829) Reprint 1968

Anglo-American China. Part 1 and Part 2. Sam Laidacker. 1954

William Adams, an Old English Potter. Turner. 1904

An Illustrated Encyclopedia of British Pottery & Porcelain. Godden.

Old China. Minnie Watson Kamm. 3rd printing, 1970

Staffordshire Blue. W.L. Little, 1969

Victorian Pottery. Wakefield. 1962

The Country Life Pocket Book of China. G. Bernard Hughes. 1965

American Historical Views on Staffordshire China. Larsen. 1950

China Classics 4. Ironstone. Larry Freeman. 1954

China Classics 6. English Staffordshire. Serry Wood. 1959 (Kamm)

Blue and White Transfer Ware 1780-1840. A.W. Coysh. 1970

Blue-Printed Earthenware 1800-1850. A.W. Coysh. 1972

British Pottery, An Illustrated Guide. Geoffrey Godden. 1975

China Collecting in America, Earle. 1892

Mason's Patent Ironstone China. Godden. 1971

Auction Supplement to the Standard Catalogue, Anglo-American China. Laidacker. 1949

Historical China Cup Plates. Richard and Virginia Wood.

Pottery and Porcelain Tablewares. John Cushion. 1976

American Glass Cup Plates. Ruth Webb Lee and James Ross. 1948

 Glossary

ACANTHUS A plant that grows in the Mediterranean region having toothed leaves. The stylized rendition of the leaves is used in architectural and classical design.

ARABESQUE Surface decoration in colour composed in flowing lines of branches, leaves and scroll work fancifully intertwined.

ASYMETRICAL Laching symetry; was identical on both sides of a central line.

BAROQUE Irregularly shaped, and/or extravagantly decorated.

BUCOLIC Pastoral, rustic; countrified.

CARTOUCHE An oval or oblong figure enclosing a design.

CASTELLATED Built like a castle with turrets and battlements.

CAVETTO The concave space between rim and well of a dish.

CONCENTRIC Having a common center; circles within circles.

CROCKET A small ornament, usually a plant or leaf form, placed on steeply inclined surfaces, such as copings of roof gables, and which turns up from the surface and returns upon itself to form a knob-like termination; seen in Gothic and Victorian architecture.

CYMA CURVE A curve that is partially convex and partly concave.

DENTIL Any of a series of closely spaced small rectangular blocks (from latin word for tooth).

DIAPER A linen fabric woven with small constantly repeated figures such as diamonds. Diaper Pattern — such geometrical or conventional pattern used to form the ground of a design.

DICED Ornamented with diamonds.

DIRK A dagger.

DORMER A projecting vertical window in the sloping roof of a house.

EMBOSSED With surface designs raised in relief.

EPI A finial, an ornament placed upon the apex of a roof.

EWER Tall slender pitcher with spout and a handle.

FLEURETTE An ornament like a small conventional flower.

FLEURON A floral motif used as a terminal point or in a series.

FOLIATED Consisting of, or ornamented with leaves or leaf-work.

FRET An angular design of interlaced angular designs.

GADROON A decoration of concave and convex flutings as found on silver.

GAZEBO A summerhouse built on a site that affords an enjoyable view.

GREEK KEY An angular design of interlaced angular designs.

JUNK A large oriental sailboat with square prow and square sails, flat bottomed and with a high stern.

LAMBREQUIN In ceramics, ornamentation consisting of solid color with a jagged or scalloped edge, a curtain-like band.

LINE ENGRAVING A technique of engraving in which all effects are produced by variations in the width and density of lines.

LOBED Having rounded projections or divisions.

LOZENGE A diamond.

MANDARIN A government official with one of nine ranks in the days of the Chinese Empire.

MAURESQUE (MORESQUE) Moorish in style or ornamental design.

MEDALLION An oval or circular panel in a decorative design.

MINARET A slender tower attached to a moslem mosque surrounded by one or more balconies for which the muezzin calls the people to prayer.

NEOCLASSIC Pertaining to a revival of styles from classical antiquity, particularly a severity of composition.

OVOID Egg-shaped.

PAGODA A temple or sacred building, especially sacred tower built over the remains of a saint.

PARAPET A low wall placed at the edge of a platform, or along the sides of a bridge to prevent people from falling over.

PAVILION Small ornamental building in a garden.

PRUNUS In oriental pottery a representation of the Chinese or Japanese species of Rosacex which contains plums, peaches, almonds, etc.

QUATREFOIL Four lobed ornament; like a four leaf clover.

ROCOCO Having the characteristics of Louis XIV or Louis V workmanship such as shell-and scroll-work.

SAMPAN A small boat propelled by a single scull over the stern, and with a roof made of mats.

SCIMITAR SHAPED Curved, resembling an arc.

SERPENTINE Characteristic of a snake in form or movement.

STIPPLED Engraved by means of dots.

STRIATED Furrowed, striped or streaked.

TREFOIL An ornamental figure representing a three leafed clover.

TREILLAGE Lattice work, a trellis.

TROPHIES Symbols appropriate to love, pastoral life, war, music etc. (such as bows, arrows, torches, and quivers).

TUSCAN ARCHITECTURE Pertaining to one of the five classic orders developed in Rome, basically simple Doric style with little decoration.

VIGNETTE Small pleasing picture or view.

Index

F – Floral

C – Classic

O – Oriental

S – Scenic

G – Genre

J – Juvenile

PC – Polychrome Chinoiserie

M – Miscellaneous

Page

Page

AMARYLLIS (F)

Made by Ralph Stevenson and Son

The rim of this scalloped platter is decorated with a wide band of alternating stylized floral panels separated by bands of dotted stripes centered with a vertical band of white coral against a dark ground. The rim pattern extends halfway into the well.

A row of triangles and hexagonal beads surrounds the central stylized drawing of two large amaryllis on a double leafed stem. Small buds, blossoms and sprigs surround the main floral group.

Marked R.S.&S. and "Imperial Stone", GMK. 3706, c. 1832-35.

"CLASSIC BOUQUET" (C)

Made by Copeland and Garrett

The object photographed is a dish strainer, which was used by inserting it in a platter so that juices and liquids from meats or fish would drain into the space below.

The geometric border pattern, resembling cubes and diamond chains is contained at the center by a wreath of scrolls. In the middle of the strainer there is a picture of a two handled vase, decorated with a scene containing two women in Greek costume. The vase is filled with a large bouquet.

Marked as above, and (ptd. and imp.) "New Blanche", GMK. 1090, 1833-47.

"CLASSIC BOUQUET" (C)

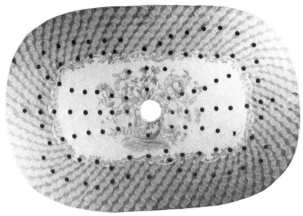

HINDU (O)

Made by Edward Walley

The edge of this ten sided plate is decorated with a narrow brocade band. The rim is embossed with ten curved lotus shapes. In each curve there is a peony and prunus or an alternate geometric trellis filled with a diamond diaper pattern and three rosettes.

The central medallion, framed by a brocade circle of laurel leaves and Chinese fret design, contains a large peony tree and other overscaled flowers set in a two handled vase. The vase is placed in a basin or basket with scalloped edge, which in turn is supported by a table-like platform. At right a small costumed figure sits midway up a flight of stairs.

Marked W., and (imp.) "Pearl White", GMK. 3990, c. 1845-56.

"MILKMAID" (G)

Made by Davenport

 The outer edge of this deep saucer is detailed with a row of white triparted leaves. The bold rim pattern consists of two or three large white flowers with very dark leaves which are separated by small sweet william or forget-me-nots. The rim design enters the well and is contained by a narrow white scalloped line.

 The milkmaid is seen at her labor at left. She kneels on the ground and milks a large cow into a wooden pail. A white sheep reclines near her, and he casts a dark shadow behind him. In the background there are bushes, trees, and other sheep lying on a hillside. In the bottom of the cup only the sheep are pictured.

 Marked as above, (ptd.), like GMK. 1187, 1820-60.

PAGODA (O)

Made by Enoch Wood and Sons

 Butterflies perch on small bouquets on the rim of this scalloped vegetable dish. Large sprays separate the bouquets. The edge is outlined with a simple dark band of darts and an inner lighter row of darts.

 The "Pagoda" of the title is at right across a river in the central scene. The left and central sections of the picture are filled with overscaled flowers and fruits which spill from an overturned oval basket. A small bird perches on the large rose at center, and another flies above the melons and cherries in the right foreground.

 Marked E.W.&S., GMK. 4260, c. 1818-46.

PAGODA (O)

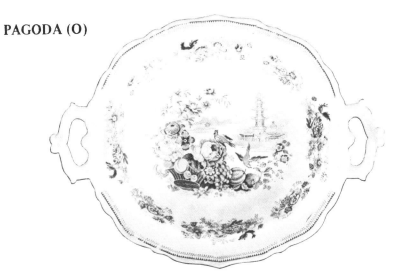

PEPPER SHAKER OR MUFFINEER (M)
Maker Unknown

This small shaker (5" high) is decorated with a very pale willow pattern, which resembles that attributed to Ratcliffe with its half sun-flowers and hooks, two men on the bridge and a figure in a doorway. c. 1831-40.

RAIL WAY (M)

Made by Enoch Wood and Sons

The white edge of this unevenly scalloped plate is decorated with a series of small curved feathers and dark diamonds. The rim design, which resembles clumps of grass on a stippled field, extends into the well where it is contained by white scallops and a deep row of diamond headed pennants.

The center scene is dominated by a pair of square towers topped with smoke stacks and connected by an Arabic arch. The towers form the entrance to a bridge or trestle. Under the archway there are two railroad tracks. A train approaches the arch at right. At left there is a church-like building. Tall trees rise at either side of the scene and there are over-scaled flowers in the foreground. This plate is printed in the same colours as Suspension Bridge and is printed on the same mold, and bears the same backstamp except of course for title.

Marked E.W.&S., GMK. 4260, 1818-46.

SEASONS (M)

Made by William Adams & Sons

This cup plate bears part of the famous "Seasons" border shown in detail in this book. The center is covered with a large full blown rose and grapes, peaches and other fruits and small flowers. The border omits three seasons and the figures and repeats, Spring, Spring, Spring.

Marked (imp.) Adams. GMK.

WOODMAN, THE (G)

Made by Joseph Heath & Co.

Oval white medallions, showing a large French Poodle carrying a basket in his mouth, alternate with panels containing a fruit arrangement on the stippled rim of this scalloped saucer. The ovals are separated by a triangular Gothic pattern topped with an acanthus leaf flanked by leafy wings and pendants. A rosette is in the center of the design and there is a trefoil at the bottom. The outer edge of the dish is enhanced by a band of rosettes, white leaves and dark diamonds. A scalloped band of diamonds contains the rim design at the bottom. Small spearpoint extends from the diamonds into the well.

The "Woodman" of the title, pipe in mouth, wide hat on head, dog at heel is placed in the center of the scene. A cottage with thatched roof is in the background at left, and a woman and child stand near the house. At right there are figures of four other men who hold sticks or poles. They seem to be frolicking on an icy pond. In the distance at right there are a church and spire a white mountain peak.

Marked J.H.&Co. and (imp.) a propeller on a beaded circle, GMK. 1994A, 1828-41.

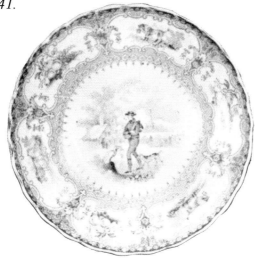

Notes

Notes

TYPESETTING BY VARI-COMP INC.

PRINTING BY REYNOLDS-FOLEY

LOUISVILLE, KENTUCKY

FRONT PIECE AND STUDIO PHOTOGRAPHS

BOB KELLOGG